DUKE UNIVERSITY PUBLICATIONS

SCOURGE
AND MINISTER

SCOURGE AND MINISTER

A STUDY OF

HAMLET

As Tragedy of Revengefulness and Justice

G. R. ELLIOTT

Æquabiliter

DURHAM, NORTH CAROLINA

DUKE UNIVERSITY PRESS

1951

To

Robert Frost

IN OLD FRIENDSHIP

AND IN ADMIRATION PARTICULARLY OF HIS
TWO RECENT MASQUES
SHOWING REASON AND JUSTICE AND MERCY

PREFACE

On "Mystery" and Method

IN THIS BOOK I have attempted a comprehensive view of *Hamlet* as a poetic drama, or dramatic poem, wherein the main character is merely the main thread of the whole weave. What light I have thrown on his "mystery" is due to my not having set out to unravel it. Nowadays we know too well that *Hamlet* is nothing with Hamlet left out. We need to know that *he* is nothing apart from the play. Surely the multifarious explanations of him ought by now to have demonstrated one fact: to isolate him in any way, in any slightest degree, from the pattern of the play is to *deform* him, and the play. Shakespeare formed him in forming the play; created him as the inextricable centrum, so to speak, of a vital complex of events, poetic tones, and persons.

The events and tones are primal. *Hamlet* is an eventful story, uniquely intense and condensed, told in lines written to be spoken aloud. The primary clue to its meaning is, simply, the sequence in which the author gives the lines, thereby and therewith giving us a specific series of happenings, physical and mental. Hence the scene-by-scene procedure adopted in my text: more exactly episode by episode, speech by speech, tone by tone; with general comments woven in at convenient junctures—a method imperfect enough in my handling of it but right, I am sure, in principle; particularly right for understanding the persons of this drama. Only in the poetic-dramatic continuum which Shakespeare has here created can we truly *see* the characters.

For example, it is significant that the first of those to be presented with any fulness is the honest, temperate Horatio. The dominant tone of his speeches in the opening scene insinuates that idea of justice or justness, which, expressly associated with him later, in a central episode (III. ii. 59 ff.), proves to

be central in the play's whole design. The next person to focus
our attention is Claudius, in the beginning of the second scene.
His rhetoric is designed to stand out in striking, even shocking,
contrast with the style of the preceding episodes. But presently
Hamlet speaks; and (in our subconscious mind at least) his
style recalls Horatio's, though now there is a new note of
imaginational intensity. We must listen to his "solid flesh"
soliloquy as climax of the first three hundred lines of the
drama, instead of assimilating it to certain subsequent moods
of his, thus reading the story backwards. In its immediate
context this great speech, so far from being subjective and morbid, conveys a very objective *feel* of honesty and justness, in
smiting opposition to the slick egoism of Claudius. In essential
quality it is close to Horatio's utterances. Accordingly it prepares for and merges into the ensuing dialogue between Horatio and Hamlet. And the penetrating verity of this dialogue
is made—with the aid of a satiric allusion to the final words of
Claudius (I. ii. 125, 175)—to emerge like a sharp, clear peak ·
above the cloudy eloquence of the king in the preceding courtly
ensemble.

Thus Hamlet's role though central is a lineament of an
intricate dramatic landscape: its intricacy or "mystery," as my
Introduction and text will show, is one with his. Here notice
that in the famous passage on his "mystery" (III. ii. 382)
Shakespeare is doubtless punning, characteristically and cru-
cially, upon the old meanings of that word: skill, craft, profession. Profession—notably that of the Players, the prince's association with whom has just now concluded.[1] That *double-
entendre*, which must have hugely appealed to Richard Burbage, the first great player of the title role, suggests that the
"heart" of Hamlet's and the play's meaning, while not a thing
for shallow-hearted persons to "pluck out," can be conveyed
to a sympathetic audience by competent actors. I have studied
the theatric aspects of this drama; I have watched the chief
performances of it from Forbes-Robertson's on. And I hope
this book will have some appeal to actors. From their stand-

[1] The words "skill" and "play" (III. ii. 378, 380) allude, I think, to their
craft. See the passage on "our mystery" in *Measure for Measure* IV. ii. 30 ff.

point, no doubt, many a passage may seem supersubtle; but Shakespeare must share the responsibility for that: he wrote this profound and complex poem ultimately for readers. But he wrote it immediately for his stage. And the "heart" of it would come out clear and strong on the modern stage if directors and actors would discard wholly a notion that Shakespeare and Burbage were happily free from, the notion of Hamlet as a modern individualist. In fact the theater is now in confused process of changing that idea. But we should "reform it altogether" (III. ii. 42); that is required by the truest principles of theatric art. Hamlet will not be less but more of a star role when it is fully integrated, as in Shakespeare's conception, with all the other leading parts, for instance, that of Ophelia. The modern misconception of her is histrionically ruinous not only for her but for Hamlet.

But chiefly I have tried to show that Hamlet as gentleman-prince, in type, is far more effective theatrically than he is as a Romantic or naturalistic genius. This play is the drama of gentility, true and false gentility, with Hamlet's personality for centerpiece. And only when we grasp that pattern may we see fully, not only his relations with each of the other dramatis personae, but also the great dramatic oppositions within his own nature. He is both a greater and a more sinful man than has been generally perceived. In slubbering the idea of sin, a fundamental factor in Shakespeare's outlook and work, romantic naturalism has "sicklied o'er" the vivid figure of Hamlet with a "pale cast of thought." The deep and violent contrast between his noblest reaches and his sinful descents is, whatever else it is, tremendously dramatic.

Since Shakespeare attained in this play the height of his power and effect, the most dramatic (and poetic) interpretation of any given passage is likely to be the right one. This bit of quickfire dialogue, this orated period, this winding stretch of soliloquy, this bit of urgent address, this sharp exclamation or question—just what is the most effective rendering of its sound-and-sense, sense-and-sound? Such must be our continual question. And of course the vital reader will wish to answer it in his own way. To him I would say: This book is intended to be

laid alongside your copy of *Hamlet*.[2] Read an act, scene, or
episode for yourself; then, please, consider my treatment of it.
If my interpretation irritates you, so much the better. Return
to your own *Hamlet* with renewed ardor of scrutiny. My best
hope, really, is to provoke your sharpest attention to the lines
of this drama, in their given sequence, and to help intensify
your delight in their force, suggestion, and beauty.

Scholars closely familiar with the literature of the Renaissance, particularly of sixteenth-century England, will perceive
that a long study of it underlies my book. But that familiarity
is still lacking to many teachers of Shakespeare. They are devoted to him, not to his milieu; their interest is in other and,
generally, more modern periods. Consequently their view of
him is largely determined by the modern literary outlook.
Most of them, to be sure, are now critical of the nineteenth-
century concept of *Hamlet*. But while rejecting many features
of it they still adhere, for the most part subconsciously, to the
essence of it. Accordingly they are apt to regard my interpretation of this drama as much too subjective, which, ironically
enough, is the very adjective applied by students of the Renaissance to modern ideas of Shakespeare.

With those teachers in view I originally intended to docu-
ment my points by giving elaborate references in the Introduction and notes to Erasmus, Castiglione, Elyot, and many others
who shaped the outlook of the earlier Renaissance.[3] But later
I discarded that design as cumbrous and supererogatory. The
spirit of an age cannot be conveyed by citations, no matter how
extensive, to persons imbued deeply, sometimes pugnaciously,
with the spirit of a different and much nearer period. Suffice
then to say that in reading between the lines of *Hamlet*, as
everyone does and must, I have been swayed by the dramatic
sixteenth century, not the lyrical nineteenth. The latter, however, was my own first field of study, and I trust I have compre-
hended its finest illuminations of the poetry—this more than

[2] My incessant references to act, scene, and line will, I hope, excite the
curiosity of readers not closely familiar with the text, and be regarded by
knowing ones with charitable indulgence.

[3] Actually I have considerably cited Spenser, whose influence on the Elizabethan drama has of late been signally recognized. To study Shakespeare in
isolation from his greatest immediate predecessor in poetry is *somewhat* like
ignoring Tennyson's debt to Wordsworth and Keats.

the dramatic art—of the Shakespearean drama. Moreover, the meaning of *Hamlet* for its contemporaries, though important as an offset to subsequent distortions, is a very secondary question for present purposes. The perennial meaning of this superb drama-poem is ever open to the general reader, i.e., one who is free from specialistic interests. A literary scholar, above all a teacher, should be also a general reader, especially of *Hamlet*.

My debt to contemporary scholars and critics is too large and various to be particularized; but it is nonetheless, perhaps all the more, real.[4] I believe this book is in line with the main trend of Shakespearean study in the present century.[5] During the past twenty years my students in Amherst College have shown keen and, I think, typical interest in the project of bringing Renaissance ideas together with perpetual dramatic principles to bear upon *Hamlet*. Dr. James G. McManaway of the Folger Shakespeare Library (owned by the Trustees of Amherst College) gave me very helpful suggestions regarding the text of the play. In a careful re-study of the original editions my main resource was a negative photostat of the Yale Elizabethan Club copy of the First Folio version of *Hamlet*. The material of my book has been presented in addresses to a number of audiences, all of them inquisitive, sometimes helpfully combative. Particularly I am grateful to President Gordon Chalmers of Kenyon College for having me lecture and confer there upon Shakespeare, Spenser, and the Elizabethan Christian Gentleman.   —G. R. E.

Brunswick, Maine
October 1, 1950

[4] A good scholar who read this book in manuscript, for the most part sympathetically, termed my conception of *Hamlet* "revolutionary." But I am sure it is a very natural evolution.

[5] Three brief and very interesting books recently read by me may be mentioned here because, while very different from each other, they are all symptomatic of that trend: Richard Flatter's *Shakespeare's Producing Hand*; S. L. Bethell's *Shakespeare and the Popular Dramatic Tradition*; and John E. Hankins's *The Character of Hamlet*. The first two titles are sufficiently suggestive. Professor Hankins's essay stresses the idea of justice. This idea is now coming to the fore again in various realms of thought after suffering eclipse in the Humanitarian movement which grew out of and succeeded the Renaissance. For Shakespeare it was basic.

CONTENTS

(The design on the title page is from *Emblemata Politica*, Nuremberg, 1617. This book is in the large collection of emblem books and related works in the Duke University Library.)

INTRODUCTION

On Pride, Justice, and the Gentleman-Prince

THE QUESTION "Why does Hamlet delay, fatally for himself, the killing of Claudius?" is inseparable dramatically from another query: "Why does Claudius delay, fatally for himself, the killing of Hamlet?" Of course there is a very obvious ground of Claudius's delay so far as the first half of the drama is concerned. The new king conciliates his queen together with "the world" (I. ii. 108) by recognizing the son of her and the former king as crown prince. But soon we learn from the Ghost that Claudius had performed a quite unique feat: he had managed to murder his mighty predecessor with absolute secrecy. Surely he may very well do likewise to Hamlet later on. That is what we feel if we credit the specter's story and if we are as much interested (very many of us are not) as Shakespeare intended us to be in his fascinating Claudius. And our premonition is justified in the second half of the drama. There the king devises two clever schemes for disposing of his nephew without incurring suspicion on the part of the queen and Denmark: first, Hamlet's healthful voyage to England, to be climaxed by the beheading of him there; then his charmingly friendly, but fatal, fencing-match with Laertes. Both schemes are wonderfully specious, but especially the second; which is apparently so designed by the king as to rule out the unforeseen accidents, very regrettable from his standpoint, that nullified the first. The upshot is, however, that Hamlet is left alive long enough to unveil and destroy his enemy before he himself succumbs. Surely, then, we are intended to perceive that Claudius's second and last murder, in contrast with his first, is brilliantly unsuccessful. It is true that Hamlet dies because he postpones too long the killing of the king. But it is equally significant that Claudius dies because he postpones too long the killing of Hamlet.

In the middle of the drama both men had been summoned by their opposite fates to take definitive action; and both had failed to do so. The Play-within-the-play convicted Claudius in the prince's eyes—and showed Claudius that he was thus convicted—of the murder of the prince's father. But in the ensuing sequence of episodes (III. ii. 282 ff.) the King's conduct is just as fatefully inconclusive as the prince's. Hamlet temporizes in his long talk with Rosencrantz and Guildenstern; but at the same time Claudius is temporizing by having those two underlings talk lengthily with Hamlet. Thereupon, to be sure, he determines to ship the prince in their charge to England. In two ways, however, this episode sharpens our sense of his procrastination. First, it is the belated fulfilment of a decision he had taken waveringly (III. i. 170-196) when he had excellent grounds for believing that Hamlet was seeking his life (line 155). Second, this episode (III. iii. 1-26) shows that even now he hesitates to destroy the prince: merely he "will fetters put upon this fear Which now goes too free-footed" (line 25).[1]

Note the stabbing irony of those lines in view of what follows. The king's "fear" is now climactic and intense. Nevertheless, the prince is "free" pending the preparations for his voyage—free to kill the king. Of course Claudius had promised Polonius to permit Hamlet to visit his mother before being sent abroad. But surely some sort of "fetters" would *normally* be placed upon his movements now by his astute, suspicious, and critically endangered sovereign.[2] Instead, the king, after a long soliloquy, kneels down alone, unguarded, to say a long prayer—while the "free-footed" prince enters and draws his sword (III. iii. 87). If it is strange that Hamlet does not kill Claudius here, it is still stranger that Claudius should have given him such a wide-open chance.

Normally the king would have himself guarded at this junc-

---

[1] On rationalistic grounds critics have read back into the present episode the later decision of Claudius for the "death of Hamlet" in England (IV. iii. 67).

[2] Polonius had previously suggested that the king might "confine" Hamlet (III. i. 194) after the conference with his mother. Why not, beforehand, "confine" him, at the least, from the one spot where the king is?

ture.[3] Normally, but the point is that in the Prayer episode, as result of the Play scene, Claudius's state of mind is abnormal, uniquely so, owing to a crucial conflict that is taking place within him. And the same is true of Hamlet. The two cases are designed by Shakespeare to play into, interpret, and accentuate each other. This design is more fully exposed in my text. Just now let us note that each of the two men in the Prayer scene is more at odds with himself than he has ever been before or will be afterwards. Each, preoccupied inwardly, is for the moment reckless of his own outward safety. The king's postponing words "prepare" and "forthwith" in the opening of the scene (III. iii. 2 f.) are dramatic antecedents of the prince's postponing words at the close, "This physic but [i.e., merely] prolongs thy sickly days." Each of the two men is determined to take action against the other "forthwith"—but not on the spot, not at this very instant. In a few minutes Hamlet tries to kill the king (III. iv. 26). Soon the king tries to kill Hamlet (IV. iii. 67). But in the Prayer scene each delays fatefully the ending of the enemy of whom, as the Play scene has just shown, he stands in deadly, instant danger.

There is general agreement that Hamlet's soliloquy here, "Now might I do it pat" etc., does not state his real motive for delay; rather, as will be shown in my text, it does not expose his *deepest* motive in true terms. But now observe that exactly the same is true of the preceding soliloquy of Claudius, "Oh, my offense is rank" etc. He has been forced to face his past crime against the prince's father; but he refuses to face his present offense against the son: his withholding of the throne from Hamlet. He reveals to us his bitter awareness that he cannot "retain" his crown and yet be "pardoned" for the murder by which he attained it (III. iii. 56). Yet he will not consider the possibility of relinquishing the throne to Hamlet. His proud ambition, even while he is ostensibly striving for religious humility, prevents him from making any allusion to the prince. His resolution to banish him persists; at the same time his aroused conscience will not tolerate here any thought

[3] As he does at Hamlet's next approach to him (IV. iii. 14), also on the occasion of Laertes' expected attack (IV. v. 97).

of murdering the son of the murdered father. That point is not stated in so many words; Claudius refuses to confront and formulate it. But it is very clearly implied, by Shakespeare's fine art, in the scene taken as a whole. In short, the king's underlying motive here for postponing the destruction of the prince—and the same will be found true of the prince's delay regarding the king—is an ungodly but very human mixture of ambitious pride and obscure conscience.

In that respect the Prayer scene results from and illuminates Claudius's treatment of Hamlet during the first half of the play.[4] Indeed this scene illuminates his treatment of Hamlet—and Hamlet's of him—throughout the whole drama.

Obviously, as already stated, the king wishes to conciliate Denmark and the queen. But there is far more to it than that. When Claudius and Hamlet first appear together (I. ii), the new king's demeanor to the prince is really genial, as well as politic. To be sure, he delights in the eloquent dialectic with which he throws discredit on Hamlet's hostile attitude and solidifies the general approval of himself. He is sleekly proud of his triumph. All the more, then, are we impressed by his vein of genuine kindliness towards the one person who so patently and fixedly hates him. We wonder. And our wonder heightens when we learn from the Ghost that the new ruler's ambition is hellishly murderous. The opening question of the drama, "Who's there?"—the symbolic quality of which is dealt with in my text—recurs with renewed force: What sort of person may this Claudius be? In the second and third acts why does he continue, despite his increasing peril, his forbearance towards his madly (so it seems) hostile nephew? Before the time of this drama many a usurper in history and fiction, including Shakespeare's history plays, had destroyed not only the sovereign but also the heir, as promptly as possible, to make assurance doubly sure. Not so Claudius. And his desire to conciliate his wife and subjects is very far, certainly, from accounting for the fact that this astutely ambitious man, when

---

[4] Of course this statement does not imply a reading of the story backwards, in contravention of a principle stated above. Continually the reader is impelled to glance back, and forth. But first of all, if his glances are not to be crooked, he must follow the action of the play precisely as the author gives it.

finally he ends the heir, ends also his own life together with sovereignty and wife.

In the beginning he poisons the father, secretly and safely. In the close he poisons the son—indirectly and almost, but not quite, secretly and safely. This failure is immediately due to certain new and external factors, above all the conduct of Hamlet. Also to such factors, above all the conduct of Claudius, is due the failure of Hamlet. But the essential cause of Claudius's as of Hamlet's ruin is not new and external: it is old and inward. It is spiritual faltering due to a subtle mixture of pride and conscience, exhibited so tellingly in the Prayer scene but clearly implied in the whole action of the drama.

Claudius's conscience is so revolted by his murder of his brother that at once he tries to hide his crime from himself, even more than from everyone else,[5] and to make all possible amends, short of giving up his gains. Hence his subtly ambiguous demeanor (missed as a rule by actors of the part) in the opening ensemble. His "auspicious" and "smiling" mien (I. ii. 11, 124) is factitious enough to betray a deep underlying uneasiness. His iterated citation of "heaven" and "love" (lines 95, 101, 110, 121) is strikingly rhetorical and overdone. He is trying to pacify "heaven," more than Hamlet, by recognizing the prince as his dear "son" and the "most immediate to our throne."[6] Here already he is humbling himself, in public, as he will later do in solitude and with climactic ostentation, before heaven's "mercy" and "justice" (III. iii. 46, 58). At the same time his pride is strident in exhibiting himself to the assembled court as a far more efficient ruler than, he thinks, Hamlet could be. Thus his pride soothes his remorse, cloaking from his own gaze the enormity of his crimes. Such is his twofold, and intensely dramatic, mood throughout the whole episode (I. ii. 1-128).

Above all, his pride-and-conscience throughout the whole

---

[5] Including even his wife. Here, I think, lies the main reason for Shakespeare's insistence, in his final revision of the old *Hamlet* play, upon Gertrude's entire ignorance of the crime.

[6] This phrase is darkly ironic. In the final scene Hamlet, again in full presence, will take the throne *immediately*—after thrusting the dead body of Claudius from it.

drama keeps him from admitting his reluctance to take action against Hamlet. For to confess that reluctance would be to confess how much he has wronged the prince as well as the prince's father. His conscience, burdened with his murderous wresting of the throne from the father, tries to elude the resultant extra burden, the guilt of withholding the throne from the son. He will not face the fact that the least real amends he could make to heaven and to Hamlet for the murder of Hamlet's father would be his yielding the crown to the prince, not in due course of nature, but right now.

He takes a keen, false comfort in the prospect of Hamlet's succession to the throne in the future. Indirectly he confesses that "comfort" (I. ii. 116) to us of the audience; but he will not confess it plainly to himself. For to confront it fully would mean confronting its falseness, as a sheer piece of "shuffling" (III. iii. 61) in the eye of "heaven." Accordingly he will not admit how deeply anxious his conscience is that Hamlet shall be his assured successor, with the full agreement of court and nation, and with the genial concurrence of the prince himself. Claudius does not tell us that the prince's initial "intent" of returning, aloof, to Wittenberg is "most retrograde" not only to the king's "desire" but to his conscience and that his conscience is richly solaced by the prospect of regarding Hamlet "as ourself in Denmark" (I. ii. 114, 122). That gleaming phrase suggests that the speaker's guilt, already much eased by the court's approval of him, would be definitively eased by the identification of the interests of Hamlet, "Our chiefest courtier," with the interests of "ourself": the prince could thus be regarded, by means of a little moral shuffling, as sharing and alleviating the dire culpability of his would-be other "self," his king-uncle-father. Claudius does not say these things; Shakespeare says them dramatically.

By the same means we perceive in the second act that Claudius's remorse, as well as his concern for his safety, is rearoused by Hamlet's insane aloofness. And when the prince gives a sudden sign of sociability, we see that the king's overemphatic satisfaction has the same grounds here (III. i. 14-27) as at the first (I. ii. 118-128). Presently we are intended to gather from an aside on the part of the king that it is mainly his "conscience" (III. i. 50), though he will not say so, which makes him reluctant to banish Hamlet. At the beginning he showed himself inordinately anxious to prevent the prince's retirement merely to Wittenberg; and now, for the same underlying reason and despite his new sense of danger, he postpones sending him to faraway England. Nor will Claudius confess in the fourth act that he shrinks (like Macbeth) from committing his second murder, as he committed his first, with his own hands. His vicarious and elaborate plotting against Hamlet, while extremely clever, as noted above, stands out otherwise in vivid contrast to the method of his initial crime. We are made to feel that only extreme desperation renders him willing to devise in the climax a poisoned "chalice" (IV. vii. 161) for his nephew, a device intended to strike us as extremely circumstantial in comparison with the "swift" venom (I. v. 66) poured in his brother's ears. We are not too much surprised when the scheme fails and betrays the schemer. With significant irony, Claudius kills Hamlet indirectly by means of the poison on Laertes' sword while Hamlet kills Claudius by a direct and mortal thrust of the same sword. The weapon, and symbol, of underhanded crime is converted into the instrument of open justice—the traditional sword of justice.[7]

The deepest irony is this: Claudius's conscience along with his proud ambition brings about his own ruin. Owing to the conduct of the prince the conscience of the king is forced, notably in the Prayer scene, to face his initial crime. But he will not face it fully; he evades the confronting of its full implications and consequences; and these bear their fruit in the final scene. He would have been a completely successful villain if he had seen betimes and acted upon the dire fact that his secret murder of Hamlet's father demanded as sequel the secret murder of the son. He equivocates with fate. It requires of him either realistic repentance or realistic wickedness; but he declines the choice. He sees that "heaven" (III. iii. 36) has exposed the

---

[7] This point, and a number of others made below, will not seem forced to readers who are familiar with the incessant use of symbolism in Renaissance literature and art. See Professor Samuel C. Chew's *The Virtues Reconciled* (Toronto, 1947).

horridness of his crime. He refuses to see, even while he *feels,* that the same supernal "justice" (line 58) will exact vengeance. My text will show that towards the end he even makes himself feel that heaven condones his conduct. Such is the blindness of his proud self-trust. Because of his pride-and-conscience he never once in the course of the play confesses to himself, much less to others, what nevertheless he betrays clearly to us: the fact that he shrinks desperately from killing the crown prince of Denmark.

Parallel is the case of Hamlet. The main plot-point that emerges in Act I is not merely the prince's delay: it is the delay of king and prince in taking action against each other, each thereby laying up trouble for himself in the future. For the opening scene makes us aware that some or other deadly event is in the offing. The next scene, however, intimates that such an event though destined will not be immediate. The king's postponing of action against the ominously hostile prince in the second scene prepares dramatically for the prince's postponing of action against the murderous king in the fifth scene. Here a crucial passage (I. v. 39 f.), generally misread by critics, as will be shown below, tells us that the crown prince, while eager to destroy the man who has murdered his father, recoils from killing the king of Denmark.[8] Hamlet despises Claudius the man. But that very respect for the kingship which aggravates his horror at the murder of the "royal Dane" (I. iv. 45), his father, makes him hate to do what his uncle has done: assassinate the sovereign of the realm.

Proudly he refuses to see the least jot of worth or ability in Claudius. At the outset the new king skilfully prevents a useless war with Norway while employing the threat of a foreign invasion as a means of uniting his people: he re-establishes and maintains order in Denmark. Shakespeare takes pains that we of the audience, as well as the subservient court, shall admire that achievement. Hamlet, however, ignores it. And if in the opening ensemble Claudius's oily attitude to Hamlet is ominous, so is the absoluteness of Hamlet's condemnation of

---

[8] This idea (like many others in my book) is of course not new; but I think it has hitherto not been stated in its right and full context.

that "satyr" (I. ii. 140), to whom here, as generally throughout the play (significant exceptions will be dealt with in my
text), he refuses the royal title. And this omen is fulfilled
after the Ghost's revelation. For from now on it appears increasingly that Hamlet employs his execration of Claudius the
man to both justify and activate his determination to do the
hateful deed of killing Claudius the king. He doth protest too
much. Commonly in Shakespeare's dramas, as in real life, a
person who proclaims his reasons for doing some feat which he
nevertheless delays, is trying to conceal from himself a strong
motive for *not* doing it. And in the case of a fine person this unveracity may be largely sincere. Hamlet puzzles himself. He
lays bare his paradox: his strange hesitation in destroying the one
whom he totally condemns. Sincerely though untruthfully he
calls himself a "coward" (II. ii. 598). And presently he faces
the truism, "conscience doth make cowards of us all" (III. i.
83); but he evades its application to his own chief task. In the
final scene he admits, fully though indirectly, that the essential
cause of his procrastination has all along been "conscience" (V.
ii. 67). The admission, fatally late, is due to a new humility
learned through hard experience. If he had earlier and humbly
looked into the depths of his "conscience," he would have found
there an instinctive, potent awe of the kingly office. But his
"mind's eye" (I. ii. 185), otherwise so keen, was blinded to that
awe by his proud, personal, revengeful hatred of the new in-
cumbent of that office.

Accordingly Hamlet never considers, deliberately, the difference between personal revengefulness and just vengeance, a
distinction clearly present to the mind of Shakespeare here as
elsewhere, notably in the companion play *Othello*. But the
dramatist with consummate art shows us that his prince's soul,
if not his mind—we would say his subconscious if not his conscious mind—is aware of that vital antithesis. At the first Hamlet's attitude to Claudius is largely, not entirely, revengeful;
at the last largely, though not entirely, impartial and just. In
between we see him proceeding, painfully and with gross lapses,
from the wrong towards the right mood.

His doubt in Act II of the Ghost's message is human and

normal; but readers are right in feeling that it is also an excuse for delay. While Claudius in the first half of the drama delays action against Hamlet, ostensibly on politic grounds but more deeply because of hidden remorse, Hamlet delays action against Claudius, ostensibly because of inadequate evidence, fundamentally because of the hidden protest of his conscience. He shrinks from killing a king, guilty or not, in a mood of personal revenge. But when Claudius has been proved guilty beyond doubt, a dreadful outbreak of that revengeful mood (III. iii. 73 ff.)—dreadful and blind just because Hamlet has not previously faced the moral question involved—results in his blind murder of Polonius. Repenting, he leaves revengefulness behind him, in the main, and seeks just vengeance as heaven's "scourge and minister" (III. iv. 175). At the same time Claudius undergoes an opposite conversion, from hesitant remorsefulness to utterly selfish villainy.

In neither case is the conversion quite complete until the end. Only when Claudius offers Hamlet "the cup" (V. ii. 294) —with a desperateness of resolution beneath his smooth manner which only a very gifted actor can convey—does he finally set himself to do what all along he has tried by every possible subterfuge to avoid: to murder with his own poison the son of the similarly murdered father.[9] Hamlet's situation is parallel. In the course of the fourth act he becomes, I believe, just as *virtually* ready to kill Claudius with sword-in-hand as Claudius becomes to kill him with poison-in-hand. Yet we are not *absolutely* certain that Hamlet, any more than Claudius, will actually do the deed until he does it. Obviously he does not succeed, despite his near-perfect resolution, in preventing Claudius from doing "further evil" (V. ii. 70): the destruction of the queen, Laertes, and himself ensues. Only when the dying Laertes cries, with biting iteration of the august title, "the king, the king's to blame"—this "king" is the original cause of all

---

[9] In the preceding act Shakespeare prepared for this climax by having Laertes instead of Claudius propose the poisoned sword and provide the poison for it. The king would have hated to do so. His own poisoned cup is a reluctant and desperate afterthought (IV. vii. 149 ff.). As for the mixed emotions appearing in the king's mien when Hamlet refuses the cup—there is a task for a royal actor!

the evil—is Hamlet's soul (as well as his mind) entirely ready for his hateful "work" (line 333) of regicide. Not until now does he *feel* fully right for the doing of it; that is what the dramatist makes the audience feel. The elaborate, black, faltering revengefulness of the Prayer scene has been left far behind; he acts now on the plain motive of righteous vengeance. In the first act Claudius certainly deserves to be killed; but only in the last act does Hamlet deserve to kill him. The king becomes immoral enough for the atrocious crime of murdering his crown prince. The prince becomes moral enough—in the largest sense of the word *moral*—for the high task of executing his king.

Thus the central plot of this drama is the story, not of Hamlet, but of Hamlet-and-Claudius; and its main motives are implicit. They cannot be stated explicitly because it is of the very essence of the story that the two protagonists will not so state them. The motivation is not, as some have asserted, outside the play; it is deeply and clearly, on the whole, involved in the action. It is not clear enough, certainly, from the standpoint of modern rationalism and the naturalistic drama; and indeed I think that at certain junctures it is really defective. In this book, however, I am eschewing criticism, the better to establish the fact that Shakespeare's general design is at once greater and more evident than has been perceived. This drama is a vital unity; but its design is so large that the dramatist-poet had to fulfil it largely by overtone and connotation.

Tacit motives are incessant in the Elizabethan and Shakespearean drama, as in real life.[10] In *Hamlet* they are employed to an extraordinary extent. They appear in the subordinate characters. Rosencrantz and Guildenstern, at the opposite intellectual pole from their prince, dissemble like him a dominant motive. They refuse to confess, even to each other, the courtly ambition, in their case cruel, that causes them to spy upon their friend in the service of the king. And Polonius in II. ii tries to hide his new ambition that his daughter shall marry the prince of the realm.[11] In short, tacit or implied motives per-

---

[10] In another book I shall bring out this sort of motivation in Iago and Othello, the immediate successors of Claudius and Hamlet.

[11] Incidentally we are never directly told but are led to assume that his ambition is presently condoned by Claudius, mainly at the instance of the

vade the whole texture of this drama; so that we are readied, or should be, to find them in the warp and woof of the Hamlet-Claudius story.

That motivation-by-implication invited the modern distorted views of *Hamlet*, though it did not cause them. Their cause, generally speaking, is a certain basic confusion. Poets and critics have read into Hamlet's character their own individualism, Romantic or post-Romantic, while at the same time recognizing the inescapable fact that he is a typical gentleman. But the gentleman and the modern individualist are two different types, each with its own peculiar values and limitations. In actual life the two types may be more or less combined in a single person;[12] but this cannot be the case in a supreme and therefore fundamentally unified work of art. And the tacit attempt of the earlier critics to combine them in Hamlet brought on inevitably the later conviction that his character, or his story, or both, lacked unity in Shakespeare's mind. But that conviction is confined to literary persons. The average reader or spectator of this drama has a persistent sense that, somehow or other, it has a great oneness, a deep and real harmony.

In fact, Hamlet is first and last and always the gentleman. He has individuality but not individualism. His great individuality is that which is proper to a great gentleman, and in the main it is not only great but noble. This adjective is traditionally pertinent to the type. At the close the prince's second worst enemy, Laertes, and his best friend, Horatio, term him "noble Hamlet" and "a noble heart" (V. ii. 340, 370). This indicates Shakespeare's constant criterion for his hero: Hamlet's conduct is at its best noble, at its worst extremely ignoble. But critics have applied to him the criterion of *genius*, in its modern individualistic sense, without perceiving its radical difference from *noble-man*. The latter may, or may not like Horatio, be a nobleman. Always, whether sociable or not, he is by nature social; whereas the modern genius, for good and for ill, is by type nonsocial. From this radical disparity spring many other

---

queen (III. i. 28-43, V. i. 267-269). Here, as frequently in the course of this play, Shakespeare is driven by the sheer bulk of his material to employ an adroit dramatic economy.

[12] Pre-eminently in Emerson—not with entire felicity.

differences. In short, the modern interpretation of *Hamlet*, from Goethe and Coleridge to A. C. Bradley and his successors, is centrally confused. It has had the effect of making over *The Tragedy of Hamlet* into a rambling, alluring, mystery-romance centering in a genteel person who is perforce inhumanly ineffectual because he is trying to be both—and succeeds in being neither—a typical gentleman and a transcendent individualist.

The predominant theme in sixteenth-century literature, whereof *Hamlet* is the consummation, was the so-called Complete Gentleman, particularly as occupant of influential office. The gentleman was the keynote figure in society, no matter how low his station; as sovereign he was the keystone of the whole social structure. His *sine qua non*, whatever his rank, was a certain kindly but firm justness.[13] This was the very essence of the noble nature. It rendered a person "gentle," i.e., gentlemanly, though of course not complete. The utterly complete gentleman was an ideal or criterion, not an actuality. In modern parlance he was the perfectly vital and all-round personality. But today, whereas all-roundness may be conceded to the gentleman, the concept of vitality has been largely expropriated by the genius or individualist. That is one way of stating our modern problem. Our word "gentle," unlike Shakespeare's, connotes softness. The modern gentleman needs to regain vitality. And perhaps a sense of the relevance of *Hamlet* to that need helps to explain its extraordinary fascination for us. This drama is built upon the principle that complete gentility implies complete vitality.

The ideal "complete gentleman," who was constantly in the minds of the moralists and poets, whether explicitly cited or not, was extremely many sided. In Ophelia's apothegm he had the "courtier's, soldier's, scholar's, eye, tongue, sword" (III. i. 159). Her main stress is upon the "scholar," i.e., thinker, with his "noble mind," his "noble and most sovereign reason"

[13] This characterizes, for instance, the simple, unschooled Orlando in contrast with Oliver in the opening scene of *As You Like It*. He is "gentle" and "noble" in character (lines 172 f.), more than by birth. His friend and counterpart is old Adam who, in modern terms, is the gentleman in servitude as his master is the gentleman in rags.

(lines 158, 165); dramatically echoing Hamlet's "noble in reason" (II. ii. 317) in his famous lines on "a man." Hamlet's praise of *man* applies equally and significantly to the *gentleman* in his most vital and lofty aspect. Polonius too has this personage in mind, though not loftily, in his well-known "precepts" for Laertes (I. iii. 58 ff.). He, like his immediate predecessor, Sir Andrew Aguecheek in *Twelfth Night,* imitates the complete gentleman.[14] The old fellow is anxious to display that interest in the "matter" of books (II. ii. 197) and that critical appreciation of poetry and drama (II. ii. 415 ff., 520 ff., III. ii. 105 ff.) which he perceives in Hamlet and recognizes as characteristic of the complete gentleman. This personage's mental, physical, social, and political traits were minutely elaborated in treatise after treatise. His circumference was vast; but his nature was not centrifugal. It revolved upon a religious and moral center.

He was a Christian humanist.[15] To be sure it was obvious, especially with the ancient classics fresh in view, that genuine gentility was by no means limited to the Christian fold. But the gentleman or gentlewoman who would be not only genuine but complete had to be, formally at least, a Christian believer: that was involved in the very idea of completeness. Hence *Hamlet,* unlike *Lear* but like Book I of *The Faerie Queene,* is saturated with Christian tradition and imagery.[16] But it is also saturated, like Book II of that poem, with pagan lore. The complete gentleman had to be conversant with ancient mythology and ethics. He must have the classic virtues: courage, temperance, prudence, and justice; the last founded on the other three but far surpassing them—a virtue at once individual and social, demanding justness in managing one's own desires as prerequisite for justness in dealing with other persons. And

---

[14] The incessant parodies of this figure, notably those by Spenser, Shakespeare, and Jonson, testify to the healthiness of the ideal: its potential absurdities were fully visualized.

[15] A brief and excellent book on that subject is Professor Douglas Bush's *The Renaissance and English Humanism* (Toronto, 1939).

[16] It is well known that Shakespeare, unlike Spenser, shows no aversion to Roman Catholicism, and some Protestant critics have termed *Hamlet* a Catholic drama. One fact is clear: Shakespeare wished his hero to be a completely representative gentleman and therefore richly flavored, at least, with total Christianity.

he must reconcile those ancient virtues with the comparatively new Christian ones, from basic humility on and up. Above all, he had to harmonize pagan justice with Christian charity.

That was an extremely difficult task, as appears, extensively, in *The Faerie Queene*. This vast fragment, issued and acclaimed in the last decade of the sixteenth century when *Hamlet* was forming in Shakespeare's mind, is an allegoric summation of the century's Christian humanism. In his central hero, Prince Arthur, Spenser planned to show forth comprehensively the complete gentleman. In Shakespeare's central hero, that ideal personage is tested by action. Hamlet may be regarded as an extraordinarily terse dramatization of the allegorical Arthur. Consciously or not, the dramatist wished to put the idea of the gentleman-prince, climactically, to the most severe and complete trial that he could conceive for it. Each successive scene contributes its quota to the complex tribulation of the hero; at the same time the various aspects of his complex nature are displayed. *Hamlet* is the unfolding ordeal of an unfolding character. And constantly in the background, as in the Shakespearean drama as a whole and in sixteenth-century literature as a whole, one perceives the question of the interrelation of charity and justice.

The ultimate criterion was charity, or love, that was just and righteous on the one hand, on the other kind and merciful. Such complete charity would characterize, ideally, the complete gentleman. It is at the heart of the "magnificence," the "perfection of all the rest" of the virtues, which Spenser designed to "set forth" in his Arthur.[17] But of course perfect charity is divine, not human; and it is the typical goal of the saint rather than the gentleman, whose differentia is justice. However— to apply here a recent line by Robert Frost—"Nothing can make injustice just but mercy."[18] The gentleman, in the Elizabethan view of him, must venerate complete charity and approximate

---

[17] This comes out clearly in Book I of *The Faerie Queene*, especially if after reading it through one reconsiders the cantos in which Arthur appears. My quotations from Spenser here and later in this paragraph are from his Letter to Raleigh.

[18] From the *Masque of Mercy*. This poem and its companion, the *Masque of Reason*, embody in fresh form the true idea of charity as distinguished from the decadent humanitarian concept of it.

his conduct to it, trying constantly to make his justice more charitable and, thus, more true and vital. His "discipline," in Spenser's words, was both "virtuous and gentle."[19] His treatment of others must be neither hard nor soft but both firm and kind. That is how Hamlet treats, or tries to treat, his mother in the Closet scene (III. iv), where he is at his best. On the other hand his attitude to Claudius in the Prayer scene is a gross and fatal violation of the spirit of firm but merciful justness proper to the gentleman-prince.

It was in the light of the idea of complete gentility that Shakespeare, aided by his predecessors, but also and mainly by his own previous writings,[20] transformed the ancient Hamlet-tale into a great drama. That idea bears upon every character in the play, though chiefly upon the two principals. These two were simple, primitive killers in the ancient story. Shakespeare transmuted them into complex modern gentlemen. Hamlet is the real and potentially complete gentleman as prince; Claudius is the pseudo gentleman as king. That central contrast is reinforced by the association of Hamlet with the limited but very genuine gentleman-scholar Horatio; and by the contrasting of Hamlet with the anti-hero, the king's creature, Laertes. This young man is the merely conventional gentleman, like his parodical understudies, as they may be termed, Rosencrantz, Guildenstern, and Osric. And the difference between Laertes and Hamlet—like that between Hamlet and the militaristic gentleman-prince, Fortinbras—is designed by Shakespeare (many critics to the contrary) to redound entirely, or almost entirely, to Hamlet's advantage. On the other hand the contrast between the prince and his intended princess, Ophelia, redounds to Hamlet's disadvantage. She, unlike her showy brother Laertes and her loquacious father Polonius, has the simple, quiet, religious strength of true gentility. Her strength has been missed by critics who have applied to her a wrong criterion and who, incidentally, have here overlooked Shakespeare's

---

[19] Hamlet's favorite word "honest" is a synonym for "virtuous."

[20] The first half of Shakespeare's work, 1590-1600, may be termed a dramatic study in gentility, as I plan to show elsewhere. An important point is that Prince Hal is an even more significant forerunner of Hamlet than Romeo and Brutus.

fixed custom of sharply differentiating the two chief female characters in each of his plays. Gertrude the queen, of highest rank in the social scale, is the infirm gentlewoman swayed by her desires; Ophelia, the lowly but firm one, swaying hers. She symbolizes the Christian charity, as Horatio the classic justice, which Hamlet needs. His rejection of her in the opening of Act II is the direct sequel of his secretiveness to Horatio in the close of Act I.[21] Her perceptive humility of spirit is the chief foil to the occasional stark blindness of Hamlet's pride.

The dishonest pride of Claudius together with his great ability enables him, despite his crimes, to essay the role of the gentleman as sovereign, wherein he is remarkably supported by the cast. We are made to feel more and more as the play proceeds that he is the natural leader of a social order pervaded with unveracity. This eats at the very roots of justice and nobility. It poisons the "pith and marrow" (I. iv. 22) of true gentility and charity. The king has the superficies of those two virtues: he is genteel and kindly, just the reverse of a ruthless tyrant. So that his gross and cruel selfishness is generally concealed, as intimated above, even from himself. And the poison of dishonesty, so concentrated in him, runs in varying degrees of dilution through the veins of his associates; by infection from him but also because of native predisposition in themselves. Significantly the poison is most thin and innocent in the king's chief initial backer, Polonius; deadliest in his obedient son Laertes, the king's chief aide at the close. The young man's sheerly external notion, encouraged by his father, of what a gentleman should be renders him in the end fatally open to contagion from his genteel-royal master.[22] The virus is entirely absent from Horatio and Ophelia—except in Hamlet's suspicious imagination. But it is not entirely absent from the prince himself.

At the very heart of this drama is the fact that its hero has

[21] To miss this point is to miss the climax of Act I. Here Hamlet disobeys one of the leading precepts set down for the gentleman-prince: he must select the best possible confidants and advisers when confronted with a great problem. Hamlet's refusal to do so would appear to the Elizabethans proudly, immorally, and insanely reckless.

[22] With rich dramatic irony Shakespeare has Claudius praise Laertes to his face as "a good child" of his father "and a true gentleman" (IV. v. 148).

a touch of dishonest pride. So has every man: Hamlet is representative. But unlike most men he is so situated that this taint has catastrophic results: Hamlet is tragic. He is tragically representative of mankind. We are made to feel that we in similar circumstances would conduct ourselves in much the same way as he, probably worse. He becomes infected with the prevalent dissimulation which he so sharply condemns. His infection is due largely to the position forced upon him by the crooked king and court; but inwardly it is due to his pride in his princely mission, a last infirmity of a noble mind. The classic precept "Know thyself"—be honest with yourself—was pre-essential for the gentleman-prince of the time as it is, surely, for all persons in positions of authority in all times. On his first appearance Hamlet is outstandingly free from seeming (I. ii. 76 ff.), but he is somewhat proud of that fact. And his pride, though entirely natural here and not in the least ignoble, comes before a fall. For the task the Ghost lays upon him is precisely one which demands of him the utmost humble clearness in scrutiny, scrutiny of the task and of himself in relation to it. And such scrutiny is obviated by his pride. Instinctively, as a gentleman, particularly as a gentleman in the position of crown prince, he shrinks from slaying the sovereign ruler of the realm no matter how guilty. But he will not confront that instinct, humbly and clearly.

That instinct is lacking, for good and for ill, in the modern individualist. As revolutionary he has killed many kings and other rulers with approval of his conscience. As Romantic critic, obtuse to the conscience of the gentleman, he has assumed that it was Hamlet's duty to kill Claudius at once. But this play embodies and appeals to the perennial spirit of gentility; the same in all ages beneath its shifting forms, and present to every normal human being: indeed it constitutes normal humanity. Act I, considered in that spirit, means that Hamlet's duty, dimly felt by him, clearly seen by Shakespeare and the audience, is precisely NOT to kill the king at once. We see that Claudius's present frame of mind, whatever his past crimes and present defects, cannot be termed that of an evil ruler; and we see that Hamlet's present frame of mind is not one in which this king should be destroyed by his designated successor. And we see that the prince is not confronting that situation. He is prevented from doing so by his very frame of mind—his confused passionateness, after the Ghost's revelation, capped by his proud sense of mission. But his unconfronted conscience, his deep moral instinct, makes him delay action. Consequently he who at the outset condemned all seeming is driven at the close of Act I to motivate his delay by dissimulation.

His simulated madness is the outward form of his inward dissimulation, his proud refusal to face his innate horror of the regicide he has undertaken. We watch with utmost fascination his continual efforts to hide that horror from himself. We note his oscillation, characteristic of wrong pride, between overweening confidence and blind self-blame. At the same time we admire the thing of which he himself is so charmingly unaware, his fundamental greatness—the unawareness is of the essence of the greatness. We see what Hamlet does not see: his profound though imperfect humanity is the ultimate cause of his delay. His exceedingly articulate hate of the man Claudius is vividly opposed to his inarticulate but all the more powerful reverence for that man's office, the royal headship of the state. Hamlet is very far from being a case of weak will and too abundant intellect. That view of him, psychologically false, is also flatly undramatic; it does not account for his theatric appeal. His main inward contrast is the very human and dramatic discrepancy between his surface activity, in emotion, thought, word, deed, and his underlying soundness and largeness of character. The dramatist with wonderful art enables us to see through Hamlet in spite of Hamlet, that is, with Hamlet's brilliant unconscious co-operation. We watch him growing, though with dire setbacks, in "virtuous and gentle discipline." This discipline prevents him—and our better nature is glad thereof—from killing the Claudius whom he hates until he can execute the head of the realm, not only with complete outward justification, but in the spirit of inward justness. His tragedy is, not that he postpones the deed, but that the ripening of his justice is delayed too much by his pride.

The tragic theme pervades, as my text tries to show, the

drama's whole atmosphere. This has two opposed strains, cosmic grandeur and insidious disease. The latter relates to dishonesty and obscurant pride. The former conveys the supernal spirit of justice, austere but essentially charitable, that broods so to speak upon the human community, inspiring awe and calling for humility, actuating Hamlet in his best moments. In the opening scene that spirit hovers dimly; in the last scene it descends and works definitively, disposing of the community. The "majestical" poetry of divine dayspring in which the first scene culminates (I. i. 143 ff.) finds, in the last scene, a human fulfilment in Hamlet's noble speech to Laertes (V. ii. 237 ff.). This speech is like a "trumpet to the morn" (I. i. 150), to the dawn of a better day on earth. Here Hamlet has the "station" of a "herald Mercury" (III. iv. 58). Tainted by cankerous dust, by "foul and pestilent vapors," he is also divinely infected: he breathes the cosmic "air" that overhangs this drama—a "most excellent canopy" (II. ii. 311 ff.).

Shakespeare has here written the perpetual tragedy of man in society. To be sure all his major tragedies are that; and in each case the catastrophe is centrally due to the hero's pride. But none of his other heroes has Hamlet's potential completeness as leader or ruler; and in none is the temptation to pride so natural and subtle, so closely implicated with great social powers. Hamlet is an intensely social person; essentially an extrovert; normally cheerful and temperate; at his best socially right, at his worst socially wrong. His critique of society, so far from being individualistic, is, like Shakespeare's, thoroughly social in its standpoint and motives.[23] His devotion to the commonweal, too intrinsic to be orally flaunted, is thrown by the dramatist into strong contrast with the loquacious zeal of others—Claudius, Polonius, Laertes, Rosencrantz and Guildenstern (III. iii. 8-23)—for what we would call "public service." At the outset Laertes talks finely upon that "sanctity and health of the whole state" (I. iii. 21) which, in the end, he does very

---

[23] For Shakespeare's political outlook, see John Palmer's excellent *Political Characters of Shakespeare* (London, 1948). Incidentally Mr. Palmer deals well with Shakespeare's use of assumptions—of facts and principles so obviously true that he does not explicitly state them. This connects with the motivation-by-implication that I have treated above.

much to ruin. Hamlet does not talk that way. Instead there is the agonized curtness of his resolve to "set it right" (I. v. 189 f.). In the end he ministers to the state by destroying its corrupters, including Laertes, and by establishing a nobler conception of its "health." His profound and therefore mainly tacit love of the state is the source of his acid loathing of its corruptions, and also of his reverence for its highest office, the sovereignty.

He is confronted with an extremely difficult *social problem.* It demands the employment of all his great abilities *in the right spirit.* This requires right relations with his associates; and here his pride makes him falter. Claudius employs his associates far more swiftly and surely. That is the chief practical way in which evil works in society more effectively than good. The able, evil leader, appealing to temporal and selfish interests, constructs a quick and for the time being a solid front. The good leader, good in the main but imperfect, has the harder task of activating the deeper instincts of humanity, in others and also in himself. He is in the main "honest," but also more or less "ambitious," sometimes "revengeful," always apt to be "proud" (III. i. 123-127): his very honesty and righteousness betray him unawares to pride. While he is mastering painfully his large and difficult social function, the evil leader (e.g., Hitler) learns his limited one with ruinous efficiency.

In short *The Tragedy of Hamlet, Prince of Denmark,* is uniquely representative and suggestive. It is *the* tragedy of civilization, of social man: of man destined to be a many-sided yet symmetrical and therefore purposeful creature; dimly pursuing, clearly pursued by, the divine Charity wherein justice seasoned with mercy is perfect; finding by hard experience the "good thing to be done" (I. i. 130) and the thing that "cannot come to good" (I. ii. 158); discovering through disaster and regeneration, though never fully in this world, the "heart" of his own "mystery."

NOTE ON THE TEXT

The First Quarto (Q1) of *Hamlet*, 1603, is a pirated and garbled version of Shakespeare's hasty revision in the later 1590's of an old play, a popular melodrama of the late 1580's. Our modern texts are derived from the Second Quarto (Q2), 1604, and the First Folio (F1), 1623. Q2 is an issue, very probably authorized by Shakespeare, of a radical revision of the old play—rather, a transmutation of it—completed by him about the year 1601. The manuscript of the new drama was too long for the Elizabethan stage. It was immediately cut for acting purposes. The stage version was the basis of the text of *Hamlet* printed in F1, the first collected edition of the poet's works, published seven years after his death. This text omits more than two hundred lines given in Q2, notably in Hamlet's longer speeches; but it contains some eighty-five lines not previously printed. More importantly, F1 has many brief but often very meaningful variations from Q2.

The question of the true text is complicated by the errors (especially in Q2) and the peculiarities of the Elizabethan printers. My own studies have served to confirm the belief, recently questioned by Dover Wilson and others, that the F1 version has paramount authority. It embodies, I am convinced, alterations made by Shakespeare himself towards heightened style and more penetrating conception. If he had lived to prepare for his readers a full and definitive text of the drama, he would surely have re-incorporated, with more or less revision, the passages given exclusively in Q2. These, therefore, are to be read in the light of the F1 text.

That view of the text has influenced my interpretation of *Hamlet* at a number of points, only a few of which could be given specific attention in the footnotes. References in the notes are generally, not always, to the F1 version unless otherwise stated. Concurrence of the later quartos with Q2 and of the later folios with F1, as noted in the Furness Variorum Edition, is indicated below by the terms "quartos" and "folios" respectively. Occasionally I have cited Q1, which, though never authoritative, is often very suggestive. In quotations from the play—usually but not always from F1—I have of course modernized the punctuation as well as the spelling, except in some cases where the original seemed to me peculiarly significant. Several times I have inserted a dash—rarely used in Elizabethan printing—where I thought the sense demanded it.

SCOURGE
AND MINISTER

Born to Set it Right

(a) *heaven and earth*   I. i

"Who's there?" These sharp
opening words of the play are presently repeated (14).* Meanwhile two other questions have been asked (4, 9). And further queries occur thick and fast as the dialogue proceeds.
Gradually, however, the rapid lines give way to longer
speeches; the scene slackens in tempo and deepens in meaning.
The inquiries become more and more significant. Eventually
they merge into a single large problem: what "good thing"
should be "done" (130)? This problem, this question, runs
throughout the whole drama.

Considered as a whole *The Tragedy of Hamlet, Prince of
Denmark*, is at once the tragedy of a prince and of his kingdom;
the two are indivisible. The underlying theme of the story is
divine justice working itself out, imperfectly but awfully, in
one small nation that is typical of human society at large.
Shakespeare's Denmark is an image of the mighty world; and
the image is extraordinarily full because it comprises, not only
the individual person and mundane society, but also the seen
and the unseen realms. We are shown "our known world"
(85) environed by the "undiscovered country from whose
bourn No traveller returns" (III. i. 79).* No actual human
person can return thence; but spirits, human or inhuman, may
come; and certainly messages, true or misleading, do come.
For the "undiscovered country," the realm of spirits, is the
realm too of intuitions and impalpable influences. It is very
close to us throughout the whole poem; yet it is strictly marked

---

* Throughout this book arabic numerals in parentheses refer to lines in
the scene under discussion. When a different scene is referred to, roman
numerals for act and scene are always given.

off from the life of flesh and blood—marked off at the very
first by "bitter cold" (8) and dread (25). It is an ambiguous
region between "heaven" and "earth" (124): the earth of common sense, the heaven of perfect charity and justice. The undiscovered country contains preternatural good and preternatural evil.

Shakespeare, while making use of the multifarious beliefs of
his time regarding the unseen world, succeeds in expressing con-
victions that spring eternal in the human breast. People in
general instinctively believe that souls are immortal; that their
concern for the earth whereon they were shaped as human
beings does not cease beyond the grave; that their sphere, like
our world but more so, is a purgatorial region of development
with hellish depths and heavenly reaches; and therefore that
all intimations coming to us *from beyond*, as we say, need to
be carefully tested. We need to question critically each mystic
messenger or message. The spirits and also our own glimpses
into the unseen have to be tried in the gradual light of human
experience and human responsibility. The spiritual world is
for us dim and questionable.

Accordingly the light of the opening scene of this drama
is, at the first, the fitful rays of lanterns in human hands and,
at the end, a faint dawn. The place, in Shakespeare's imagination, is the narrow platform of the watch high up on the battlements of a royal castle with shadowy turrets around.[1] And the
questioning mood, as indicated in the first paragraph above, is
dominant. In the opening lines, while a bell far within is
tolling twelve faintly, we are startled by an oncomer challenging, irregularly and nervously, a sentry on his beat:

BERNARDO Who's there?
FRANCISCO Nay, answer me: stand and unfold yourself.

Presently we wonder why Francisco, "honest soldier" (16), is
"sick at heart" (9) on so quiet a night, "Not a mouse stirring"

[1] The usual stage-direction at the head of this scene, "*A platform before
the castle*," originated by eighteenth-century editors, is not in keeping with
the atmosphere of scenes i, iv, and v as conceived by Shakespeare. The question of Elizabethan stage usage, which did not and could not conform fully
to the dramatist's imagination, is not involved.

(10). Moving off quickly while Bernardo gives him a slow
and reluctant "good night," he pauses at the muffled sound of
feet that may be, or may not be, the feet of expected friends
approaching in haste: "I think I hear them—Stand! who's
there?" Relieved in a double sense, Francisco passes entirely
out of the drama, uttering a repeated (16, 18) and meaningful
"Give you good night."

With the coming of Horatio and Marcellus interrogation
intensifies. "Who hath relieved you?" . . . "What, is Horatio
there?" . . . "What, has this thing appeared again tonight?"
Bernardo is pointing to one nameless star above (36), and below
in the castle the bell is beating one—the very star and bell of
the previous visitation, emblemizing heaven and earth—when
the "dreaded sight" comes again. "Looks it not like the king?
(43) . . . Question it, Horatio (45)." Now, however, the
rhythm of the questioning rises to the stately movement of the
armored phantom:

> What art thou that usurpst this time of night
> Together with that fair and warlike form
> In which the majesty of buried Denmark
> Did sometimes march? By heaven I charge thee, speak!

The Ghost is a symbol—necessarily an imperfect symbol, in
contrast with "heaven"—of summoning justice; noble in its
way, but limited and dubious. Its "form" requires this doubtful "time of night"; its stalk and frown (50, 62) denote human
frailty; it is reminiscent of the might and passion that belong
with human trials of right (61-63). It rouses "fear and wonder" (44), not the *awe* that attends supreme right; and like
those feelings of fear and wonder it is transient; it passes away
now. The abiding question is "What think you on't?" (55).

But that theoretic question cannot be answered apart from
the practical problem, mentioned in the opening paragraph,
which Horatio urges upon the Ghost when it reappears (130):

> If there be any good thing to be done,
> That may to thee do ease, and grace to me . . .

The quality of spirits, whether in or out of the flesh, as intimated by Horatio's emphatic "thee" and "me," may be surely

known only by issuant deeds, by the actions which these spirits perform or inspire.[2]   And the question from now on to the very end of the play is as to the "good thing to be done."   Sometimes the question is explicit; more often it is implied.   Here it is very explicit; and Shakespeare gives it prominence by placing it between two significant dialogues, the first concerning "our state" (67-125), the second regarding "the god of day" (142-175).

(1) The Danish state is a very organic society.   At the outset it is shown confronting that particular kind of crisis which, more than any other, produces a display of national unity: the threatened aggression of a foreign power.   The kingdom is preparing speedily and thoroughly for war.   The speakers in the scene are "Friends to this ground" and "liegemen to the Dane" (15); they are taking part in a watch that is "strict and most observant" (71).   The nation, made up of many ranks (72-78), has in its foreground the soldier and the scholar, representing opposite poles of society.   The function of Horatio here is to render, not merely the appearance of the Ghost, but also the unity of "our state" convincing and vivid.   Such is the import of his long speech upon the violent injustice towards Denmark of the present procedure of "young Fortinbras" of Norway.   Horatio, the patriotic scholar, can meet ordinary citizens such as the blunt soldier Bernardo upon the ground, important for national solidarity, of plain rights and obvious causes.

All the more striking then is Horatio's persistent feeling that such causes, no matter how real and pressing, cannot fully account for the Ghost.   It "bodes some strange eruption to our state" (69).   Later, "A moth it is to trouble the mind's eye" (112).[3]   That brooding line opens a passage wherein the scholar, moved by the "prophetic soul" (I. v. 40) characteristic

---

[2] This idea is recurrent and basic in the Shakespearean drama.   Cf. *Measure for Measure* I. i. 35: "Spirits are not finely touched But [i.e., unless] to fine issues. . . ."

[3] The stress in this line is upon the almost dissyllabic word "mind's" ("mindes" in the original).   The "moth," which may mean also "mote," implies elusiveness, not triviality.   It denotes a phenomenon difficult to locate and envisage, filmy and spectral, like the "motes and shadows" in *Pericles* IV. iv. 21.

of this drama, perceives dimly a relation between the "mightiest Julius" and the late king of Denmark, unaware that the latter too, though differently, suffered a foul ending which will prove to be the beginning of tragic troubles, the "precurse of fierce events" (121). The speaker is sure only that "heaven and earth" (124) have in some sort "demonstrated." They will continue to demonstrate throughout the poem. Again and again the author will make us feel the presence of the heaven above and the earth beneath, commenting with "secret influence" (Sonnet 15) upon the dramatic action: heaven with its night and day, stars and sun, gods and God, grace and justice; earth with its stolidity and passion, evil and lovely growths, sickness and health, hells and purgations. The story has a cosmic background, a living frame of earth and heaven.[4] The present brooding passage (112-125) in its imagery and rhythm sways between heaven and earth in the region of spectral intimation. Interrupted, and intensified in its meaning, by the second entrance of the Ghost and Horatio's questions as to what should be done, this speech leads us on and over from the plain common sense of the preceding dialogue towards the superb mythic poetry of the final episode of the scene, centering in "the god of day."

(2) In the final episode the majesty of the Ghost is again emphasized; but also, and more than before, we are made to feel its imperfection and evanescence. It is airlike (145), and "it started like a guilty thing Upon a fearful summons" when it heard "the trumpet to the morn" (148-150). "It faded" (157). Its kind of nobility concedes to—is dissolved by these celestial verses into—the nobility of the coming "god of day." And this god is related to the Christian dayspring from on high:

> Some say that ever 'gainst that season comes
> Wherein our Saviour's birth is celebrated,

[4] The old Scandinavian story of Amlothi (Hamlet) is mythological; and Shakespeare seems instinctively to retain something of the ancient mythic theme of man's divine parents, Heaven and Earth. In this connection Gilbert Murray's *The Classical Tradition in Poetry*, chap. viii, is suggestive. However, the important point is that in *Hamlet*, as in its predecessors *Romeo and Juliet* and *Julius Caesar*, the poet's imagination has cosmic reaches, and that in *Hamlet* he develops particularly the motif of "heaven and earth."

> The bird of dawning singeth all night long:
> And then, they say, no spirit can walk abroad,
> The nights are wholesome, then no planets strike,
> No fairy takes, nor witch hath power to charm;
> So hallowed and so gracious is the time.

And now from the high battlements is seen the faint red of dawn touching the moist, pale foliage of a lofty hill, one of those heights that later in the poem will occasionally rise at the rim of the scene in the mind's eye:

> But look, the morn in russet mantle clad
> Walks o'er the dew of yon high eastern hill.

These light feet, now, instead of the dark footsteps heard at the beginning of the scene! This walk, far beyond the Ghost's walk, mystic yet firm! That presence in the eastern heaven, faint at first but ever clearer![5] The demanding purity of heaven above—the earth beneath troubled with "fierce events" and doubtful omens! The urgent question is "If there be any good thing to be done."

Clear as dawn is now the first thing to be done: all that has occurred must be imparted to "young Hamlet . . . as needful in our loves, fitting our duty" (170-173). The thought of him, thus linked to love and duty, comes with the suddenness of inspiration in response to the questioning mood of the whole opening scene together with its vision of heaven and earth. "Young Hamlet" is ushered in by "this morning" (174), and he will partake of the god of day's nobility and truth. But as the clear beauty of this day was preceded by an ominous night, so Hamlet, when the scene opens down from the high battlements of the castle to the royal council-room below, is preceded by Claudius.

[5] The sense of "that presence" will be strong in readers who, like Shakespeare himself, have in mind Aurora or Eos, goddess of the dawn, together with the Christ-god of Light and the sun-god Apollo or Hyperion, banishing wandering spirits (154, 161) and other creatures of the night. Thus the "presence," at once pagan and Christian, is composite and inclusive: it is cosmically representative.

(b) *things rank and gross*   I. ii. 1—159

Claudius is a seductive thing of night: dark and ugly, fleshy and ill-shaped, but wonderfully clever and affable, with a charming smile—in a word, bewitching.[6] The present episode shows fully the "witchcraft of his wit" (I. v. 43). His opening oration is smooth and balanced, "In equal scale weighing delight and dole" (13), studiously dignified, but utterly devoid of true majesty. It violates while seeming to cherish the image of the departed king.

> We do it wrong, being so majestical,
> To offer it the show of violence . . . (I. i. 143)

That royal movement of style and manner has now given place to this:

> Though yet of Hamlet our dear brother's death
> The memory be green, and that it us befitted . . .

In those opening verses and throughout this scene the new king subtly makes the old king remote; the latter's nobility is now indeed a ghost. Still more remote is the "hallowed" and "gracious" time that hovered at the close of the preceding scene. The present time belongs to Claudius: he hath "power to charm" (I. i. 163).

He has maintained the unity of "Our state" (20) while lowering its tone grossly. Though legalized, he is a usurper, spiritually and politically. The preceding scene made us expect that the dead monarch, old Hamlet, would be succeeded, in accordance with custom and in response to the call of the whole situation, by "young Hamlet"; there was no mention of Claudius. So that when he comes on, crowned, we are taken by surprise:

[6] Claudius is not in the least stodgy, as too often he appears on the stage. I think Shakespeare has in mind the figure of his earlier Richard III, though with actual deformity omitted, sensuality added, and subtlety much deepened. In the opening scene not only was Claudius unmentioned—deliberately ignored, as it now seems, by Horatio and his companions—but we were allowed to assume, if we would, that "young Fortinbras" had succeeded his father of the same name on the throne of Norway and that the case of "young Hamlet" in Denmark would be parallel. Not until Hamlet's uncle is shown in the present scene as king of Denmark are we told that the present king of Norway is Fortinbras's uncle (28).

the play's initial questions recur, "Who's there? . . . What art thou?" Gradually we gather that Claudius got possession of the throne with full show of correctness and expediency by taking shrewd advantage of every element in the situation created by Fortinbras's threat of war upon the death of the warlike king, while young Hamlet was still a student at Wittenberg. Claudius secured the "election," as it is termed later, i.e., the votes of Polonius and the other councilors; staved off diplomatically the demands of Fortinbras; married his brother's queen, "Th' imperial jointress of this warlike state" (9); and, above all, proclaimed Hamlet his adopted son and heir, sole and immediate successor to the throne. Thus all possible factions are appeased. "Our state," which "by our late dear brother's death" appeared to be "disjoint and out of frame" (20), is united—but upon an ominously low level.

The chief omen now, succeeding the portents of scene i, succeeding in particular the Ghost's frown, is Claudius's smile. The warlike state with its rude justice has given way to the regime of a specious affability that nullifies the first requisite of justice, honesty. The new king can "smile and smile" (I. v. 108). After a decorous struggle with a "brow of woe" (4) his smile shines gratefully upon the whole court (16); then tightens to a satiric gleam for the naïve "young Fortinbras," who held "a weak supposal of our worth" and "hath not failed to pester us. . . . So much for him. Now for ourself" (26). The smile sobers into easeful triumph. The new king performs his first act of state, the sending to Norway of a peaceful mission which, we anticipate, will be successful. Thus the martial preparations of Denmark in scene i, here not even alluded to, appear in retrospect a feature of adroit policy. The Danish nation is now assured of that which any nation can so easily love above all else, peace with pleasure. Symbol of that new situation is Laertes, fashionably attired and eager to return to France. His name is caressed with iterative Lydian sweetness by the tongue of Claudius while the royal smile plays fulsomely upon the loyal young gentleman and upon his basking father, whose instrumentality in the enthroning of Claudius is alluded to with flattery (47-49).

"But now" (64)—instead of the "And now" (42) that introduced Laertes—the king concenters upon his heir the kindliness that, in Hamlet's view, is "less than kind" (65), is hatefully insincere.[7] We, however, perceive that the smooth benevolence of Claudius for Hamlet has in it a genuine touch (to be discussed later) which helps him to keep the upper hand in the ensuing verbal contest with the hostile crown prince; a contest for position, political and moral, in the eyes of the court and, by implication, of the whole realm. Claudius wins that contest but, in our eyes, loses a greater one. He is displayed by Shakespeare's consummate skill as the merely genteel gentleman over against the real gentleman, Hamlet. Claudius, in spite of his strain of good will, is on the whole insincere and selfish. Hamlet, in spite of a touch of egotistic histrionicism, is on the whole veracious and unselfish. The one is the politician who, successful for the time being, degrades the nation fatefully; the other, the true statesman who looks into moral and social reality. By the end of scene ii Hamlet stands revealed as potentially the sovereign who, naturally succeeding but surpassing his father, would have raised the "warlike state" to a higher level of national life.

Thus Hamlet and Claudius are indeed "mighty opposites" (V. ii. 62), two perennial types that largely determine the course of political society. And now Shakespeare brings out the universality of his theme by recurring to the motif begun in scene i of "heaven and earth." The ensuing speeches give a series of cosmic images ranging from sun and clouds to dust and earth. Claudius asks why "the clouds still hang on" Hamlet, who replies ironically that he is "too much i' th' sun." His mother, after entreating him with soft impatience to cast off his "nighted colour" and lift his eyes from "the dust," refers in lines of languid, mournful charm to the unseen world (72):

---

[7] "A little more than kin and less than kind" alludes of course to Claudius's relationship to Hamlet, but mainly it stigmatizes, as the whole context shows, his unveracity. The noun "kind" means, or at least connotes, nature in the sense of *the truth of nature* as in III. ii. 23. Claudius, a hateful uncle who has secured Hamlet's throne, is now showering him for reasons of policy with sunshiny favor (67): the situation is unnatural, unreal, false; so is Claudius. Thus Hamlet's first and keynote line in the play points at the dishonesty and injustice which he is to attack throughout.

> Thou knowst 'tis common, all that lives must die,
> Passing through Nature, to Eternity.

But her son summons the winds and rivers of the natural world
to rebuke her sighs and tears of unreal grief (79-80). Thereupon the king, expanding the queen's religious allusion with
elaborate unction, overcrows Hamlet with "heaven" and "nature" and "earth" (95-107). In the climax he declares that
the prince's apparent submission, his consenting to remain at
Elsinore,

> Sits smiling to my heart; in grace whereof
> No jocund health that Denmark drinks today
> But the great cannon to the clouds shall tell,
> And the king's rouse the heavens shall bruit again,
> Respeaking earthly thunder.

Against the background of that cloudy cosmic showiness
comes the lightning thrust of Hamlet's great soliloquy, passionately sincere and *active*. Its opening verses, designed in
vivid contrast with the slow rhetoric of the lines of Claudius
above, come forth, after a little silence, with a rush:

> Oh that this too too solid flesh would melt,
> Thaw and resolve itself into a dew,
> Or that the Everlasting had not fixed
> His canon 'gainst self-slaughter. O God! O God!

The Eternal, previously cited with public glibness by the king
and queen, is real and commanding to this young man alone,
now, in its presence. For a passing moment he yearns that the
grossly solid flesh which he wears in common with all those who
have just left him (the word "this" is accompanied, I think,
by an inclusive gesture) could be escaped by him or transmuted
into a pure "dew"—recalling for us the "dew" of the eastern
hill this morning (I. i. 167).[8] But divine law[9] has fixed him

---

[8] Instead of "solid" the quartos have "sallied," which as Dover Wilson
argues may well be a misprint for "sullied." But if this was Shakespeare's
original word he later changed it, I think, to "solid" for the sake of the cosmic suggestion described in my text, and because the sullied or polluted condition of the "flesh" is sufficiently implied by the whole context. Hamlet is
thinking not just of his own body but of the fleshly life common to him and
the others, particularly his mother. The word "dew," in the present passage,
is of course not literal; it means a dewlike, spiritual essence.

[9] The Everlasting's "canon," spelled "cannon" in Q2 and F1, plays upon

in this society to which he belongs and for whose welfare he is deeply concerned. Hence his rejection, above, of a romantic wish to get away again to Wittenberg. Hence the tragic vividness with which he sees "this world" of Denmark as an "unweeded garden" (135) overrun by gross growths coming to seed and, by implication, to tragic fruitage later, dominated by a grinning "satyr" instead of the former "Hyperion" (140), an unnatural region under "the winds of heaven," between "Heaven and earth" (142).

Hamlet's mind (like Shakespeare's) is at once poetic and morally realistic—prudent, in the Elizabethan ethical sense of the term. Accordingly he seizes upon and holds in the foreground a single, concrete, dark fact: the unnatural haste of the queen's second marriage. This, exactly, is the irreducible minimum of the whole bad situation. Political expediency could justify the union itself but not the "little month" (145-153) between the funeral of the late king and the wedding. The indecency of this haste stands in ironic contrast with the piety of Claudius in rebuking Hamlet as "incorrect to heaven" (95). Whatever may be correct, the haste of this wedding is not: "O heaven, a beast that wants discourse of reason Would have mourned *longer*" (150). This dark fact is aggravated for Hamlet by his natural love for his mother, her apparent love and grief for his father, the flagrant inferiority of her new husband, the incestuous nature of the union from the Catholic standpoint, and, above all, the fact that she as queen represents Denmark. His chief thought, stressed at the beginning and at the end of the soliloquy, is the degradation of the kingdom. It is now enslaved by what he will later call "damned custom" (III. iv. 37). Its uses, its ways and habits, are "weary, stale, flat, and unprofitable" (133): it has lost true social vitality. And all of its "rank and gross" condition is summarized and symbolized by the "dexterity" (157)—a wonderfully well-chosen word—of this marriage:

> It is not, nor it cannot come to, good.
> But break, my heart, for I must hold my tongue.

Claudius's "cannon" above, in the Elizabethan fashion of tragic punning, thus linking the two speeches closely. Hamlet is satirizing the cosmic showiness of his uncle's speech.

The heartbreaking fact is that there is nothing he can say, much less do, to remedy the situation. When he publicly rebuked the new regime on its most vulnerable score, its slight mourning for the great dead king, no one made the faintest gesture of assent. His dramatic citation of the "customary suits of solemn black" (78) laid aside by the court so soon, in gross defiance of good custom, fell on deaf ears. (On the stage that speech should be followed by a dramatic silence in which Hamlet and Claudius glance about the court, the latter with rising complacency.) It merely gave occasion for the final triumph of Claudius in his superbly politic oration (87-117) making Hamlet out to be overswayed, at present, by unworthy emotion, "obstinate condolement" (93)—capable, however, of fitting himself for his future kingship if only he will accept the realities of "the world" (108). To that speech Hamlet made no reply. The reason is fully apparent by the close of his soliloquy: there is nothing further he can say that can "come to good." Any further adjurations on his part would appear to "this world" (134)—the phrase satirically echoes that of Claudius above—merely further ebullitions of a "sweet" (87) but weak idealism, together with a sullen disappointment, hiding itself under grief for his father, at not obtaining his father's throne (106 ff.). Such is the specious character put upon Hamlet by the bewitching satyr Claudius and fully accepted by the court. It forces the prince to hold his tongue.

And there is nothing he can do. He is no "Hercules" (153), no demigod able to cleanse an Augean kingdom with miraculous power. And he is no revolutionist. His very metaphors show his conviction that society is an organic growth, like a "garden" (135), to be weeded and fostered by honesty and good custom, not uprooted. Never in the whole course of the play does he question the *legal* right of the council to choose Claudius for king instead of himself. Later on, because he is very human, he will emit flashes of personal resentment against that deed; but, because nobly human, he does not do so here. His first and chief thought in his first soliloquy—demonstrating the dishonesty of all the insinuations of Claudius to the contrary—is not for himself. Obviously he has a personal hatred

of the new king; his every glance was unfriendly to Claudius
(69). But in his soliloquy we find, with surprised admiration,
not a single touch of disappointed personal ambition: his hostility to the new king here is entirely on behalf of the queen and
the realm. However, he has neither the wish nor the opportunity to unseat by force this sovereign who, not criminal in
any eye except Hamlet's, has responded so successfully to what
this nation deems its present needs. Claudius is an organic,
though evilly organic, outgrowth of this human "garden."
Hamlet, tacitly accepting his own legal position of crown prince
under the new monarch, knows that until he himself is king he
can do nothing effectual, but that in the meanwhile his kingdom
is bound to grow increasingly "rank and gross."

(c) *my revenge*   I. ii. 160—I. v. 31

That desperate situation prepares the way for a desperate
undertaking on the part of Hamlet. So far, along with his
passionate sincerity, he has maintained the prudence of a prince
and gentleman devoted to the commonweal: whatever others
do he wills to do nothing that "cannot come to good." That
very prudence was claimed by Claudius for himself. His every
word and gesture were designed to show that he had it, in contrast to his nephew, to whom he denied it in accusing him of
"impious stubbornness . . . unmanly grief . . . a will most incorrect to heaven, A heart unfortified, a mind impatient, An
understanding simple and unschooled" (94-97). The whole
picture is false. But two of the features, so nicely woven in as
to lend color to the whole, have some truth in them, namely
the "heart unfortified" and the "mind impatient." Considering
his weight of troubles Hamlet has shown a remarkable degree
of patience and fortitude; for though young he possesses precisely that which Claudius was most anxious to deny him, an
understanding schooled and wise. By means of this understanding Hamlet normally reins in his temperament, which,
however, is proud, emotional, and impatient when allowed the
upper hand. And we are made to feel that a further and more
fearful blow of fate, foreshadowed by scene i, may breach his

princely prudence: his mind and heart *may* become, for the time being, "impatient" and "unfortified."

I. ii. 160-258

For that crisis Horatio innocently prepares the way now. He is welcomed with pathetic eagerness by his lonely prince. A college companionship is ripened quickly into friendship by Hamlet's need and Horatio's truth. The newcomer, pressed by the other's shrewd inquiries, makes gradually and fully evident that, as suggested in scene i, he is not a favorer of the new king. He did not come to Elsinore to see the royal "wedding" (178) nor, obviously, to show his "duty" (53) like Laertes at the coronation. But it is not his part as a humble, loyal subject of the realm to criticize the anointed sovereign in the presence of the crown prince. Horatio has the true blend, greatly admired by Hamlet, of decorum and honesty. Unlike all the courtiers, he assents to the prince's condemnation of the indecent haste of the marriage (179). But he refuses to speak either indecorously against the new regime or politely and insincerely in appreciation of it, though Hamlet lures him by declaring pointedly, with satiric use of the royal plural, "We'll teach you to drink deep ere you depart." Ignoring that matter, Horatio rejoins simply, "My lord, I came to see your father's funeral" (176).

Hamlet is pierced by the words "see" and "father." Dropping his friend's hands, which he had caught up, he looks far off and speaks in a low, intense tone. He sees again in bitter vision the "funeral baked meats" and the "marriage tables" (180 f.) just as he had recalled, a few moments ago alone, his mother's "shoes" (147), new for the funeral and still new for the wedding. "Thrift, thrift, Horatio." But those sights, more mean and cold than the face of an everlasting "foe" (182), are quickly put away by the presence of the living friend—and then suddenly another, warmer sight, instigated by Horatio's words, comes to the fore (184):

> HAMLET My father, methinks I see my father.
> HORATIO Oh where, my lord?
> HAMLET In my mind's eye, Horatio.

HORATIO I saw him once, he was a goodly king.
HAMLET He was a man, take him for all in all,
       I shall not look upon his like again.
HORATIO My lord, I think I saw him yesternight.
HAMLET Saw? Who?
HORATIO My lord, the king your father.[10]

Horatio is exactly the sort of person to convince Hamlet of the fact of the ghostly apparition, but in so doing he is influenced by his more percipient friend. Hamlet (like Shakespeare) is realistic; he is not visionary but intensely visional. Because he seizes the *actual* facts with a devouring eye—as shown throughout scene ii, climactically in his cross-questioning of Horatio and the two soldiers—his memory is sharp and his imagination truthful. At the beginning of the dialogue quoted above he sees his father with a closeness of recollection that opens towards the supernatural. Horatio, startled, is made to recall vividly his own memory of the "goodly king." Then, deeply moved by Hamlet's sense of utter loss, he declares with new conviction, "I think I saw him yesternight," and later, "I knew your father, These hands are not more like" (211); a quite Hamletian image and gesture. Horatio, under the spell of Hamlet and of Hamlet's affinity in character to his father, is strongly inclined, as not in scene i, to identify the Ghost fully with the actual person of the late king.

On that point Hamlet himself, prudent though strongly moved, suspends decision, obeying the gentleman's precept presently to be enunciated, though not well obeyed, by Polonius: "Take each man's censure, but reserve thy judgment" (I. iii. 69). This time it is Hamlet, not Horatio, who bears in mind the fact that an alien and perhaps evil being may have usurped his father's form (244; I. i. 46-49). But also, unlike Horatio and the two soldiers, he perceives that if the apparition is really his "father's spirit in arms," it may signify "some foul play"

---

[10] This extraordinary bit of dialogue, as suggested in the ensuing paragraph of my text, is full of the mystery that there is in human seeing, outward and inward seeing. Our outward world when vividly seen, as it is by Hamlet, can lead into the visional realm of the "mind's eye"; and this, into the illusive sphere of the supernatural, which, apprehensible only in terms of the other two realms, may be truly interpreted just in so far as human beings utter and compare, honestly, their experiences of it. Cf. note 3, above.

(256), something akin to but worse than the "things rank and gross in nature" on which he has brooded alone. He masters, however, his rising excitement. The last two lines of the short soliloquy that ends the scene are the sequel of the last two lines of his long soliloquy above. There (159) he said, "I must hold my tongue." Here (257) he exclaims, ". . . sit still, my soul." Here the premonition of coming evil is much stronger; so is the hero's self-command—so far.

I. iii

While Hamlet is setting out for an unknown awful shore of the spirit, Laertes, the anti-hero, is setting out for—Paris. The present scene resumes the court air of pleasure and smooth propriety, beneath which Hamlet saw an "unweeded garden" (I. ii. 135). But now we are informed of a certain growth in that garden which at first seems very surprising, Hamlet's love for Ophelia. "What art thou?" She rearouses the play's initial questioning mood. She is lovely but, at the outset, somewhat faint; not a fit wife, seemingly, for the prince we have been watching. Yet it is as impossible for us as it is for her, though natural for her brother and father in the atmosphere of this court, to believe that Hamlet is merely "trifling" (5) with her.

Her exclamation "No more but so?" (10) is smilingly incredulous, like her preceding question "Do you doubt that?" (4) in regard to the matter of writing letters to Laertes during his coming absence. For her, Hamlet's love is no more doubtful than her own affectionate care for her brother. Therefore Laertes' claim that Hamlet's devotion is "not permanent" (8) falls on ears so deaf that he, trained courtier as he is, shifts his ground at once. He hedges (14), then proceeds (17) to question, effectually, the political possibility of a marriage between her and the crown prince. This consideration, unlike the other, moves her deeply, so deeply that she cannot speak when her brother pauses for her to do so, after his culminating phrase "the main voice of Denmark" (28). Taking advantage of her silence, he proceeds to urge, again, the danger threatening her chastity. But now she smiles again, and presently gives him a playfully satiric rejoinder with a real sting in it (45-51).

Nor is she in the least impressed by the grosser animadversions which her father later in the scene makes upon the
supposed immorality of Hamlet's passion for her (90 ff.). Her
mien here is abstracted. She is still reflecting upon her brother's
contention regarding the "voice of Denmark," which she promised him faithfully to keep in mind (85). Probably the new
king, for political reasons, will wish the prince to make a far
more lofty alliance. Therefore Hamlet's "tenders" of *marriage*
must, for the time being at least, be doubtful: "I do not know,
my lord, what I should think" (104). With this admission
contrast the assured tone of her lines upon Hamlet's "affection"
(100) and "love" (110) for her. During all the chatter of
Polonius upon her imperiled chastity she hears one motif only:
"Lord Hamlet is a prince, out of thy star" (II. ii. 141). For
this reason, and this alone, she obeys her father's strict command to break off all communication with Hamlet.

Precisely because she allows herself to be overborne by her
two monitors in the matter of political propriety, her utter rejection of their view of Hamlet's love is very striking. He has
been importunate, indeed, but perfectly honorable in his wooing
(32, 111): he has urged her to marry him, and to do so very
soon. He has uttered "holy vows of heaven" (114), recalling
to us the intensely religious view of marriage in his first soliloquy. Nor is his love the romantic result of young and long
association with Ophelia. Shakespeare not only avoids any
suggestion of that but shows in many ways that "this hot love
on the wing" (II. ii. 132) is recent as well as real. Twice we
are told that it has developed "of late" (91, 99), that is, during
the time of the coronation of Claudius and his marriage with
Hamlet's mother. And over against that background the paradox of Hamlet's love for Ophelia is solved. Also the flower-
poetry with which the dramatist introduces her takes on a rich
signification. In verses "so sweet the sense faints picturing
them" (to apply a line from Shelley) we are told that this
love is

> A violet in the youth of primy nature (7) . . .
> And in the morn and liquid dew of youth (41) . . .

The "dew" of vital purity that previously imaged "young Hamlet" (I. i. 167, 170; I. ii. 130) is here bestowed on Ophelia
too. It is clear that he turned to her—her name in Greek means
"help"—as the sole really natural and congenial growth in the
"unweeded garden." And his choice of her for his princess,
eventually his queen, was right and reasonable. She is deliberately put before us in this scene as the antithesis of the
present queen: she is what Hamlet once believed his mother to
be. Frail and dependent like that mother (I. ii. 143), Ophelia,
unlike her, is strong in her sense of duty and in the fixity of her
love. Clinging to and united with Hamlet's strength of mind
and purpose, her strong purity would help him overcome the
"things rank and gross" in the soil of Denmark. For him, she
is the flower, the *violet*, that he needs. And for her, he is—
what he is not for Laertes or Polonius or anyone else in Denmark—"The expectancy and *rose* of the fair state" (III. i. 160).

For that very reason, however, her unselfish and dutiful
humility has made her hesitate to become his wife, the consort
of "Lord Hamlet" (123) so far above her. The impression
given us is that, swayed by his passionate and democratic urgency, she had come close to accepting a betrothal just before
the preceding scene, i.e., just before he learned of the Ghost.
Hence the poignant premonition aroused in us by the present
scene. If she were already plighted to the prince, with all the
sacredness which betrothal had of old, especially in the view of
persons such as Hamlet and herself, she would now be closer in
his confidence and, in her way, a greater *help* to him than his
friend Horatio; and she would be under the direction of the
prince instead of Polonius and Laertes. But now her silent
belief in Hamlet's great destiny is worked upon, while she
weighs her decision, by these words of her brother (17) vivid
in her memory:

> His greatness weighed, his will is not his own;
> For he himself is subject to his birth:
> He may not, as unvalued persons do,
> Carve for himself, for on his choice depends
> The sanctity and health of the whole state.

For us, that last line is an ironic counterpart to Hamlet's suspicion, a minute ago, of "foul deeds" (I. ii. 257). Laertes'
speech establishes a tragic irony regarding Hamlet's mission
and Ophelia's fate that persists throughout the scene. We feel
that there may indeed be for this girl a "steep and thorny road
to heaven" while, as her brother treads the "primrose path"
(48-50)—the images are in sequence to the flower-verses above
—her lover embarks on his spectral mission on behalf of the
"sanctity and health of the whole state." Her laconic response
to Polonius at the end of the scene, so far from being soft, is
painfully, quietly firm; she has made an unselfish and costly
decision in renouncing the prince: "I shall obey, my lord."

I. iv

Those words of hers stay in our ears ominously while Hamlet enters, exclaiming, "The air bites shrewdly; is it very cold?"
He knows not yet how cold for him the air of Denmark is. On
these ghostly battlements he is far above the courtly propriety
which, obeyed on noble grounds by his loved one, is dividing
her from him—and which, on a far lower level, approves the
drunken wassail now proceeding within. This is a time-honored
"custom" (15), but the prince's comments upon it are "nipping"
and "eager" as the air (2). For this old custom, followed with
new zest by the new king, symbolizes for Hamlet all that is
now wrong in Denmark (I. ii. 125, 134, 175). It is one of the
"weary, stale, flat, and unprofitable . . . uses of this world."
Moreover it provides an instance of how the fame of a nation
or a person may be corrupted by one outstanding fault (17-38).
A "dram of eale" (evil) may reduce the whole "substance" of
a "noble" reputation to its own baneful level, i.e., to "his own
scandal." Here the great speech is abruptly stopped by the
coming of the Ghost, and that fact is full of dramatic suggestion.

Hamlet could have said much more, as will appear later,
upon the subject of "addition" (20) and "attribute" (22), i.e.,
fame, standing, reputation. These, for a noble person, are
mainly important as the medium, not of worldly success, but
of his impact upon the general morale. The "censure" (35),
the judgment, that people form of him determines the good or

ill effect of his example. So far Hamlet himself, at a time of great crisis, has set a right example to his people, in contrast with Claudius and his creatures. The prince has followed the precepts so glibly retailed by Polonius to his son in the preceding scene; hence the dramatic significance of that long oration, especially the concluding lines (I. iii. 78):

> This above all: to thine own self be true;
> And it must follow as the night the day
> Thou canst not then be false to any man.

Hamlet, true to his best self, has been true to the best interests of others. His fine quality of prudent justness, demonstrated in scene ii, was further brought out by his implied contrast with Laertes and Polonius in scene iii; and the first part of the present scene brings to the fore his temperance. This may be termed the gentleman's modal virtue since all his other values depend upon it. Temperance means that his "blood and judgment," his passion and reason, must be "well co-mingled" (III. ii. 74); he must not permit the "o'ergrowth" of any tendency that will break down "the pales and forts of reason" (27); otherwise his "virtues else" (32) will all suffer. Thus the "dram of eale" speech is climactic. It completes Shakespeare's picture of Hamlet so far. It shows him, against the background of the trumpeting royal revel within and below, aiming at self-control and good reputation, the inward and outward marks of a truly royal prince. But now this character, which has so well withstood the everyday world, is to be dreadfully tried by the other, the unseen world—"Look, my lord, it comes!" (38).

No wonder Hamlet, preoccupied in his great speech with the fact that all virtue is always in imminent danger even if "pure as grace" (33), cries out now, "Angels and ministers of grace defend us!" Supernatural grace is what he needs here. The query to the Ghost in scene i, "What art thou?," becomes a cosmic moral problem here:

> Be thou a spirit of health or goblin damned,
> Bring with thee airs from heaven or blasts from hell,
> Be thy intents wicked or charitable . . .

The visitant is silent: it can speak only to solitude and credence. "If," said Hamlet earlier (I. ii. 244), "it assume my noble father's person . . ." Now he is convinced of identical form but not yet of personal identity: "I'll *call* thee Hamlet, King, father, royal Dane"; the final title indicating the grandeur of the realm under the former king. Tentatively he gives these names; for if this form is real, it violates the forms of religion and nature, the peaceful sacrament of burial, and the peaceful beauty of night (47-54). What could be the meaning of such a horrid convulsion? Finally, and above all, "what should we *do*?" (57).

That final question instantly causes the Ghost to "*beckon*" Hamlet; for as in the case of Horatio (I. i. 130 ff.; I. ii. 215-217) the spectator's willingness to act, denoting abeyance of doubt, gives the specter new power. But whereas Horatio said to it warily, "*If* there be any *good* thing to be done That may to thee do ease and *grace* to me," Hamlet with unwary impatience omits the provisos, crying desperately, "Say, why is this? wherefore? what should we do?" Thus he puts himself under the sway of the Ghost. From now on he is more and more entranced by it. As it moves away slowly with eyes fixed upon him, he follows step by step, hypnotically. And the audience is intended to sympathize entirely with the strenuous and prolonged efforts of his companions to restrain him. We admire his great courage here, but we see that it is reckless and intemperate (64 ff., 81 ff.). Horatio, through the medium of an old superstition, warns Hamlet against "toys of desperation" (75), i.e., desperate fancies; and, as the prince follows the Ghost off stage, declares he "waxes desperate with imagination" (87).

I. v. 1-31

Not yet entirely desperate. "Where wilt thou lead me? speak, I'll go no further." Here Hamlet holds up the cross-hilt of his drawn sword (drawn, above, to keep off his restraining friends) between himself and the Ghost. But his hypnotic stepping is succeeded now by hypnotic listening. And it is in this state of mind that he accepts the preliminary suggestion of

"revenge" (7) as well as the full identity of the spirit with his
"father" (9). The sublime horror of purgatory seizing upon
his pity (4) and upon his strong religious sense—the cross in
his hands merges into the Ghost's picturing of his father in those
relentless fires (11-13)—prepares him to accept a task which
is normally abhorrent to him but which can seem, in his present
ecstatic mood, sublime. And now comes an intense appeal to
his filial love (23), and then the abrupt command, prepared for
by the suggestion of "revenge" above, to revenge his father's
"foul and most unnatural murder." Hamlet's response is indeed "desperate with imagination":

> Haste, haste me to know it,
> That with wings as swift
> As meditation or the thoughts of love
> May sweep to my revenge.[11]

Those lines mark the first great crisis of the play. Hamlet
undertakes immediate and open vengeance upon an unknown
murderer; he swears it (I think) with both hands grasping the
cross-hilt of his sword. Without any basis of actual knowledge
he has rashly accepted the word of a specter in solitude. Such
evidence is distrusted by mankind proportionally with the at-
tractiveness of the apparition to its solitary hearer. Therefore
the words "haste" and "know" in the first line are charged for
us with a foreboding that rises with each succeeding phrase. We
have seen that Hamlet's "meditation" and "thoughts of love,"
prior to the Ghost's coming, were "swift" indeed but sound and
true. His present decision, on the contrary, is violently swift
and wrong. Of course we had felt in the previous scenes that
some great action on the part of the prince would be called for;
but also that such action, if he kept on being "true" to his "own
self," must be lofty and well weighed, not prompted by a sudden, desperate desire to "sweep to my revenge." Here Hamlet
is guilty of the "hideous rashness" (*Lear* I. i. 153) that is char-

---

[11] The "haste" explains the omission of the first personal pronoun before
"May." The Q2 version of these lines is metrically smoother but less expressive of Hamlet's "desperate imagination":

> Haste me to know't, that I with wings as swift
> As meditation or the thoughts of love,
> May sweep to my revenge.

acteristic of Shakespeare's later tragic heroes. Like them he has a tragic flaw in his character. Near the close of the play he says of himself truly, "though I am not spleenative and rash Yet have I in me something dangerous" (V. i. 284). Normally not rash at all, he is capable of extreme rashness when provoked extremely. The "something dangerous" is the proud impatience that there is in his otherwise noble sense of public mission.

That "particular fault" (I. iv. 36) was admitted by the prince subconsciously, as we would say, in the "dram of eale" speech; there he was steeling himself to control it in the emergency just ahead of him. But his self-control, like that great speech itself, was broken into by the Ghost. The difficult temperance with which he had succeeded in facing *"this* world" (I. ii. 134) yields to the pressure of the *other* world. Beforehand he was prepared to yield; for this ghost responds, just as fully as the merely psychic ghost in *Macbeth* (III. iv), to the repressed emotions of the hero. Hamlet's hate of the present *public* state of affairs predisposes him to believe in a *private* and worse evil: beneath the "things rank and gross *in nature"* there might well be something grossly *unnatural;* something "foul" (I. ii. 256, 257) or even, as the specter claims, "most foul, strange, and unnatural" (28). And his loving admiration of the father still living so vividly in his "mind's eye" as a great human being against the background of the subhuman court (I. ii. 180-188) is overpoweringly appealed to by the appearance now confronting him. Therefore that humane "reason" which a few moments ago he had praised so well (I. iv. 28) and whose "sovereignty" Horatio had urged him to maintain (I. iv. 73) yields now its "pales and forts" to a sweeping passion. Hitherto his intense yearning to set things right in Denmark has been governed by princely prudence aided by his love for Ophelia, she being a true image of his unselfish patience. But now all the repressed vehemence of that yearning flames out into one wild, egotistic resolve— *"my* revenge." That resolve is the commencement of his "antic disposition."

(d) *antic disposition*   I. v. 32—191

I. v. 32-112

The Ghost's pat comment upon that resolve is heavy with Shakespearean irony:

> I find thee apt,
> And duller shouldst thou be than the fat weed
> That rots itself in ease on Lethe wharf
> Wouldst thou not stir in this.

That "weed" succulent with deathly oblivion, is the acme of the "unweeded garden That grows to seed" (I. ii. 135); it is the extreme projection of Hamlet's own thought and imagery. It symbolizes all the ills that he has inveighed against, inhuman forgetfulness, complacent decay, "heavy-headed" indulgence (I. iv. 17). It has the effect of exacerbating by contrast his own proud impatience, the opposite extreme, exactly, from that "fat weed." Thus the specter confirms the prince's desperate mood —then tells him the thing withheld until now: the murderer is the present king (39).

"O my prophetic soul—my uncle?"[12] Hamlet staggers back, astounded and dismayed, letting the point of his sword fall. His "soul"—the word is resumed from the close of scene ii—had suspected "*some* foul play," vaguely though intensely, without the slightest *conscious* reference to Claudius. But also his "soul" had hated his uncle, hated him prophetically for the increasing degradation to which the kingdom was doomed by the evil "dexterity" of the new regime: it could not "come to good" (I. ii. 157 f.). And now this definite hate, and that vague suspicion, rush together in one line. The line is an outcry of horrified incredulity shaken by new conviction. The conviction is emotional, however, not mental. For the thought of Claudius as murderer, a role at first sight totally

---

[12] After "soul" Q2 has an exclamation point and F1 a colon. Both end the line with a question mark. This, in Elizabethan printing, could mean merely an exclamation; but I believe the whole context demands the question mark. The line, printed as one verse in the quartos and folios, and wrongly broken in two by editors, gains emphasis from the Ghost's antecedent, designedly curt half-line: "Now wears his crown."

incongruous with the character of that genteel and kindly politician, is intended, on sheer theatric as well as higher grounds,
to be equally surprising to Hamlet and to the audience. Therefore his present exclamation, a broken pentameter, is at the
opposite pole in tone and rhythm from his preceding speech,
"Haste, haste me to know it. . . ." Those four lines had a
mounting rush and thrust. His present single line conveys
involution and recoil. The stabbing final phrase of the previous speech, "my revenge," is paralleled and anticlimaxed by
the querying phrase "my uncle?"

Here, then, begins the delay of Hamlet's vengeance. In
regard to his "soul," and everybody's soul, we are supposed to
know what Polonius a little while ago claimed to know, "When
the blood burns, how prodigal the soul Lends the tongue
vows . . ." (I. iii. 115-120), and how soon such vows may become "extinct" when "blood and judgment" are again commingled. But whereas we perceived that Hamlet's vow to
Ophelia was veracious, we are made to feel, in dramatic contrast, that his present vow of quick revenge is not. It contra-
venes his character as a temperate and public-spirited gentleman.
No wonder he recoils in dismay upon discovering that, after
decisively if reluctantly accepting the position of crown prince,
he has undertaken to be the instant killer of the uncle and
anointed sovereign to whose throne he will succeed. Claudius,
to be sure, according to the Ghost's story, has obtained the
throne by killing a king. But that is a main motive for Hamlet's not doing likewise; the ways of his uncle are precisely
those that the prince is most reluctant to follow. All of this
has been put by Shakespeare into clear though oblique words,
enabling us to enter now into his hero's great, and therefore
dumb, dilemma.[13] The audience has been carefully prepared
to understand the "mystery" (III. ii. 382) which Hamlet himself cannot express.

But just as striking as the "mystery" of Hamlet is that of

[13] The prince's dumb dilemma accounts for his silence during the Ghost's
ensuing fifty lines. It is a natural temptation for the protagonist to interrupt
that long speech on theatric grounds; Garrick gave line 80, "Oh horrible"
etc., to Hamlet. But Shakespeare conceives his hero as utterly speechless here
from inner turmoil.

Claudius. Two questions regarding him confront us now, both implicit in Hamlet's startled exclamation, "my uncle?" First, how can a man so temperamentally averse to deeds of violence be conceived as the killer of a very martial king? The Ghost provides the answer in his ensuing long speech (41-91). Shifting the theme at the outset from murder to adultery, a crime much more readily associated with Claudius, he explains the beautiful queen's quick marriage to this "satyr" after the death of her "Hyperion," to whom, as Hamlet wonderingly recalled, she had clung so fondly (I. ii. 139-145):

> Must I remember? why, she would hang on him
> As if increase of appetite had grown
> By what it fed on.

That picture supports the specter's story. It is clear, now, that she did not cling to the strong beauty of virtue: she was lustful, and her unsatisfied "appetite" could shift from her husband to Claudius, lust seeking lust; though her conscience resisted until it was overcome by his "gifts" and "wicked wit" (43-57, 86-88). And the "witchcraft" of that wit, having found a way to the royal bed, could also, as we are now ready to believe, find the far harder, murderous way to the king's couch in the orchard— could find the *one* method of ending him, at the height of his power and in full health, without suspicion and without any use of physical force. Claudius's poison, that "juice of cursed hebenon" (62), that "leperous distilment" (64), strikes us as the distilled evil essence of all the herbal imagery of Act I. Hamlet's "unweeded garden" had in it a foul juice beyond his thought, though sensed vaguely by his "prophetic soul." The Ghost's picture is immediately convincing (later it can appear unconvincing for the very same reason) because it deepens and darkens lines already drawn by Hamlet himself. The murder is exactly the sort of murder, the sole sort, that the oily, poisonous Claudius, if strongly urged by conjoined love and ambition, could and would commit.

But the second question regarding him, one that will presently come to the forefront of Hamlet's mind, is at first baffling. The instinct of all criminals who have any touch of conscience, and Claudius is far too human to have none, is to keep aloof from those they have wronged. But Claudius after committing, if the Ghost be believed, the three worst possible sins against Hamlet—seduction of his mother, murder of his father, theft of his throne—cultivated his presence, not only on politic grounds but with a certain sincere warmth. In human nature, how could this be? The answer, never explicitly given, becomes perfectly clear in Act III, scene iii. The conscience of Claudius was so utterly revolted by his fratricide that from the first he strove to appease it by making up to the son, as crown prince, the crime against the father as well as the crimes against Hamlet himself (I. ii. 106-117), essaying thus a measure of penance and restitution, hoping to show a "will" not entirely "incorrect to heaven" (I. ii. 95). And in Acts II and III he will continue to mollify his conscience by delaying, so long as possible, self-protective, eventually vengeful, action against his hostile nephew.

Parallel to that delay is the delay of Hamlet's vengeful action against his hated uncle. The reason, never directly given, becomes perfectly clear towards the close of the play. There the prince exclaims to Horatio regarding the imminent killing of Claudius, "is't not perfect conscience?" (V. ii. 67). His conscience, elaborately displayed by Shakespeare in the opening scenes of the drama as that of a moral realist and true statesman, is revolted by the vow of "my revenge." Right *vengeance* upon a wicked ruler, the deliberate execution of him in the mood of justice, is one thing; quite another is personal, precipitant *revengefulness*. This difference is clear enough to normal spectators, who would therefore be aware that it must be known to Hamlet himself in his heart of hearts. For him, however, it is obscured by his proud quick passion. Although at once he begins to delay "my revenge" in response to the promptings of conscience, he will not admit that fact to himself, much less to others; hence it cannot be explicitly stated. Thus the audience—and this is the author's immediate purpose—has the keen dramatic pleasure of understanding Hamlet and, similarly, Claudius better than they understand themselves. To us it is clear that the troublous friendliness of Claudius for his nephew

and also Hamlet's troublous postponing of his revenge upon
his uncle are due to motions of conscience not confronted by the
two men themselves.

Accordingly the mounting agony of Hamlet in the present
scene is caused, like the highest distress of the human heart
everywhere, not by a single passion, but by an unconfessed conflict of passion and morality. King Lear (II. iv. 267-289) is
brought to the verge of madness by the struggle within him,
but not clearly envisaged by him, between the spiritual patience
which he is beginning to learn and the fury against his evil
daughters which he cannot yet control. Hamlet is torn, and
driven more and more into an "antic disposition," by his deep,
unavowed discord of revengeful passion and the spirit of temperate justness.

Both of those contrary motives are invoked by the Ghost
in the close of his long speech. First, revengeful passion. Here
(74-81) his appeal is made to and through intense personal
emotion, culminating in a return upon the "tormenting flames"
(3) that at the first caught Hamlet's pity:

> Cut off even in the blossoms of my sin,
> Unhouseled, disappointed, unaneled,
> No reckoning made, but sent to my account
> With all my imperfections on my head:
> Oh horrible, oh horrible, most horrible!
> If thou hast nature in thee bear it not—

That heaping iteration of the blackest personal aspects of the
crime, capped by a summons to "nature" in Hamlet, would
naturally impel him to "cut off" Claudius at once, even now
while he is carousing below in the castle with all *his* "imper-
fections" on *his* "head." The Ghost's next word, we may well
expect, will be, for the third time in the scene (see 7, 25),
"Revenge"—But no! Instead, the ground of appeal shifts
abruptly, reflecting Hamlet's divided soul. The specter now
(81-91) invokes the prince's higher "nature,"[14] his justice and
temperance; emphasizing public instead of personal motives,

---

[14] The ambiguous word "nature" in the last line of the quoted passage is,
thus, transitional: it denotes Hamlet's *impulsive* nature in the preceding, his
rational nature in the succeeding, context.

suggesting that the vengeance may not be swift but deliberate; and leaving in the foreground, not the brutal wickedness of Claudius, but the religious problem of the queen's conscience:

> Let not the royal bed of Denmark be
> A couch for luxury and damned incest.
> But, howsoever thou pursuest this act,
> Taint not thy mind; nor let thy soul contrive
> Against thy mother ought; leave her to heaven
> And to those thorns that in her bosom lodge
> To prick and sting her. Fare thee well at once;
> The glow-worm shows the matin to be near
> And 'gins to pale his uneffectual fire,
> Adieu, adieu, Hamlet, remember me.

Thus the speech rises from personal passion towards the lofty and therefore dim height of mercy seasoning justice, from the grim "bear it not" to the meek "leave her to heaven," the heaven in whose faint light, now, the glowworm must pale its little earthly "fire."[15]   Here the Ghost, who had previously frowned "revenge," shows a "countenance more in sorrow than in anger" (I. ii. 231 f.). And his parting behest is as dubious as the faint dawn in which he fades: "remember me."

What, in particular, is the agonized prince to "remember"? Kneeling alone in the dim light on the high battlements— while we recall the very different dawn at the close of scene i— he appeals to a cosmos echoing with that enigmatic command. He appeals to the "heaven" above him and to the "earth" beneath (91)—"And shall I couple hell?"   Later he will actually couple "heaven and hell" in the renewed impulse of "my revenge" (II. ii. 613). But now that swift, inadequate passion, faded like the glowworm's fire, is tacitly thrust aside along with the thought of "hell": "O fie, hold, hold, my heart. . . ."   Not "revenge" but "remember me" is the final injunction laid upon him, from without and from within. "Re-

---

[15] Shakespeare's fine instinct kept him from using the word "fire" in the interval between "fast in fires" (11) and "uneffectual fire" (90). The result is that the present suggestion of *earthly* fire (the glowworm's) and *heavenly* fire (the dawn's) has a background, in our memory and imagination, of the hellish or purgatorial fire (hell and purgatory are often merged in Elizabethan literature) which the Ghost spoke of at the beginning of this scene. Three kinds of "fire"!

member thee?" The words ring again and again in his tur-
moiled head, "this distracted globe" (97). He dedicates himself to the hard task of fulfilling that commandment, so vague,
and yet so full of meaning for all the rest of his life on earth.
It means, at the least, that he must now wipe from his memory
all trivial and remote matters (99); it means he must keep
mainly in mind—what? The implied question is answered by
these rushing words:

> yes, yes, by heaven:
> Oh most pernicious woman!
> Oh villain, villain, smiling damned villain!
> My tables, my tables; meet it is I set it down
> That one may smile, and smile, and be a villain,
> At least I'm sure it may be so in Denmark.
> So, uncle, there you are. Now to my word:
> It is, "Adieu, adieu, remember me." I have sworn't.

In other words, to remember the Ghost is to remember a
fact which, though awfully reinforced by the spectral vision,
was known to Hamlet beforehand: hypocrisy and dishonesty
now rule in Denmark. More pernicious than all the crimes
that have been committed is the hypocrisy concealing them.
The queen is a "most pernicious" person because she is, as the
Ghost said, "seeming-virtuous" (46).[16] And the same is true
of Claudius. He is "damned," not chiefly because of his adultery and murder, but because he has covered all his wickedness
with a genial, virtuous smile (as in I. ii. 87 ff.). And his
spiritual poison is working in the public body exactly as his
"hebenon" (62) worked in the body of the murdered king: it
is corrupting the "wholesome blood" (70) of the state. The
real life of the state is justice; its chief foe is smooth dishonesty,
masking wrong.[17] Genial crookedness kills the soul of a nation
smilingly. Therefore the ultimate evil revealed to Hamlet by
his own spirit and by a supernatural spirit—the horror which for

[16] Cf. the "most pernicious" Angelo and his "seeming, seeming" in the
contemporary *Measure for Measure* II. iv. 151. In Q1 the word "pernicious"
is applied by Hamlet to Claudius instead of Gertrude. Of course it really
applies, Hamlet knows, to both.

[17] See the trial of Duessa, Fair Falsehood, as the foe of Justice in *The
Faerie Queene*, Book V, canto ix.

him, as Prince of Denmark, must overtop the most horrible of domestic crimes—is that in Denmark "one may smile, and smile, and be a villain."

I. v. 112-191

That evil, though Claudius is the head and center of it, is general and national; "for mine uncle is king of Denmark" (II. ii. 380). Such is to be Hamlet's leading thought from now on. A nation gets the kind of ruler that it more or less deserves: Claudius can flourish here. Hence the rationality, along with the bitter irony, of the "wonderful . . . news" (117-124) which Hamlet presently confides to the questioning Horatio and Marcellus: "There's ne'er a villain dwelling in all Denmark But he's an arrant knave." When Horatio exclaims that no ghost "come from the grave" is needed to tell us that, Hamlet rejoins, "Why, right, you are in the right." News from the region of the dead, from the "undiscovered country" (III. i. 79), is too dubious to be our primary consideration. The message of a specter, ambiguous in the upshot even to him who *heard* it—and doubtful in retrospect, as Shakespeare is now suggesting, to the audience who have *overheard* it—must be entirely dubious when retold to others. Hamlet says in effect: All I can tell you is what you can know without supernatural news, what I myself knew before and now know better than ever: there's plenty of concealed wickedness in Denmark. Our nation is at present full of smiles: we have had a coronation, a royal wedding, a remarkably quick recovery from public grief, a new policy of cheap international peace, and a renewed zest in carousing. Denmark can smile and smile, yet every villain dwelling therein is an arrant knave.

> And so, without more circumstance at all,
> I hold it fit that we shake hands and part;
> You, as your business and desires shall point you,
> For every man hath business and desire,
> Such as it is; and for mine own poor part,
> Look you, I'll go pray.

That piercing last line is the sequel of Hamlet's successive appeals in the course of Act I to the cosmic powers: the Everlasting, God, angels and ministers of grace, heaven, earth. But now he *names* no power; his word is simply, and for the first time, "pray." He must find out, alone and prayerfully, his own "business and desire." He moves off a few paces from his two companions. The good Horatio's "business and desire," however, is to help his distraught prince, whom he follows, inviting a private conference. And for just a moment it seems that Hamlet, "sorry" for the effect of his "wild and whirling words" (133 f.) upon his friend, will take him into close confidence, as a gentleman in such case is expected to do: "The friends thou hast, and their adoption tried, Grapple them to thy soul with hoops of steel. . . . Give . . . few thy voice" (I. iii. 62-68). Properly Hamlet would give his voice to Horatio now—instead of much later, as actually happens—"touching this vision here" (137). He needs desperately the counsel and aid of his friend now. But Horatio's deportment seems intrusive in the eyes of his proud, overwrought prince, who soon therefore ends their private dialogue with rude abruptness. Merely assuring Horatio that the "ghost" is "honest" (138), in implied contrast to Denmark (123), Hamlet bids him overmaster as well as he may his "desire to know." Thus Horatio's earnest desire to help is rebuffed. He who was recently "my good friend" (I. ii. 163) is held aloof, relegated with Marcellus to the category of "good friends . . . friends, scholars, soldiers" (140). With very tragic results, which will appear in later scenes, Hamlet resolves, proudly and religiously ("I'll go pray"), to find his difficult way absolutely alone.

That extreme resolve produces his extreme insistence on the secrecy of his companions; and, presently, it *re*produces the Ghost. First, Hamlet demands, "Never make known what you have seen tonight." The two give their solemn assent; then, upon his urgency, they add their oath, "in faith": this should be sufficient among gentlemen. But going further, over the dignified protest of Marcellus (146), Hamlet makes them swear "upon my sword," the sword with which he himself had sworn fealty to the Ghost (112). Instantly, therefore, the *"Ghost cries under the stage,"* "Swear" (148). Responsive here as ever to Hamlet's mood, the supernatural realm abets the secretiveness not imposed by it but adopted by him on his own responsibility. The apparition, while giving his message to him alone, since only he could receive it, did not forbid him to impart it to others and to seek their aid in carrying it out. Therefore the prince's present resolve for absolute secrecy takes the supernatural, so to speak, by surprise.[18] The Ghost must, however, support his first determinate step in the fulfilling of its indeterminate command, "remember me." Consequently when the prince imposes secrecy upon his companions and obviously, at the same time, upon himself—three persons grasping the sacred cross-hilt of the sword—the spectral voice must echo, "Swear." Here Hamlet's wayward will reproduces the Ghost.

Not the Ghost at its best. Not the being that uttered the great poetic speech (42-91) so rich in humanity and culminating in a note of heavenly charity. Not that voice; nor, on the other hand, the initial "sulphurous" one (3) demanding "revenge."[19] The present voice is neither heavenly nor hellish nor humanly normal. It is sepulchral and grotesque, reflecting Hamlet's mood of eccentric, morbid secrecy. This mood brings him into sudden ironic relation with that realm of ghosts "come from the grave" (125), that eerie underground region of popular belief, which is repugnant to his normal mind. Previously the Ghost had been entirely *above ground;* now he is entirely beneath, but, at the same time, genuine enough because of the subjacent seriousness of the business in hand. Accordingly the voice from below is at once real and absurd, disconcertingly honest even while ridiculous: "Art thou there, truepenny? (150) . . . this fellow in the cellarage. . . . old mole (161). . . . worthy pioner."

Abnormal secrecy (like Othello's jealousy) breeds upon itself. Hamlet must repeat, enlarge, and itemize the oath with fantastic scrupulosity. Horatio's exclamation, "O day and night, but this is wondrous strange" (164), restores for a

---

[18] Previously the Ghost has commanded: "howsoever thou pursuest this act, Taint not thy mind . . ." (I. v. 84). There Hamlet was warned against intemperate conduct, particularly towards his mother. Here he is acting intemperately, and tainting his mind, in regard to his friend Horatio.

[19] Many of the audience would have been delighted if Shakespeare, contravening Hamlet's present state of mind, had permitted the Ghost to cry "Revenge," *"under the stage,"* in good Elizabethan fashion.

moment the lofty cosmic note so prominent earlier.   Hamlet
rejoins in the same vein:

> And therefore as a stranger give it welcome.
> There are more things in heaven and earth, Horatio,
> Than are dreamt of in our philosophy.

"But"—this is Hamlet's next word—against that cosmic background, so lofty and equable and comprehensive, the wild solitariness of his own present posture comes out starkly. He, too,
is a "stranger," under "day and night," betwixt "heaven and
earth"; but far more so than Horatio because of the new
"things" which, unlike "*our* philosophy" in college days, he has
refused to share with his friend.[20] His secret is dividing him
more and more from Horatio; in the near future it will cut
him off from all intimate companionship. His demeanor is
"strange or odd" (170) in the eyes of Horatio and Marcellus
now: "hereafter" (171), he foresees, it will appear, in the eyes
of everybody, odd and wild to an extreme degree.

Already the courtiers, swayed by Claudius, deem the attitude of the crown prince very abnormal, "incorrect to heaven,"
because the honest gentility to which he adheres has become for
them an unreal thing, a mere ghost. The rank indecency of
the hasty royal mourning and marriage was invisible to them,
despite his dramatic efforts to awaken their perception of it.
And now, more awfully than before, he has "that within which
passeth show" (I. ii. 85). They who rejected the insight of
their distinguished prince regarding "things rank and gross in
nature" would obviously not accept his revelation of things "most
foul, strange, and *unnatural*" (28). The message of the Ghost
if declared by Hamlet would seem to them simply a morbid
extension of his previous unnaturalness, "a fault to nature, To
reason most absurd" (I. ii. 102). So for the present he must
continue his heartbreaking silence (I. ii. 159) upon the invisible
crimes of the new regime while striving more than ever (as he
will in Act II) by dramatic suggestion to stir the public conscience in preparation for the public deeds he will eventually do

[20] Hence "our philosophy" of F1 is a fine improvement upon "your philosophy" of Q1 and Q2.

when he shall have found what deeds can "come to good" (I. ii. 158), the "good thing to be done" (I. i. 130). The immediate result will be that his bearing, seemingly so abnormal already, will appear to the court nothing less than "antic" (172), downright mad.

Therefore "perchance" it may be "meet," for the twofold purpose of secrecy and public effect, "To put an antic disposition on." But that euphemistic phrase "put on," uttered by Hamlet with uneasy casualness, makes us, too, uneasy. This is the man who declared at the first proudly, "I know not 'seems' " (I. ii. 76), who has found that the sin of sins in his uncle, his mother, and Denmark is, precisely, seeming. *Now* he admits that he himself may feign. Of course he is upright in purpose, and he is hard beset; doubtless he must fight fire with fire. All the more reason, then, that the Ghost's revelation regarding Claudius should be confided to Horatio, if not also to Marcellus, now.[21] That confession is demanded by the essential honesty of Hamlet's soul, as well as by the dictates of friendship and of princely prudence, in view of the dubiousness of his coming public conduct. But he refuses to confess. Instead he insists now (179) with histrionic meticulousness that both his companions shall give no least hint by word or gesture

> That you know ought of me: this not to do,
> So grace and mercy at your most need help you,
> Swear.

Thus the final form of the oath, in sequel to "I'll go pray," above, is intensely religious: "So grace and mercy at your most need help you." And a passing moment of profoundly beautiful peace ensues: "Rest, rest, perturbed spirit!"—pronounced by Hamlet outwardly to the Ghost, inwardly to his own spirit. This peace belongs, by divine "grace and mercy," with heroic dedication to a great task. But here it quickly disintegrates because the hero, in so dedicating himself, has devoted himself

---

[21] To adduce here the traditional secrecy of the revenger is to miss Shakespeare's divergence from that tradition in favor of the convention of the gentleman, according to which a friend must not keep vital secrets from a friend. As to Marcellus, a study of his lines and of Hamlet's lines to him in Act I will show the reader that Shakespeare designed him as a gentleman well worthy, along with Horatio, of Hamlet's confidence.

also to a proud, inhuman, and irreligious solitude. The remainder of the speech shows the prince's perturbation reasserting itself and rising in a climax while, with acute inner conflict, he yearns *humbly* for the intimate companionship which, at the most essential point, he continues *proudly* to refuse:

> So, gentlemen,
> With all my love I do commend me to you,
> And what so poor a man as Hamlet is
> May do t' express his love and friending to you,
> God willing, shall not lack: let us go in together,
> And still your fingers on your lips, I pray,
> The time is out of joint—oh cursed spite
> That ever I was born to set it right!—
> Nay, come, let's go together.

He still clings to the two friends who have partaken so much, and yet so little, of his dreadful experience. All three shall go in "together": then he must go his own way alone. His "love and friending" are theirs; but his task, he wrongly believes, cannot in the least be shared with them. A sorrowful tune runs through the words "love," "you," "go," "together," "I," each repeated twice and the last thrice. A moment ago he had forced his friends to take a spectral oath—spectral in the fullest sense because the friends are now to disappear like ghosts, Marcellus entirely, Horatio till Act III—not to "know ought of me." And now: "still your fingers on your lips, I pray,"[22] The time is out of joint." He feels overwhelmingly that the disjointed time is disjoining him from his friends;[23] the bitterest feature of his heavy, complex task is that he must do it alone, "oh cursed spite. . . ." This parenthetic cry of princely isolation, causing his friends to hold back in deferential awe, sets off the clause, half command, half entreaty, in which the first phase of the drama closes: "Nay, come, let's go together."

[22] The comma after "pray," changed to a period by editors, is in Q1, Q2, and F1, and it is essential for Shakespeare's meaning here.

[23] The same sequence of ideas, though in lighter vein, appears in Portia's exclamation concerning herself and Bassanio: "Oh, these naughty times Put bars between" etc. (*Merchant of Venice* III. ii. 18). In Elizabethan literature the "time" is often blamed, as Portia and Hamlet blame it, for dividing friends or loved ones from each other.

The two final words symbolize the active and social character of Hamlet: he has an urgent disposition to "go together"
with others, so urgent that, when frustrated, it breeds an "antic
disposition." If his nature were in the main contemplative,
there would be no tragedy. But the "book and volume" (103)
of his "brain" (a metaphor of a sort often applied in Renaissance
literature to very practical persons) was stored, alike by reading
and by experience (100-101), with matters making for practical
action in society. That fact was displayed particularly in the
"dram of eale" oration, which, given immediately before his
meeting with the Ghost, prepares for the soliloquy given immediately afterwards, "O all you host of heaven. . . ." The two
speeches are complementary. The first argues that "one de-
fect," growing and working, may corrupt the whole "substance"
of society and the individual. The second—resuming the theme
broken off by the Ghost's advent but illumined by his revelations and capping the moral argument of the first speech with
spiritual vision—declares that the most "pernicious" dram of
evil is smiling villainy, genial hypocrisy.[24] And, seeing this,
the prince must clear his mind of "all trivial fond records," all
that bear merely upon minor matters of conduct. What he
must now mainly remember and set right is smooth dishonesty.
This has become for him the chief social evil, the "something
rotten in the state of Denmark." Horatio and Marcellus have
also sensed it (I. ii. 179; I. iv. 90) and are providentially present to help him overcome it; in this matter Hamlet and they
would properly "go together." A *social* sin cannot be remedied
by a *single* person. Properly he who first perceives it seeks at
once the aid and counsel of at least one other whom he can trust.
The tragedy of Hamlet rises in large measure from the fact
that he, an eminently social person, sets out to remedy an eminently social wrong *alone*.

He does so because of his pride of mission; a trait in the
main noble, but carried by him to a false extreme, under the

---

[24] Compare Spenser's treatment of Hypocrisy in the opening canto of *The
Faerie Queene*, and also Milton's words in *Paradise Lost* III. 682:

> For neither man nor angel may discern
> Hypocrisy, the only evil that walks
> Invisible, except to God alone. . . .

pressure of extreme circumstances. Born to be a king and highly fitted for that office, but wrongly set aside, he shows his royalty of character in being less concerned for himself than for the commonweal. His natural pride in his own integrity is over-topped by his grief for the degradation of the realm. With a sort of proud humility he determines at first to bide his time as crown prince, as king to be, bridling his impatience with the dic-tates of temperance. However, his repressed anger and eager-ness for action break bounds upon the first intimation of his father's murder: he vows *immediate* revenge. This seems to be his mission, suddenly and supernaturally revealed; and when further insight shows that purpose to be wrong, his pride, now passionate and confusing, keeps him from clearly repudiating it. He does not revoke his vow of quick revenge; he lets it lapse silently while he resumes his complete mission on behalf of Denmark. But that complete mission, now so awfully compli-cated that his primary need is friendly help, seems to him con-fined, awfully, to himself. The energy that broke out into the wild vow of swift, open revenge actuates, in recoil, the far wilder oath of fixed and absolute secrecy. Repeatedly precluded from public action, he is driven by his pride of mission into violent isolation.

Isolation, not seclusion; isolation within society: there is the tragedy. He is intensely social, and he is Prince of Denmark. By deepened insight and supernatural revelation he knows now that this kingdom is not merely an "unweeded garden," a growth "rank and gross" yet nevertheless organic: it is *in*organic, really, a framework "out of joint" (189). This phrase echoes with rich dramatic irony the image used by Claudius in rejecting Fortinbras's view of the Danish state as "disjoint and out of frame" (I. ii. 20). There Claudius uttered involuntarily the truth that is now fully plain. Denmark is a society so disjoined and crooked, at center, so utterly devoid of the spirit of justice that it can have no inward union and growth. But it is Ham-let's nation. Born to be its leader, to "go together" with it, though the time and his pride have thrust him into singularity, he must stay with it and find what he can best do on behalf of

it. He refuses, until later—indeed until too late, as will appear
—the excellent aid that providence offers him in the person of
Horatio within that very society.   But he cannot seclude himself from Denmark.   He was "born to set it right."[25]

[25] These five words should be read together as a single phrase bearing a
single though mounting emphasis: "born-to-set-it-RIGHT."   Modern mournful
individualism has inspired a wrong stress upon the preceding "I" and a wrong
pause after "born."   Hamlet is not bewailing the fact of his birth.   He is
relieving himself by heartily cursing, even while accepting, the lonely singularity of his situation.

Catch the Conscience

(a) *my soul's idol*   II. i—II. ii. 167

II. i. 1-73

THE appearance of Polonius immediately (in Shakespeare's conception of the performance) upon the exit of the prince recalls to us his strict "charge" to Ophelia at the close of Act I, scene iii regarding "the Lord Hamlet." Hence the ludicrous effect of the old man's opening line, "Give him this money and these notes, Reynaldo." The "him" could refer to Hamlet: "so poor a man," as he termed himself a moment ago (I. v. 185), could surely do with "this money"—an allowance, mayhap, from the public treasury to the crown prince? Certainly it is "*his* behavior" on which we are now intent and concerning which we shall do "marvellous wisely" to "make inquiry" before we again "visit him" (3-5). However, the object of the present inquiry is soon revealed to be another young gentleman, resident along with other Danes in Paris (7), Polonius's "son" (11). This absent son figures here in a curious, relieving parody of Hamlet that runs through the whole dialogue of Reynaldo and Polonius.

The anti-hero, Laertes, a very social person, a young gentleman who certainly desires to "go together" (I. v. 191) with society, is also a "son" (his proper name is effectively omitted throughout this scene) haunted and admonished, like Hamlet, by the spirit of his father. But the haunting, so bizarrely tragic in the case of Hamlet in the preceding scene, is here wonderfully humorous. The prince's incremental oath of secrecy is parodied by Polonius's dilative insistence upon "indirections" (66). But still more allusive is the underlying theme of the old man's "lecture" (67), the same theme really as that of his earlier "precepts" (I. iii. 58), i.e., gentlemanly or, rather, gen-

teel temperance.   Here, carrying the subject into moral detail,
he fully displays his remarkable ordinariness.   "Usual" custom
(22), instead of Hamlet's *good* custom, is his criterion.   From
Hamlet's standpoint usual custom is "unprofitable" (I. ii. 133)
because it is oblivious of real good and real evil.   Virtue "pure
as grace" (I. iv. 32) is no more "dreamt of" in Polonius's
philosophy than devastating sin.   Once, indeed, he mentions
(33)

> The flash and outbreak of a fiery mind,
> A savageness in unreclaimed blood . . .

These strong lines, premonitory of the deeds that Laertes and
Hamlet will later perform, leap out of their chattering context
—even more than the earlier "to thine own self be true"—by
Shakespeare's art, not at all by the intention of Polonius.   His
notion is merely that a young gentleman in his dissipations
should *appear* very spirited but not *be* extreme—a ticklish balance.   Hamletian temperance, as in the "dram of eale" speech,
is real and difficult; Polonian temperance, requiring drams of
evil to be genteel, is difficult and unreal.   Reynaldo wonders
just how often Laertes may visit a "brothel" (61) without
being "open to incontinency" (30).   Reynaldo is apparently
about to demand full light on this point when Polonius, hastily
overriding his listener,[1] plunges proudly to his main goal: "By
indirections find directions out" (66).

   That is the Polonian principle.   His secretiveness is a parody
of Hamlet's secretiveness in the preceding scene; it is also an
ironic foreshadowing of Hamlet's indirectness in the scenes just
ahead.   In theatrical terms: the comic old gentleman of the
play prepares a ludicrous moral trap for the anti-hero, Laertes,
while the hero himself is preparing to "catch the conscience"
(II. ii. 634) of the villain of the play, Claudius.   But Hamlet
aims also to catch the conscience of the whole society which he
was born to set right.   Presently by "indirections" he will "find
out" the "direction" of each of a series of persons representing
that society; first of all, the heroine, Ophelia.

   [1] Reynaldo, I think, is opening his mouth to speak while Polonius is saying
"so forth" (61).   Polonius, checking him peremptorily with upraised finger,
hurries on with "See you now. . . ."

II. i. 74-119

The sudden oncoming of the "affrighted" Ophelia, challenged sharply by her father's questions, has the effect of recalling the tone of the opening lines of the play while initiating the second and main phase of the action. In the opening scene Horatio, calm and unanticipative, was suddenly harrowed with "fear and wonder" by the appearing of the Ghost. And now Ophelia, passively "sewing" in her private room, has seen a very strange, silent apparition of "Lord Hamlet"—a ghost indeed of the prince, gentleman, and lover known to her previously. Throughout the scene as reported by her he retains his wonted dignity of spirit. But his face is pale as the shirt bared by his unbraced doublet; his attire is in wild disarray, his "knees knocking each other";

> And with a look so piteous in purport
> As if he had been loosed out of hell
> To speak of horrors, he comes before me.

Those three lines are redolent of an episode unknown to her but graphic in our memory: with the very same "purport" the Ghost gazed upon Hamlet at the beginning of their private colloquy. There (I. v. 2-5), however, the apparition's "piteous" look "as if he had been loosed out of hell" was followed by an actual speaking of "horrors." Here, only the "look" speaks; the ghostly silence remains unbroken. Hamlet and the shade of the father he loved could speak to each other. Hamlet and the woman he loves, at a fateful crisis in their relationship, exchange not a single word.

Normally the prince, divining the banal agent of her sudden repulse of his wooing, would have gone at once to her father with frank, patient, tactful assurances; that was the gentleman's course. He did not take it. The passage quoted above, conjoined with the final speech of Act I, tells us that Hamlet on leaving the stage, extremely in need of "love and friending" but resolved not to confide his "horrors" to Horatio, was seized in his desperate solitude with a great yearning to "speak of"— not fully unfold—those horrors to Ophelia. She like Horatio is discreet, unselfish, and devoted. This parallel between the hero's friend and the hero's loved one came out in the transitions from I. ii to I. iii and from I. iii to I. iv. And now Hamlet, having unwisely dismissed his friend, turns all the more cravingly to his loved one: now, indeed, she can be what her name implies, his help. He thinks that now, without further hesitation, she must grant him her full acceptance of his suit. It is precisely now, however, that his letters to her are returned unopened and all his attempted visits refused (108-110). Properly he would go to her father; actually he determines to make his way forcibly to her alone.

But, as suggested in the first half of this scene by the obvious lapse of time,[2] and by the emphasis upon "indirections," Hamlet delays unduly his visit to her, brooding morbidly upon *her* indirectness to him. In so doing he is devious himself; but, humanly enough, he is severe upon his own fault in another person, a loved person. He knows as well as we do that her present withdrawal from him, like her former delay in agreeing to a betrothal, is entirely altruistic and that she cannot break the silence imposed on her by her father without violating, not only current convention, but that very flower-like modesty and reticence which he loves in her. Nevertheless he allows his pride to become deeply hurt; and thus his view of her is fatefully dimmed. Brooding unhealthily in the solitude so uncongenial to him, and needing her desperately, he resents her continued silence. He fancies it is due to a touch of Polonian indirectness in her own character. And eventually she, even she, comes to seem to him heavily tainted with that general dishonesty from which he had believed that she alone was free and which it is his destiny to oppose and set right. Therefore he must renounce her.

She is not, he tells himself—and will keep on telling himself—the helpmeet for him as avenging prince, as one "born to set it right," as "scourge and minister" (III. iv. 175). But *as a man* he loves her all the more intensely now that he decides he must lose her. This is the "after-loss" (Sonnet 90)

---

[2] A good example of the wrong way of interpreting this drama is the common assumption that the lapse of time in the first half of II. i means that Hamlet is weakly delaying the killing of Claudius. Shakespeare's whole emphasis here is upon his delay *in going to Ophelia*.

that completes the dreadful tale, set forth in Act I, of all his sufferings. Yet when he visits her alone, for the last time, there is nothing he can say to her, though he yearns to say much. His vow of absolute secrecy concerning his ghostly vision, which might have been relaxed in her presence earlier, for her sake and his own, has by now become morbidly fixed: he must not give her the least hint of the mission which she cannot share. And his silence on that point debars him from explaining his changed attitude towards her. A sheerly conventional princeling could say: Though as a man I love you still, as crown prince I have decided that, as you yourself have apparently concluded, as your treatment of me shows—and "many such-like As's of great charge" (V. ii. 43)—a marriage between us would be, on public grounds, undesirable. Prince Hamlet, however, can find no right words, none that would be free from dishonesty and cruelty. At the same time his craving to speak with her becomes overwhelming. And this conflict within him brings him close to insanity, closer than anywhere else in the course of the play.

Here he is indeed "mad for" her "love" (85), utterly distraught by the "strong conception" (*Othello* V. ii. 55) that he must renounce her, and must do so dumbly. We of the audience perceive that his plight here is due initially to the solitude and silence imposed upon him by others: "break, my heart, for I must hold my tongue" (I. ii. 159). But also we know that it is due, directly, to the intemperate oath of secrecy that he imposed upon himself and his friends in the close of the preceding scene. His "mad" conduct *now* is an intensification of his "strange" bearing *then*. At that time, unaware of Ophelia's closed door, he spoke at random of putting an "antic disposition" on; and fate has taken him at his word with a vengeance. His present condition is far worse than "antic" and "put on." He is not at all conscious—he will become so later, in retrospect—of his wild demeanor. Unlike the mad lover in romance, who occurs at once to the mind of Polonius (102 ff.), Hamlet does not in the least flaunt his disordered attire; he is unaware of it. Unlike his "inky cloak" so dramatically fingered in public (I. ii. 77; III. ii. 137), his present attire has no part in his gestures:

> He took me by the wrist, and held me hard;
> Then goes he to the length of all his arm;
> And with his other hand, thus, o'er his brow
> He falls to such perusal of my face
> As he would draw it. Long stayed he so. . . .

"Long" indeed is his "perusal" of that "face" because he is trying to "catch the conscience" within. He hopes to discover some sign of penitent awareness on her part that she has been, as he conceives it, dishonestly devious. But she knows, as we know, that she has done nothing of that sort, nor indeed anything that could make him act as if "loosed out of hell to speak of horrors" unless, for the time being, he has lost his sanity. Therefore her sole feeling is a terrified and sorrowful concern for *him*. That feeling is conveyed to us by her very first word to her father, her anguished "Alas!"[3] But Hamlet, utterly heedless of his mad appearance and of its inevitable effect on her, searches vainly for her "conscience."

> At last, a little shaking of mine arm,
> And thrice his head, thus, waving up and down,
> He raised a sigh so piteous and profound
> That it did seem to shatter all his bulk
> And end his being. That done, he lets me go;
> And with his head over his shoulder turned
> He seemed to find his way without his eyes
> For out of doors he went without their help
> And, to the last, bended their light on me.

That final line concentrates the spectral tone of the whole episode. The word "last," repeated from the first verse of the passage, together with the "sigh so piteous" that seems to "end" his being—sequel of the "look so piteous," above (82)—signifies the finality of his division from her. At the same time the lingering of his gaze suggests that one outspoken word of loving

---

[3] Q1 elaborates Ophelia's primary concern for Hamlet by having her say here (75):

> O my deare father, such a change in nature,
> So great an alteration in a Prince,
> So pitifull to him, fearefull to me. . . .

With the whole episode compare *Othello* III. iv, where the suspicious hero and the selfless but helpless heroine are in essentially the same situation as Hamlet and Ophelia here.

appeal from her (as will appear in III. i, when it is too late) could break through his proud defenses. But the sort of girl, say a Juliet, who could be expected under the circumstances to make that appeal would not in the first place have won the devotion of the sort of man, so different from Romeo, that Hamlet is. Hence the "profound" (94) quality of the present love-tragedy. Two almost, not entirely, inevitable silences meet here; hers due to a strong (not soft) retiredness; his, to a too proud and secretive sense of mission. The result is that henceforth his undying love for her will be spectral— "ghostly" in the old sense of that word: spiritual—intense but not kind, aloof and haunting, bending ever its "light" on her.

Polonius comes blindly close to the mark in exclaiming that Hamlet's "ecstasy of love" (102) has in it a "violent property" that "leads the will to desperate undertakings." The old man's conscience, so easy in the first half of the scene, is sharply smitten now. Lovably he repents of not having shown better "heed and judgment" (111) along with his "discretion" (117). These terms are nicely applied by him. Hamlet has an intellect that better understands the function of those three qualities—heed, judgment, discretion—for true temperance; but—such is the suggestion here—he has also a "will" that can be led by passion into undertakings far more "desperate" (104; cf. I. iv. 87) than Polonius can foresee. Our forebodings are deeper than those of Polonius.

II. ii. 1-167

So are the king's. At once we are struck by his "hasty sending" (4) for Rosencrantz and Guildenstern and his hurried welcome of them, so out of keeping with the smooth deliberation of his official manner when we last saw him (I. ii). His demeanor tells us, and them, that he is extraordinarily disturbed by "Hamlet's transformation." Otherwise he would pronounce it due to an "impious" prolongation of that "unmanly grief" which he announced at the first as the cause of the prince's "incorrect" behavior: we can easily imagine Claudius enlarging unctuously, here, upon the sad result of that "fault to heaven" (I. ii. 92-101). Instead, he wonders broodingly "What it should be, More than his father's death (7). . . . Whether aught to us unknown. . . . That, opened, lies within our remedy" (17).

Rosencrantz and Guildenstern show by significant looks that (as they will later demonstrate in words) they understand the king to be alluding to the ever-embarrassing subject of Hamlet's not succeeding his father on the throne. That matter, no doubt, is in the mind of Claudius but along with a great deal "More." This word and the final phrase of his speech, "within our remedy," indicate for us the distress of his conscience. He had hoped to "remedy" his misdeeds, while serving his own purposes, by large and patient kindness to "my son" . . . "our son" (I. ii. 64, 117). But now that paternal attitude is lost in self-protective anxiety together with pain of conscience; he omits the "son." While the queen talks with loving pathos of "My too much changed son" (36), the king sits in grim, uneasy silence. This covert difference between the two sovereigns is well noted by the newcomers, whose responses are carefully designed to please "Both your majesties" (26).

The queen, wrapped up in her own sad thoughts while her eyes follow the retreating forms of Hamlet's two schoolfellows, pays no heed to the oncoming of Polonius. His declaration that he has found the "very cause of Hamlet's lunacy" makes the king start visibly,[4] exclaiming, "Oh speak of that, that do I long to hear" (50). For the first time Claudius is patently off his guard, which, however, he recovers at once, aided by the unruffled mien of Polonius; who is both his understudy and his mentor in the art of covertly hunting "the trail of policy" (47). And now for a fleeting moment, singular and significant, while Polonius retires to usher in the ambassadors returned from Norway, we are shown Claudius and Gertrude conversing entirely alone:

> KING   He tells me, my sweet queen, that he hath found
>   The head and source of all your son's distemper.

[4] Similar is the heavier start of Macbeth and his adjuration to the Witches to tell him more (I. iii. 50-70). In *Hamlet* there are many situations that Shakespeare repeats with intenser stress in his later tragedies, and which therefore throw light back upon the dramaturgy of *Hamlet*.

QUEEN   I doubt it is no other but the main,
              His father's death and our o'erhasty marriage.
KING   Well, we shall sift him.

His attitude to her is at once doting and, in marked contrast
with his exclamation to Polonius above, carefully guarded. He
is hiddenly, deeply disturbed by her present thoughtful aloofness. With silky sibilance his words—"tells," "sweet," "source,"
"son's distemper"—investigate whether she shares his own
sense that Hamlet's present state cannot "all" be attributed to
manifest causes. Clearly, however, she does not share it. We
see she has no doubts regarding the manner of her first husband's death; she credits Claudius's public explanation of it.
And its suddenness, unmentioned here, is entirely overshadowed
in her conscience-pricked mind by the haste of the ensuing marriage. For that unnatural haste, because of its apparently
maddening effect upon her son, with whose grief she was at
the first impatient (I. ii. 68 ff.), she is now heavily remorseful.[5]

The return of the ambassadors, whose sending signalized
the triumph of Claudius (I. ii. 26 ff.), is a remarkable anti-
climax. His diplomacy has been successful; peace is assured.
Fortinbras has submitted to his uncle, the king of Norway,
who was thereupon "overcome with joy" (72). Not so the
king of Denmark, uncle of Hamlet: he has attained peace without while losing it within. His greeting to his successful emissaries is brief, correct, and flat: "It likes us well . . . at night
we'll feast together." How different from the cosmical rhetoric
that celebrated the "unforced accord of Hamlet" (distantly
parallel to the submission of Fortinbras) with "clouds . . .
heavens . . . earthly thunder" prologuing the initial feast (I. ii.
123-128)!

Claudius's word "night" (84) is echoed (88) in the ensuing
speech of Polonius:

> What majesty should be, what duty is,
> Why day is day, night night, and time is time. . . .

reminding us, parodically, of the cosmic background of the
drama. During the old man's tedious exposition of the prince's

---

[5] With the king and queen in this episode, compare the guilty, alert king
and the less guilty, listless queen in *Macbeth* III. ii.

love and madness we watch the faces of the king and queen. She is hurt to the quick: she is so far out of her son's confidence that she has known nothing of his addresses to Ophelia. "Came this from Hamlet to her?" she exclaims of his letter sharply (114), then keeps silent. In the end the king, still investigating her silence, has to offend the old lord by asking her, "Do you think 'tis this?" Her reply is bitterly listless, "It may be, very likely" (152). She thinks that very probably this love affair became an incidental cause of Hamlet's madness when added, as her soul is now adding it, to "the main" cause confessed by her above (56). Her conscience is still more unhappy.

Thus this scene tells us that the absent Hamlet has, beyond his will, affected Claudius and Gertrude deeply. In Act I he appealed repeatedly to "the Everlasting" (I. ii. 131) under various forms and, so it seemed, ineffectually. But now Shakespeare makes us feel that by means of Hamlet's "madness" which, as Polonius remarks with unconscious irony, "all we wail for" (151), the divine Justice is shaping the ends of the prince and all the others in this Denmark. At the beginning Hamlet appealed deliberately to the moral sense of the realm (I. ii. 76 ff.) without avail. Now, involuntarily, he has begun to catch the conscience of the realm's king and queen.

They are not at present in the foreground of Hamlet's mind. It is occupied with Ophelia, "the celestial and my soul's idol" (109).[6] This phrase from his letter, recalling to us, unlike Polonius, the "holy vows of heaven" that the prince made to her (I. iii. 114), is intended here to signalize the permanent part, the pure "soul," of his love for her. It is no longer "hot love on the wing" (132); but it is as abiding as Hamlet asseverated in the rest of the letter and as his demeanor showed us in the close of the dumb-show episode with Ophelia above: the "light" of his love stays with her (II. i. 100). Moreover, Polonius's account of the growth of the "madness" together with his cocksureness regarding its origin (146-167) is deeply

---

[6] This sort of language, more or less Platonic, was commonly addressed to the beloved one of the lyrists and sonneteers of the 1590's. At best it was sincere, as in Spenser's *Amoretti*. Shakespeare has in mind that part of Hamlet's love for Ophelia which is "permanent and free from frail corruption" (*Amoretti*, 79).

amusing just because it is a true parody: it is partial and histrionic, but it is close to the actual truth. Thus we are forewarned by the dramatist that when Hamlet reappears his "soul's idol" will be in the forefront of his thought, though not of his conversation. We learn that "sometimes he walks four hours together Here in the lobby" (160). And now he enters *"reading on a book"*—the last thing that the sociable prince would ordinarily do in such a place of resort, as his mother knows well: "But look, where sadly the poor wretch comes reading" (168).[7] His renunciation of Ophelia has brought him to the extremity of silent, wretched loneliness. But now his attire is orderly though somber, as usual; the insane discomposure of the dumb-show episode is over. In what follows he will be seen focusing his mind more and more on the Denmark that he must set right—without the companionship and help of his "soul's idol."

(b) *heaven and hell*   II. ii. 168—634

II. ii. 168-331

Ophelia's father is the very last person with whom Hamlet wishes to talk at the present juncture. It is obvious that the old politician is ready now to welcome a marriage between his daughter and the crown prince if such an extraordinary event could come to pass without the least appearance of Polonius's instigation. Hence the careful elaborateness with which, above, he informed his sovereigns of his discovery and stern interdiction of the love affair; deliberately playing down Ophelia's part in it, omitting the fact that she had taken Hamlet's vows for "sterling" (I. iii. 107); and finally proposing, casually and grossly, to "loose my daughter to him" (162)—privately he phrases it "contrive the means of meeting" (216)—as though Hamlet's sexual passion merely, not his marriage, were in question.[8] We, however, know that the old man is entirely con-

---

[7] His "reading" here, so far from being a sign of bookishness, is exactly the contrary. Books are normally for him a source of precepts for the active life (see the first paragraph on page 39 above). Here only is he shown reading a book for relief from life—to emphasize his great grief regarding Ophelia.

[8] Thus Polonius in II. ii. 86-167 is less asinine and more artful than he is

vinced that Hamlet desired to wed Ophelia (II. i. 111 ff.) and will still so desire if he recovers his wits when allowed to resume his wooing. Then it will be for the good king and queen, who are so far noncommittal on this point, to decide whether they will approve such a union; probably, for the sake of Hamlet's sanity, they will.

All this, divined by Hamlet,[9] appears in the obsequious concern of his would-be father-in-law for the mental health (171, 173) of the princely suitor so recently turned away. Hamlet responds with the assurance that he is sane enough to recognize "excellent well" Polonius as a "fishmonger," i.e., a go-between, a bawd. Polonius replies, "Not I, my lord," with vigorous head-shakings. Thereupon Hamlet expresses the wish that this politician who is trying to conceal his interest in his daughter's coming promotion were "so honest a man" as an actual fish-peddler or even, maybe, as an out-and-out bawd.

> POLONIUS   Honest, my lord?
> HAMLET   Ay sir, to be honest as this world goes
>   Is to be one man picked out of two thousand.[10]
> POLONIUS   That's very true, my lord.
> HAMLET   For if the sun breed maggots in a dead dog, being a
>   good kissing carrion—Have you a daughter?

Polonius's facile "very true" impels Hamlet to translate his maxim into a brutally concrete image: the sun—"the god of day" (I. i. 152), giver of light and truth—mates with the earth to produce swarms of dishonest men, like the maggots in a "carrion" which that very sun can deem "good" stuff for "kiss-

---

usually regarded. His prologue (86-105) is designed by him to stress his own simplicity so much that his two hearers will conclude from what ensues that he does not perceive, as they themselves can, the seriousness of Hamlet's love for Ophelia. His art conceals the "art" which he disclaims (96). But the reader may perceive it fully if he notes in detail the differences between Polonius's words regarding Hamlet here and his words on the same subject when alone with Ophelia in I. iii and II. i.

[9] Dover Wilson's contention that Hamlet must have overheard Polonius's final speech to the king, above, goes counter to the dramatist's intention of bringing out, here and elsewhere, even at the expense of stage-probability, Hamlet's almost *spectral* power of divination.

[10] Q2 gives this speech in verse form as above instead of prose, thus bringing out its aphoristic flavor. But the "two thousand" of F1 is more piquant than the conventional "ten thousand" of Q2.

ing." Such is the intent of the speech. But Hamlet suddenly breaks off the simile, wasted upon so flat a listener, and makes a direct thrust at his conscience with the word "daughter."[11] She must not be permitted to walk "i' the sun" (185, cf. I. ii. 67) of princely favor lest Hamlet, following the bad example of the sun-god, may prove to be an illicit breeder, as Polonius had earlier believed he would. "Friend, look to 't."

That injunction uttered very gravely and accompanied by a fixed gaze, which Hamlet at length withdraws to fasten upon his book with an air of finality, is a fair warning to Polonius that his hidden hope is vain: his daughter is not to be the consort of the prince. The warning is as explicit as it can be made under the circumstances. In lieu of publicizing the Ghost's visit, the ultimate cause of his division from Ophelia, Hamlet must work upon Polonius's fears for his own and his daughter's honor. But this point, formerly so sensitive in the old man (I. iii. 105 ff.), is calloused now by his secret ambition. Delighted to find that Hamlet unprompted is "Still harping on my daughter" (188), he waives the note of indecency in the other's speech as due to the frustration of honorable love: probably the book that the prince is so intent upon has to do with youthful sufferings "for love" (190-193). But no; Hamlet declares he is perusing a satire upon old men, notably their "plentiful lack of wit" (202). This is a sharp reinforcement of his grave warning above; but it is lost upon Polonius. He sucks nourishment for his hidden hope from the "method" (208) that he thinks he perceives in the other's "madness": the prince's meaningful replies suggest that if he presently meets "my daughter" (217), he will respond more effectively (as indeed he does in III. i, though not in the way Polonius hoped) than if he were in full possession of his "reason and sanity" (214) to control his emotion. Polonius swells inwardly with the thought of the high honor which may then descend upon her and upon

---

[11] Ophelia's name is not uttered in II. ii outside of Hamlet's letter (110, 120). His present use of "daughter" is a satiric echo of Polonius's incessant repetition of it above (106, 124, 134, 162). The old man's secret ambition makes him think of her as his progeny and chattel—"*my* daughter" (lines 189, 217, cf. line 428 below)—not as a human person with a beautiful and significant name.

her humble sire: "My honorable lord, I will most humbly take my leave of you."

"You cannot, sir," Hamlet rejoins with an elaborate imitation of the old gentleman's low bow, "take from me anything that I will more willingly part withal—except my life, my life" (221).[12] The last five words are uttered with a sudden mad grimness designed, successfully, to scare the old fellow into beating a hasty retreat. A moment ago the prince had hinted that he was readier to walk into his "grave" than into the court with Polonius (210); and a short time before that he had parted from Polonius's daughter with a sorrow that "did seem to . . . end his being" (II. i. 95 f.). The tragicomic situation is that Hamlet, saddened to death because of Ophelia, is bored to death by her father. Polonius emblemizes all the "tediousness" (91) that old age, which ought to be wise, can acquire and display in this decadent Denmark: "These tedious old fools!" (223). But now two tedious *young* fools, surely, are approaching; that is the impression they made a few minutes ago upon us. Therefore we are deeply touched when Hamlet, with a quick and utter change of mood, greets them very warmly: "My excellent good friends—how dost thou, Guildenstern? O Rosencrantz! Good lads, how do you both?"

Those "lads" were "brought up with him"—unlike Horatio and Ophelia—and remained the intimate friends of his "youth" (11 f.). Recently in his mother's presence he has "much talked" of them, clinging fondly to the thought of them (19-21). Consequently he now assumes that, learning of his unhappiness, they "in the beaten way of friendship" (277) have come to pay him "a free visitation" (284). And he is ready to take great comfort from their naïveté, so different from the Polonian sort. They are, he believes, unlike Polonius, utterly free from "craft" (290) and self-seeking. They can bring him, from a region outside the dishonest court, that honest simplicity which he loves and which was always so congenial to him, so "neigh-

---

[12] The more elaborate version of the quartos, "except my life, except my life, except my life," was perhaps intended to accompany three long strides with which Hamlet should back Polonius off; compare Touchstone's treatment of William in *As You Like It* V. i. 51 ff. In any case it is clear that Hamlet does not utter the words "except my life" in a tone of heavy, lingering, romantic despair. His mood is sharply saturnine, not suicidal.

bored to his . . . humor" (12), in them. All this is in his mind when he greets them with simple, full-hearted warmth and trust.

But to his surprise, instead of resuming like him the old frank relationship, they respond, jauntily uneasy, with smart court talk of fortune, contentment, moderation. He perceives that their heads have been turned; they long for that advancement at court which they are pretending to despise (232, 267). He guesses what we already know: summoned hither by "the good king and queen" (291), basking in royal favor, suddenly raised from obscurity to the high status of "helpful" (39) friends of the mentally ill crown prince, the two young gentlemen have put their heads together—hence their comic unanimity on the stage—to play this golden opportunity for all it is worth. The tragic comedy of their dealings with Hamlet is that of a Polonius gone "like a crab . . . backward" (205 f.) into youth; like him they have a fain-to-be-hidden ambition at court.

It is clear, however, that Hamlet is ready to forgive and tolerate their ambition and also their inquisitiveness regarding his own supposed "ambition" (258) if only they will resume their old-time simple frankness when in private company with him. But they will not do so. Like Polonius they can mouth the great word "honest" (242) even while violating its meaning; and, as in the preceding episode (176), the utterance of that word renders Hamlet somber and monitory. He will catch their conscience. He casually introduces (244) and gradually presses the question (278), "what make you at Elsinore?" —thus repeating his initial tactic with Horatio (I. ii. 164, 174), but with an opposite result. There he found honest friendship; here he uncovers dishonest obsequiousness. The two young gentlemen are eager to "wait upon" him (273) but only in the royal service. They are forced to admit they were "sent for" (303); and they are embarrassed, but only by their unlucky strategic situation. They give no sign of that which Hamlet is seeking in them, the conscience which is at the very heart of real affection; the just (285), the "even and direct" (298) dealing that must appear in the face and manner, more than in the words, of a true friend. The prince's final appeal to their

hearts is extraordinarily intense and humble. Laying aside
every tinge of bitterness and satire, returning to the warmth of
his initial greeting of them, but with climactic gravity, he con-
jures (294) them "by the rights of our fellowship, by the con-
sonancy of our youth, by the obligation of our ever preserved
love, and by what more dear a better proposer could charge
you withall. . . ."[13]

That last clause is a disarming confession of his own shortcomings as an exponent of the "perfect ceremony of love's
rite" (Sonnet 23). He himself is far from being a perfect
"proposer." He knows he has been secretive in his way as they
have in theirs. Their conceited sense of mission as royal emissaries investigating the crown prince is a parodical counterpart
of his own pride of mission as investigator of king and court.
Shakespeare makes us feel this parallel, and the suggestion is
that some awareness of it on Hamlet's part facilitates his meekness here. By example he invites his boyhood friends to penitent frankness. But their words and their eyes remain guarded;
not at all because of mental stupidity—no wit is needed to
grasp such offered affection—but because they have wilfully
stupefied their hearts. Their ambitious, cocklike vanity, along
with their "secrecy to the king and queen," wishes to "moult
no feather" (306), as Hamlet implies in a satiric thrust that
denotes the end of his patient, fruitless efforts to win them.

The ensuing lofty elegy upon nature and man in poetic
prose is, not an outbreak of disillusioned idealism, but the peak
of Hamlet's loneliness. The initial stage of his isolation, due
to causes outside himself, was prepared for in the first scene of
the play and exhibited in the second. Afterwards it was tragically heightened by his own conduct, his absolute secrecy regarding his spectral vision, and his consequent separation from Horatio and Ophelia. Having lost those two, he turned all the
more hungrily to his two schoolfellows. Their simplicity al-

---

[13] Many other passages in Shakespeare and in Elizabethan literature have
the same intent. See, for instance, Helena's appeal to Hermia in *A Midsummer
Night's Dream* III. ii. 198 ff. In the current philosophy of gentility true
friendship was regarded as a prime *virtue*, as in *The Faerie Queene* Book IV.
This matter, as shown in my text, is of great importance for the right interpretation of the climax of the first act.

lured him extremely—so the dramatic sequence tells us—because of its extreme contrast with what he conceived to be the indirectness of Ophelia and the intelligent intrusiveness of Horatio. But the two newcomers have proved to be both indirect and intrusive and, finally, hard of heart, utterly rejecting his offered "love and friending" (I. v. 186). Otherwise he would have confided his troubles to them; to what extent, is left to our imagination. Patently he yearned to tell them somewhat of the "bad dreams," not attributable to mere "ambition," by which he is "most dreadfully attended"; on this matter he wished to speak to them in "friendship" and "like an honest man" (258-277). He staked upon these two "lads" his last hope of intimate and genuine companionship.

Now, in their very presence, their specious presence, he is more than ever alone with his awful troubles. The world and Denmark are for him a manifold "prison" (247-253), recalling to us the secret, fiery, fasting "prison-house" of his father's spirit (I. v. 11-20). Yet even now he is not in the least doubtful of the essential rightness of the universe. He knows that the world is "goodly" (251); it is a prison merely "to me" (257); he could be as free as "infinite space" except for his "bad dreams" (260-262); "for there is nothing either good or bad but [i.e., unless] thinking makes it so" (255-257).[14] Our "thinking," our state of mind, determines, not goodness and badness, but whether any particular thing shall seem good or bad to us at any given time. Accordingly all the gloom, personal and intermittent (as we have seen) in Hamlet's present state of mind, is gathered and emphasized in certain personal and intermittent lines of his elegy, namely those beginning at the margin in the arrangement given below. The inset lines, couched in the cosmic mood of the drama and recalling the final

---

[14] Cf. *Troilus and Cressida* II. ii. 52:

> TROILUS What is aught but as 'tis valued?
> HECTOR But value dwells not in particular will;
>   It holds his estimate and dignity
>   As well wherein 'tis precious of itself
>   As in the prizer . . .

In other words the value of anything is indeed determined by thinking but *not* by individualistic thinking—"not in particular will." Hamlet like Hector knows that "the general censure" (I. iv. 35) must be taken into account when we are aiming at the value which a thing has "of itself."

episode of the opening scene (I. i. 143 ff.), tell what the universe and man, Hamlet's present mood aside, really are.

> I have of late, but wherefore I know not,
> lost all my mirth, forgone all custom of exercise;
> and indeed, it goes so heavily with my disposition that
>   this goodly frame, the earth,
> seems to me a sterile promontory;
>   this most excellent canopy, the air, look you,
>   this brave overhanging firmament,
>   this majestical roof fretted with golden fire,
> why, it appears no other thing to me
> than a foul and pestilent congregation of vapors.
>   What a piece of work is a man!
>   how noble in reason, how infinite in faculty,
>   in form and moving how express and admirable,
>   in action how like an angel,
>   in apprehension how like a god:
>   the beauty of the world, the paragon of animals;
> and yet, to me, what is this quintessence of dust?
> man delights not me—

Woman is of course comprised in "man" and in "the beauty of the world"; but with sudden particularity, parallel to his shift a few minutes ago from the "world" and "man" to Polonius's "daughter" (178-183), Hamlet adds bitterly: "no, nor woman neither, though by your smiling you seem to say so." The undercurrent of his lonely thinking keeps setting towards Ophelia. He betrays that fact to us—as he will again presently, for the third time in this scene (422 ff.)—by his very endeavor to hide it from himself and from his listeners. Hence his extraordinary misreading here of the "smiling" of Rosencrantz and Guildenstern. They have no thought of Ophelia; merely, they are trying to banish from their minds the thought of his declared, deep unhappiness. They have listened to his moving speech with a growing embarrassment which in the end they relieve, after the custom of cooled friends, by simpering at his immoderateness, as it seems to them, and by desiring to change the subject. His finale, "man delights not me," draws from them an uneasy "laugh" (326) smothered at once into "smiling" (323). His "lenten" mood (329) as Rosencrantz terms it—the word "lenten" nicely blunts the poignancy of his misery while glossing over his schoolfellows' part in causing it—will spoil, amusingly, the reception of the Players who are coming to offer him their "service."

II. ii. 332-634

However, the idea of that "service," so different from the sort offered him by his two false friends (273), gives Hamlet a quick, warm delight. The word "delight" is iterated (321, 327, 328, 341) in the transition from his elegy to the subject of the Players. We are made to feel that his melancholy, now in its apogee, can be relieved only by the vital pleasure of plain, honest "fellowship" (294) with persons absolutely outside the courtly and political sphere. Hence his very great interest in these "tragedians of the city." He wishes to know their fortunes in minute detail before they arrive on the scene. And he intimates (387 ff.) that his "entertainment" of them, so far from being "lenten," will have all the reality of welcome forfeited by Rosencrantz and Guildenstern, to whom he assigns with delicious fitness "the appurtenance of welcome," mere "fashion and ceremony." He accompanies this speech with histrionic gestures, bowing ironically to the two "Gentlemen," as he now for the first time terms them, and then taking their hands very formally, in contrast with the simple warmth of his initial greeting to them (228) and of his coming welcome to the Players (441 ff.). To these, when they at length enter, he speaks intimately, scrutinizing their faces one by one intently. They, direct opposites of the insincerely chattering Rosencrantz and Guildenstern, make no replies, at least none audible to us. Their silence sets off the significance of his scrutiny of them. In their honest, quiet, friendly looks he finds what he wants. In these actors, as human persons, he sees the same quality which he loved in their "excellent play" (460) and which he has not found at court: no "affectation" but "an honest method, as wholesome as sweet" (465).

And in finding the great relief of honest fellowship Hamlet begins to find also a way towards solving his great problems.

Allusions to these, at first remote, become more and more pressing as the episode proceeds. At the first when the prince exclaims, "He that plays the king shall be welcome . . . and the
lady shall say her mind freely" (332, 338), he is unconsciously
getting relief from the unwelcome "king" Claudius and the
mute "lady" Ophelia. The theme of Ophelia recurs when
Polonius re-enters. That "great baby" (400) sets up to be a
judge of actors (415 ff.). He is therefore dubbed by Hamlet
"Jephthah, judge of Israel" (who sacrificed his daughter to his
own worldly ambition) and warned, covertly but extensively,
to have enough judgment and also enough Christian piety[15] to
cherish the welfare of his daughter, that "treasure" (422-438).
And upon the Players' entrance we note the prince's humorously
tender attention to "my young lady and mistress" (445), i.e.,
the boy who plays the heroine's parts. He hopes "her" voice
will still ring true like an uncracked goldpiece; as, above, he
wanted the "lady" to "say her mind freely." His conscious and
subconscious allusions to Ophelia make a transition from his
former meeting (II. i) to his coming meeting (III. i) with her.
Meanwhile, for immediate purposes, the thought of Claudius is
brought to the fore urgently.

It appears that the reputation of these Players, like the
fame of Hamlet's father, has suffered from an "innovation"
(347). Though still as proficient as ever in their art (353),
they have been ousted from public favor by the competition and
satirical attacks of a strange new company, mere child-actors.
Like these "boys" (377 ff.), Hamlet reflects bitterly, his uncle,
formerly despised, is now as "king" highly regarded. Many
will even go to any expense to own "his picture in little"—a
miniature of him whose very looks were repulsive to them
"while my father lived." Such power has false custom to
distort plain nature! " 'Sblood [i.e., God's blood],[16] there is

---

[15] Contrast the paganism of the previous warning (181-187). That
warning failed to impress Polonius; hence the religious sharpness of Hamlet's
present admonition.

[16] The "s'bloud" of Q2 was omitted in F1 because of an Act of Parliament
(1606) against blasphemous profanity on the stage. But the Eucharistic oath
is essential to Hamlet's thought here: the mystery of preternatural evil in men
is as nonplusing to "philosophy" as the mystery of supernatural good ("God's
blood") in Christ. Compare Lear's thought of Regan: "Is there any cause
in nature that makes these hard hearts?" (III. vi. 81).

something in this more than natural"—something more than
"things rank and gross in nature" (I. ii. 136)—"if philosophy
could find it out." Hence Hamlet's sympathy with the Players
is intensified. They have undergone like his father an unnatural oblivion; and they have come to him, the crown prince
—not to the new king—in the hope that he, unlike the fickle
public, will favor them as formerly (341).

Accordingly his thoughts go back to an old play or interlude
of theirs which he "once" (454) heard them rehearse, a work
of classic excellence, in his judgment, but immediately rejected
by the public. He dwells upon that antithesis. The play was
"caviare to the general." For "the million" are not pleased by
a work "very much more handsome than fine"; they prefer a
play with "sallets in the lines"; as they now prefer his uncle's
to his father's picture. This latent comparison is conveyed to
us by Hamlet's resuming the tone in which he spoke of the
miniature (383) above, in contrast with his intervening banter
and jocularity: now again he becomes serious and deliberate.
And this tone intensifies when he comes to the "One speech"
(467) which he had "chiefly loved" in the unpopular play. It
describes Pyrrhus's "slaughter" of Priam. Hamlet's "prophetic
soul" (I. v. 40) is aware, although he does not say so, that
this speech is "something like the murder of my father" (624).

"Something like." The *un*likeness, so manifest in the antique speech as a whole, gives sharp point to the covert, piercing
likenesses. Claudius is no Pyrrhus. But this militant, open
killer was secret (like Claudius) at the first, "When he lay
couched in the ominous horse." Hence Hamlet's preliminary
shift of similes: he withdraws his violent phrase for Pyrrhus,
"like th' Hyrcanian beast" (472), i.e., a desert tiger, in favor
of the simile "did the night resemble" (475). These four
words convey the very spirit of Claudius. And in the ensuing
lines, recited by Hamlet with a growing tenseness that fascinates
his listeners, the obvious horridness of Pyrrhus bodies forth the
prince's horror of the secret "hellish" (485) evil of Claudius.
The prince's personal emotions stop him, forcing him to turn
over the rest of the speech to the First Player, when he comes
to Priam (486)—"methinks I see my father" (I. ii. 184). His

father, though the antithesis of the weak old king of Troy, lay helpless too before his killer, according to the Ghost's story. In the same tense silence with which he heard that story in I. v Hamlet listens now to the First Player's equally circumstantial narrative. The present situation is a distant but real reflection of that ghostly scene on the battlements. The resemblance is spectral; designed, we are made to feel, by the invisible powers. The unseen Ghost of his father is present to Hamlet now. The symbolism is intense. The sudden "hideous crash" (498) of the citadel of Troy intimates the downfall of the moral order of Denmark. And the ensuing pause represents the pause we have been watching since Act I in the drama of Claudius and Hamlet:

> But as we often see, against some storm,
> A silence in the heavens, the rack stand still,
> The bold winds speechless, and the orb below
> As hush as death, anon the dreadful thunder
> Doth rend the region, so after Pyrrhus' pause
> Aroused vengeance sets him new a-work. . . .

Those lines, leaping out from the antique mold of the speech into the cosmic vein of *The Tragedy of Hamlet, Prince of Denmark,* prepare us for a quick renewal of the vengeance-action. The prince's silent tension is now extreme. It is momentarily relieved, but indirectly increased, by the inane comments of Polonius upon the First Player's speech: the old courtier represents all those who, oblivious of the late king and devoted to Claudius, are accordingly insensible to noble drama, preferring "a jig or a tale of bawdry" (522). Therefore Hamlet urges the Player to proceed at once to Hecuba, who is the reverse of oblivious. This "mobled" (muffled) queen, so vividly the opposite of the queen of Denmark in every detail of appearance and conduct, becomes an allegorical figure of grief, of mortal and heaven-moving (540) mourning.

Hamlet, deeply brooding, says to the First Player: " 'Tis well, I'll have thee speak out the rest, soon" (545).[17] But

---

[17] The quarto version, "the rest of this soon," is inferior dramatically. The F1 version, "the rest, soon," implies that Hamlet makes a significant pause after "rest," emphasized by the harsh sequence of "st" and "s," in order to hint that "the rest" will be something very important, indeed different—a different play, perhaps, though concerned also with the subject of vengeance.

presently (562) when the two are alone we learn that "the rest" means, now, another play, the *Murther of Gonzago*, including a few lines to be inserted by the prince himself: it shall be performed "tomorrow" before the court and king. Thus Hamlet has experienced through his fellowship with the Players a mystic revelation of his immediate duty. While listening to his "old friend" (443, 562) the First Player and under the influence, as Shakespeare makes us feel, of the supernatural realm the crown prince has discovered what he himself should at once do as first player, as leading actor, in Denmark's drama.

But now, before proceeding to act, he gives way, in the first part (575-610) of his ensuing soliloquy, to an unprecedented outburst of wild emotion—to be ridiculed immediately afterwards by himself. Its prelude is "Now I am alone"; spoken, not with quick gratification, but very slowly in a tone of brooding gloom that culminates and dwells in the final word "alone."[18]   He has just parted from the First Player, the "old friend" in whom as in none else he has found great practical help, but whom, after a moment of private converse which the other was obviously ready to continue, he has dismissed abruptly, with assumed lightness of manner (570 f.).[19]   Even that reliable friend-at-need Hamlet will not take into further confidence. So now he is indeed "alone." This word, here uttered by him for the first time, marks the climax of his secretive isolation and prepares for a unique outbreak of repressed confession. Having painfully concealed the Ghost's message from all the individuals with whom he has come in contact he is now, on the verge of public action, seized with a wild yearning to reveal it at once *to the whole nation.*

[18] The whole line in F1 reads: "I so, God buy'ye: now I am alone." The first half of the line, addressed to Rosencrantz and Guildenstern, is light, quick, impatient; the second half, in contrast, very slow and weighty. ("I" stands for Ay, "God buy'ye" for goodby.)

[19] The importance of the First Player is blurred for the modern reader, but should not be for the spectator in the theater, by the fact that he has no name, like a number of other important personages in Shakespeare's plays. Of course his inferiority to the prince in rank does not in the least account for Hamlet's failure to take him into full confidence; that motive is excluded by Hamlet's intimate treatment of him in the foregoing episode. Incidentally, the intimacy between noblemen and distinguished actors, including Shakespeare himself, in the late sixteenth century, was well known to the contemporary audience.

Of course he will not do so. He knows that the Ghost's message, even if it were free from doubt in his own mind, would be instantly rejected by Claudius's Denmark. But that fact, repeatedly intimated to us and presently to be faced again by the prince, is swept aside for a minute by the loosed torrent of his feelings and imaginings. He fancies that this Denmark, deaf even to his plea for a merely decent mourning for its onetime idol, the late king, would actually believe the spectral story of his murder if it were told by his son with passionate dramatic power. Such is Hamlet's momentary delusion; and he can "force his soul," like the Player, "to his own conceit" (579). Therefore, especially as he is now moved by an underlying sense (which I shall presently discuss) of his own *real* faults, he heaps blame upon himself for the *imaginary* fault of not yet having publicized the ghost-and-murder story. We listen, half amused yet with deep sympathy, while the gentleman-hero calls himself a "rogue and peasant slave," a "John-a-dreams," and finally even a "coward" (598). He has his "cue for passion" (587). A few minutes ago, starved for utterance, he demanded of the Players "a passionate speech" (452) and threw his soul into the opening lines of it. Now he is resuming and completing that dramatic recitation in his own style. He throws himself into the role of a player on "the stage" (588) of Denmark: he would fain "drown" it "with tears,"

> And cleave the general ear with horrid speech,
> Make mad the guilty and appal the free,
> Confound the ignorant, and amaze indeed
> The very faculty of eyes and ears.

In plain reality, however, he "can say nothing" (596).

Those three words, for us of the audience, not for Hamlet himself in his present mood, render a hard fact of fate. Intemperately he declares himself responsible for that fact. In actuality his oath of secrecy with Horatio and Marcellus in the close of Act I was intemperate. Now he has gone from one extreme to the other: the proud resolve to hide his secret from those two friends is the cause of his mad craving now to proclaim it to the public. After yearning in vain to confess something of it to Ophelia, and thereafter to his two schoolfellows, his secret "horrors" (II. i. 84) and "bad dreams" (262) found indirect vent in the Pyrrhus-Priam-Hecuba oration. Thus in the climax of Act II the experience that formed the climax of Act I is paralleled, with the First Player replacing Horatio as sympathetic friend. But this Player, unlike Horatio, is closely congenial to the emotional and imaginative side of his prince, and the prince's need of a confidant is now extreme. On the other hand his pride of mission has become in the meantime "a habit that too much o'erleavens The form of plausive manners" (I. iv. 29). All the precepts of right manners and morals for a prince, all the sixteenth-century dictates governing the conduct of the gentleman, would normally prompt him now to confess his pent-up secret to his ultimate friend, the honest and devoted First Player. To do that would be human, prudent, and gracious. But his pride seals his lips. So presently, false pride giving way as so often in human life to false humility, he paints a melodramatic picture of himself as a "coward" deserving public insults (598-605). He chose to "say nothing" of his secret to close friends when Providence gave opportunity. Therefore by way of reaction, and in passionate confusion of mind, he vilifies himself for the ineluctable silence in public that fate has forced upon him. To the present public, which loves the new king's picture and is bored with the old moving tragedy of "Priam's slaughter," Hamlet "can say nothing," nothing that would be in the least convincing.

In the climax of his passion his theme leaps suddenly from saying to doing (606-610):

> I should have fatted all the region kites
> With this slave's offal, bloody, bawdy villain,
> Remorseless, treacherous, lecherous, kindless villain!
> Oh vengeance!

He is beside himself. Those lines are "bloody" melodrama, obviously echoing his Pyrrhus speech above with its "blood of fathers," etc. (480), and utterly unlike anything he has hitherto said. The initial passage in which he willed to "sweep to my revenge" (I. v. 29-31)—our thoughts go back to it because in the long interval the word "revenge" has never once been on his lips—was equally sudden and brief; but it was very restrained in comparison with the present lines, which terribly contravene his character and conscience. We are made to realize how very much, in the meantime, his inhuman secrecy has rendered him liable to inhuman emotion. His violently repressed desire to speak becomes, in a moment, brutal desire to act. And this desire, though sensationally expressed, is brutally sincere. For Hamlet has now let loose in himself, for the first time, that primitive nature which, subsisting in all of us, rouses when we lose our humane control, especially when we fear that we are soft, "pigeon-livered," lacking "gall to make oppression bitter" (605 f.). At this moment he is quite oblivious of his just "cause" (595-598). He is concerned only with self-satisfaction. He rages with the Pyrrhus sort, actually, of "aroused vengeance" (510, 610).

Then he struggles to pull himself together, almost wondering for an instant who it was that spoke so wildly: "Who? What an ass am I! Ay sure, this is most brave. . . ."[20] He proceeds to re-identify his true self and cause: "the son of the dear father murdered. . . ." who should not "like a whore unpack my heart with words. . . ." Those blatantly illegitimate "words" of his he now revokes; but at the same time he admits they came from his "heart." And just because of that outbreak of heartfelt primitive passion he utters now, by way of sequel, the ominous line: "Prompted to my revenge by heaven and hell" (613). This verse packs together in passionate confusion three things that were formerly apart, "my revenge," "heaven," and "hell" (I. v. 31, 92, 93). He does not hesitate now, as he hesitated then, to "couple hell." He does not distinguish hellish revengefulness from the kind of vengeance that partakes of heavenly justice when a man is "noble in reason" and "like a god" (316-319).

---

[20] In Q2 the line reads: "Why what an ass am I, this is most brave." This version, like the initial revenge passage in Q2 (see note 11, Act I), is smoother and less suggestive than the F1 version, which reads in the original: "Who? What an Asse am I? I sure, this is most brave." The second "I" (Ay) stresses punningly Hamlet's sense of self-division. In both versions the word "ass" mocks the melodramatic sibilants of his preceding lines, and "brave" echoes the *b*'s of "bloody, bawdy villain."

But that vital distinction, blurred for his "judgment" by his "blood" (III. ii. 74), is not lost to his "soul." We perceive it at work there when, after recovering himself further, after quieting his "heart" and exerting his "brain" (617), he develops his just and excellent plan for employing the *Murther of Gonzago*. He hopes this play will strike Claudius "to the soul" (620). His own soul has been moved by the supernal spirit of justice. That is why he now mistrusts the "spirit that I have seen" (627). He doubted it at the first: it might be a bringer of "airs from heaven or blasts from hell" (I. iv. 41), though it soon laid his doubts asleep by looking and saying what his own feelings had predisposed him to see and hear. For, as he now declares, "the devil hath power To assume a pleasing shape" (628). Hamlet, who from the first has been looking into the "pleasing," specious feelings of others—all the way from the politic kindness of Claudius (I. ii. 65) to the hollow friendliness of Rosencrantz and Guildenstern—is looking now into dubious emotions of his own. He is mainly concerned with his present state, not his condition in Act I. He alludes with extreme brevity to the apparition of his father because he knows, as we know, that he is excusable if he was deceived at the time by its strong appeal to him. The crucial point now is that "the devil," once admitted by us, however innocently, proceeds to increase his power, using subtler ways; appealing to us, no longer through visible spirits, but through wrong "spirits" within us, our own deceptive feelings:

> yea, and perhaps
> Out of my weakness and my melancholy,
> As he is very potent with such spirits,
> Abuses me to damn me.[21]

[21] In Q1 the present tense of the verb is still more emphatic: "Doth seeke to damn me." To read back Hamlet's *present* weakness and melancholy into his first soliloquy (I. ii. 129 ff.) is to miss the dramatic development which, since then, notably in Act II, has brought him to his present state of mind. However, we must remember that when Hamlet first saw the Ghost he perceived the evil possibility of its "pleasing shape" (629). This phrase is surely intended to echo the initial phrase, "questionable [i.e., inviting] shape" (I. iv. 43). In accordance with the old belief that the devil or one of his demons might assume the form of a deceased loved one to ensnare and damn a man by inducing him to commit a mortal sin, Hamlet was immediately aware that the, for him, uniquely alluring form of the specter could be the work of a "goblin damned" (I. iv. 40).

These "spirits," so much subtler than the outward specter of the past, are the "weakness" and "melancholy" which, growing upon him in his proud solitariness, culminated a moment ago in the "bloody" cry for personal "vengeance."

That cry, Hamlet knows, was "weakness," a word nowhere else in the play applied to him by himself, or by anyone else, and here very significant. For he also knows the evil nature of the passion vented by that cry, the primitive revengefulness. His *soul* confesses that fact. But his *mind* does not; and nothing is effectually real to a man unless and until his "thinking makes it so" (256). Hamlet's intellect grasps all else with extraordinary clarity; in self-knowledge the other Shakespearean tragic heroes are childlike compared to him. All the more striking, then, is his *mental* evasiveness regarding his own proud revengefulness. In this particular matter he "hath ever but slenderly known himself" (*Lear* I. i. 296). That is what Shakespeare intends "the judicious" (III. ii. 31) to say of his prince at the present juncture, as at certain later crucial moments. The dramatist's thought is that even Hamlet (like his fore-study, Brutus) must be as naïve as lesser minds at the point where his self-knowing is blinded by pride. "I know not," he said truthfully in regard to the "wherefore" of the gloom exposed in his great elegy (307). He did not *know* his melancholy's deepest cause. Nor does his *mind* grasp it now, though he goes so far as to confess "weakness" in addition to "melancholy." His melancholy's deepest cause, his real weakness, his "dram of eale," is his impatient, secretive pride of mission.

That pride has effected the sharp division in the present soliloquy between his passion and his brain, his "blood" and his "judgment." Like "the time" he himself is "out of joint"; and he is the vital center of the time. He can "set it right," as the whole course of the drama will show, only in so far as he himself is set right: "This above all, to thine own self be true" (I. iii. 78). Denmark is dishonest.[22] The prince of Denmark, hating that vice, has it subtly in himself: his vengeance-motive

---

[22] In Shakespeare's time "honesty" had a wide range of meanings, from mere propriety and negative chastity up to positive and lofty righteousness; but always the word implied genuineness or veracity. In *Hamlet*, particularly, the denotation of genuineness holds the foreground.

is confused and unveracious. Hence his present intemperate-
ness. The radix of it is ingrown pride.

Therefore his prime need now is a new access of humility.
And this need, though but dimly seen by his conscious mind, is
felt by his "prophetic soul"; as Shakespeare shows us with
consummate art in the end of Act II and the first part of
Act III. Hamlet is now aware that like every man he himself
is very faulty: "use every man after his desert, and who should
'scape whipping?" (554). That exclamation prepared for the
outburst of self-blame in the first part of the ensuing "peasant
slave" soliloquy. And there, even while he still seems so sure
of Claudius's guilt, he is planning to test it by the *Murther of
Gonzago:* his new self-condemnation is making him question his
hasty condemnation of his chief enemy. He evades, wrongly
and fatefully, the ultimate issue, the conflict of justice and
revengefulness, of "heaven and hell." Should Claudius prove
to be guilty, "I know my course" (627), he says with evasive
vagueness. But though he compromises with the "hell" of
revenge, he repudiates the possible "devil" of delusion regarding the king's guilt; he must have firm rational "grounds" for
believing the murder. In this great matter his perception cuts
through illusive feelings. His inner sight has been sharpened
by his new humility. Hamlet's own conscience deepens while
he proceeds to "catch the conscience of the king."

(c) *beget a temperance*   III. i—III. ii. 281

III. i. 1-55

We, unlike Hamlet, know that Claudius's conscience has
already been caught in a preliminary fashion. "And"—the
king's suggestive opening word in the present scene—his conscience is much troubled now, as the average human conscience
is, by an external threat which persists in being vague. His
nephew's mental state is more mysterious than ever; therefore
it appears, to Claudius's uneasy soul, no longer just a "transformation" due to something that "put him . . . from . . . himself" (II. ii. 5-9), but a "turbulent and dangerous lunacy" that
he himself "puts on" (2-4). That word "dangerous," sending

our thoughts back to Hamlet's threatening soliloquy above, is thrown up by "the conscience of the king." Nothing "dangerous" appears in the ensuing report of Rosencrantz and Guildenstern. This report, to be sure, is couched by them in euphemistic terms for the sake of the listening queen, suggesting, in connection with the king's opening "And," that they have privately informed him of Hamlet's most disturbing remarks to them.[1] Their smooth account in Hamlet's mother's presence of his evasiveness when they questioned him (5-9) and his effortful politeness (10-14) recalls to us, and doubtless to the informed Claudius, Hamlet's discovery that they were the king's spies and, more importantly, his refusal to give a direct denial to their suspicion of his desire for the throne: he left that question painfully suspended in air (II. ii. 258-272). But that is an old question. The king's growing pangs of conscience (as will be presently shown in his own words) are the main cause of his present very painful suspense regarding what Guildenstern terms the "crafty madness" (8) of Hamlet.

Therefore Claudius welcomes warmly (24) the coming Play, relieved that the Players have occasioned in the prince "a kind of joy" (18); just as he was much delighted at the first (I. ii. 121 ff.) when Hamlet's accusing grief seemed to abate a little. Then as now his conscience was soothed by a touch of good humor in the young man he has wronged. Now, however, that relief is comparatively faint and only serves to intensify his need to express in words his growing inner anguish. The dramatic irony here is complex and profound. The situations of the sovereign and the crown prince are parallel. The king, like the prince in the preceding scene though far more guiltily, is burdened with an inhuman secret. The king too has "a kind of joy" in the thought of the coming Play—the very instrument which is designed to catch his conscience fully

---

[1] Present repetition of those remarks is excluded by the dramatic economy of Shakespeare, skilfully employing the excuse of Gertrude's presence. The last of those remarks, deeply disturbing from the standpoint of Claudius, was: "when the wind is southerly I know a hawk from a handsaw" (II. ii. 396). Whatever else this passage may mean, it is clear from the whole context that "hawk" alludes to the spying of Rosencrantz and Guildenstern in the service of the king. Thus the passage directly prepared for the opening lines of the present scene.

while fully satisfying Hamlet's: the king helps to "drive" the prince's "purpose on" (27). And just now the king is approaching an emotional outburst which, like Hamlet's above, comes suddenly and astonishingly, though it has been in process of preparation ever since his first appearance on the stage. The prince's outburst, above, is touched off unwittingly by a speech of his old friend the First Player; the king's by an unwitting speech of his old friend Polonius. Here the irony is acute. The old courtier—styled by his master "the father of good news" (II. ii. 42)—now covertly delighted by the queen's apparent approval of a marriage between Ophelia and the prince (37-42), is inspired by his cheerful conceit, together with a prayer book (44), to utter a smug truism that cuts his patron to the quick:

> We are oft to blame in this,
> 'Tis too much proved, that with devotion's visage
> And pious action we do sugar o'er
> The devil himself.

Indeed it is "too much proved" (too much a matter of experience). "Oh 'tis too true," the wretched Claudius exclaims aside. The terms "devotion's visage" and "pious action" render with dreadful precision the mien he exhibited in his triumphant initial scene (I. ii). And now, in a crucial soliloquy, parallel to the prince's above, the king's confession, brought about gradually by the overruling Justice, rushes forth suddenly:

> How smart a lash that speech doth give my conscience!
> The harlot's cheek, beautied with plastering art,
> Is not more ugly to the thing that helps it
> Than is my deed to my most painted word:
> Oh heavy burthen!

We think of the "painted," artful, ingratiating public smile of the lowest and the highest figures in Danish society: the whore on the street, the king on the throne.

The profoundest irony, however, is that the crown prince as well as the king of this Denmark has essayed, though far more excusably, to "sugar o'er the devil himself." A few minutes ago we saw Hamlet, at the nadir of his "peasant slave" soliloquy, trying to paint the devil of revengefulness in attractive colors. That devil is as "ugly," from the standpoint of supernal Justice, as the king now declares his crime of murder to be. And the parallel is intensified by the image of the harlot common to both soliloquies, applied confessionally by each speaker to his own misconduct. The king sees her engaged in her "plastering art"; the prince heard her "fall a-cursing," unpacking her heart with words (II. ii. 614 f.). In both cases Shakespeare feels the ugliness, whether in "drab," "scullion," king, or prince, of the prostitution of humanity to evil passions, above all when these are disguised, sugaring-over "the devil himself."

However, the devil must be given his due. We, unlike the prince, know now that "the devil" (II. ii. 628) did not in the least deceive him regarding the king's guilt. We foresee that very probably this guilt, pressing so heavily now upon his conscience, will be manifested through the agency of the Play. What then? For us that question is urgent now. The center of dramatic interest is already beginning to shift from the prelude to the postlude of the coming Play scene. Will Claudius's present remorse be followed, then, by full repentance? Will Hamlet, who mistakenly called him "remorseless" (II. ii. 609), kill him in the revengeful mood displayed above, thus heaping crime on crime, not really setting the time right? Claudius in six lines has clearly confessed his "burthen"; Hamlet in sixty lines, above, did not clearly confront his. His burden is of course far more complex; but so in his case is the "devil." The prince, unlike the king, has a deep devotion and piety; but these can be so distorted as to sugar-over the devil of proud, personal hatred and revengefulness. The dramatist shows this situation working, unclearly but really, in Hamlet's soul during the "To be" soliloquy and the ensuing "nunnery" scene. Desperately he needs, and struggles inwardly to achieve, a new self-mastery, a deeper temperance.

III. i. 56-196

The prince re-enters with firm step, intent upon a manuscript in his hand to which he has been adding some final touches, the *Murther of Gonzago*. Finishing with it he halts, lowers it, and looks beyond it, into the future; which is very dim because he has evaded the question of the right and wrong of "my revenge." He does not see just what he will do after the Play; and he cannot know what may be done to him. The vagueness of the situation gives him, like Claudius above, a sharp sense of danger. He may lose his life. He feels, and faces, personal fear, as a brave soldier will in the moment before battle, and as he himself did before following the Ghost (I. iv. 64-67). Well, is life or death better? That classic and popular enigma, normally uncongenial to Hamlet's morally realistic way of thought, forces itself upon him now. His mind seizes it and plays with it. Further lowering his manuscript, emblem of very real and urgent questions—which, however, may eventuate in his death—he admits with a smile, "To be, or not to be, that is the question. . . ." Standing erect and still (not mournfully slumped in a chair, nor ambling romantically about the stage) he proceeds in a swift-flowing style.[2]

The first and longer part of the speech, down to "know not of?" (82), goes very trippingly on the tongue. It is "Words, words, words" (II. ii. 194); beautiful words, but coming close in their tenor to the mere "saws of books" which hard real experience caused him earlier to "wipe away" (I. v. 99). This flow of comparatively superficial words gives needed relief to Hamlet, and to us. It helps him to put personal fear aside and to face the dim future with re-established resolution. His hidden dilemma, the problem of how to achieve right and just vengeance, rises close to the surface at times but not above it, as in the question, "Whether 'tis nobler in the mind to suffer . . ." Here he touches, fleetingly, the noble-sounding but inadequate doctrine of Stoic passivity. It would lead him to the ignoble extreme of retiring to a life of meditation, relinquishing

[2] Doctor Johnson rightly perceived that Hamlet is here concerned with the danger ahead of him and not, as in the popular interpretation, with the question of suicide. His strain of life-weariness is very literary and light, here, compared with what it was in his first soliloquy. Even there, however, he did not really contemplate "self-slaughter" (I. ii. 132). Merely he was human enough to express his great unhappiness by exclaiming, in effect, "I wish I were dead, I'd like to kill myself."

vengeance altogether.   He turns swiftly, incoherently to the
alternative:

> Or to take arms against a sea of troubles,
> And by opposing end them, to die, to sleep. . . .[3]

His incoherent state of mind is exactly rendered through the
famous mixed metaphor and the syncopating onrush from the
thought of action to the thought of death; by opposing his
troubles militantly, in and after the coming Play scene, he
may end them simply by losing his life.   Then there would be
peace for him—*if* the peace of death is really peace.   But is it?
All men, pagan and Christian, agree that death, whatever else
it may be, is a sleep.   But all know that sleep brings "dreams";
and these, he has special reason to know, are often very "bad
dreams" (II. ii. 262).   There's the "rub" that makes us cling
to our "mortal coil"; there's the "respect" (consideration) that
makes "calamity" (i.e., an unhappy person) willing to live
so long on earth.   Otherwise who would bear all the miseries
of life when "he himself" (75)—not leaving the issue to fate,
not waiting to die in conflict with the "sea of troubles," not
"taking arms" against it, but against himself—might make his
"quietus" with a mere "bodkin"?   All this on the assumption
that death, in itself, is a dreaming sleep; but what comes "*after
death*" (78)?   We human beings have, really, not just an
uneasiness about the "sleep of death": we have a great fear of
something more and beyond—

> the dread of something *after death*,
> The undiscovered country, from whose bourn
> No traveller returns. . . .

No "traveller," no actual human being, can return to enact
again his earthly travel, and travail, in the light of "those ills"
beyond death "that we know not of."[4]

---

[3] The comma after "them" is from Q2 and is in keeping with the synco-
pative speed of Hamlet's thought here.   The fourth quarto and the folios have
a colon.   Editors have substituted a question mark, or a period, or even a
period and a dash, followed by a new sentence.

[4] The words "travel" and "travail" were closely associated in Shakespeare's time because of the toil and danger of contemporary traveling.   The
"undiscovered country" is reminiscent of "that vast shore washed with the
farthest sea" in *Romeo and Juliet* II. ii. 83, the sea being the Pacific Ocean.

Why do we so dread those ills? Obviously because of "conscience" (83). We cannot forget our "sins" (90).[5] "Thus," in the upshot of our broodings upon the unseen world, "conscience doth make cowards of us all." Here (83) Hamlet's tone shifts from dreaminess to severity. Hard experience has taught him that the human conscience, his own included, is a mixture of truth and deception. Hence the paradox that our wholesome moral fear of what comes *after death* may foster a sickly pensiveness weakening the "native" will-power which is a fundamental factor in true morality *upon earth*. Thus conscience which, naturally, "puzzles the will" (80) with the thought of troubles in the *unseen* world may keep us, unnaturally, from fighting "outrageous fortune" (58) at the risk of our lives in the *seen* world:

> And thus the native hue of resolution
> Is sicklied o'er with the pale cast of thought,
> And enterprises of great pitch and moment
> With this regard their currents turn awry
> And lose the name of action—[6]

The "To be" soliloquy, as a whole, is beautiful and true in itself. But in it Hamlet glosses over, as in the "rogue and peasant slave" soliloquy, his essential problem, the nature of "my revenge." It is this problem, at bottom, which is stirring his

---

From the distant shore of a newly discovered country a sixteenth-century traveler might eventually return, though commonly he did not, after a long, deathlike absence. But from the "bourn" of the "*un*discovered country," eternity, "*No* traveller returns." Here "bourn" suggests at once a "vast shore" and an inviolable boundary or confine.

[5] The underlying connection between "conscience" and "sins" is clear in the syncopated closing lines of the soliloquy as given in Q1:

> Ay that, O this conscience makes cowards of us all,
> Lady in thy orizons, be all my sins remembered.

And near the beginning of the soliloquy Q1 has these lines:

> For in that dream of death, when we awake,
> And borne before an everlasting Judge. . . .
> The happy smile, and the accursed damned. . . .

If the dramatist had something of that sort in his first version of the speech, he removed it later because its religious literalness, though in keeping with some of Hamlet's utterances elsewhere, conflicts with his present mood. The speaker's emphasis here is upon the judge within us, conscience, not the "Judge" above.

[6] The phrase "this regard" (87), referring to a wrong fear of death, is antithetical to "the respect" (68), referring to a right fear of death.

conscience; but he does not face it. His projected "enterprise,"
that of the Play, is indeed of "great pitch and moment," but it
is ominously incomplete. If he catches the conscience of the
king, what will be his ensuing "action"? He avoids that climactic question. Not thinking enough (so far from thinking
too much) he suddenly reacts from "pale" thought, as we are
all apt to do in like case, into warm feeling. However, he
does not react into the extravagant passionateness of the "rogue
and peasant slave" outburst. He is now begetting a temperance
(III. ii. 8), aided by the fact that the enterprise of the *Murther
of Gonzago* is, so far as it goes, a sound and right action, a
"good thing to be done" (I. i. 130).

However, though more temperate than before, he is letting
his tone rise towards stridency (lifting high and shaking his
symbolic manuscript) while he utters the phrase "name of action"—when he catches sight of Ophelia, kneeling at a *prie-dieu*.
He checks himself; he gazes upon her for a moment, breathing
deeply, as fixed and still as she. She is rapt in her devotions.
Upon her father's departure she had disregarded his commands
(44-46): she had knelt, instead of walking, and had closed the
hypocritic prayer book. She is praying, as we and Hamlet
divine—and as she will presently do aloud (138)—for him.
He knows he needs her prayers, now more than ever. "Nymph
. . ." the word, as he tones it, has something of its ancient mythic
solemnity along with the courtly formality which he must now
use to her. He is no longer her wooer, but she is still "celestial
and my soul's idol" (II. ii. 109). And his new humble sense
of his own guilt appears in his first sentence to her. This sentence is transitional: it alludes to the deepest intent of his foregoing soliloquy and, at the same time, gives the keynote of the
ensuing dialogue with her. "Nymph, in thy orisons Be all my
sins remembered."

She, however, knows nothing of his "sins," excepting his
wild strangeness to her; for which he is apparently expressing
contrition now, in process of regaining his self-control. That
is what his gentle words, in contrast with his mad silence at
their previous meeting (II. i. 75 ff.), must mean to her. Still
kneeling she trembles with joy; her prayers have been an-

swered, it seems. She had put an end to his suit at her father's command because she doubted her worthiness to be the consort of this prince. But now she is sure he needs her: it seems plain now that his love for her was indeed, as his mother has intimated, the "happy cause" of his "wildness" and that she, Ophelia, can "bring him to his wonted way again" (38-42). She rises quickly; she comes to him with glad self-giving eagerness—and, for us and for him, with heart-breaking pathos. "Good my lord, How does your honor for this many a day?" He can scarcely speak; he thanks her faintly, his face averted. And she thinks that to help him regain "his wonted way" she must appeal to his sense of responsibility, answering his plea, above, to remember his "sins": his word "remembered" (90) suggests her word "remembrances" (93). With a loverly rebuke of his long absence from her—"longèd long" (94) echoes the yearning of "this many a day" (91)—she takes from her neck and bosom the rich jewels he gave her and offers to return them to him.[7] He, she is sure, will press them back upon her, adding to them again his "words of so sweet breath composed" (98), his former "holy vows" (I. iii. 114). His protest, "I never gave you aught" (96), uttered with voice still faint and averted face, seems to her, naturally, a further confession of self-blame. Meekly bold she resorts to aphoristic speech, inciting him *not* to "prove unkind":

> Take these again, for to the noble mind
> Rich gifts wax poor when givers prove unkind;[8]
> There, my lord.

He, however, exclaims (not with angry vehemence, as some actors use, but in a low, intense tone of dismay), "Ha, ha, are *you* honest?" Her innocent adage has struck him as not inno-

---

[7] Keats's "warmèd jewels" unclasped by his Madeline in "The Eve of St. Agnes," stanza 26, may come to our minds here. Ophelia avoids mention even of the word "jewels," but their sensuous appeal to her lover is certainly implied; it intensifies his pain in breaking with her. Probably Hamlet receives them into his hands when she says, "There, my lord" (102), and drops them when he declares, "I loved you not" (120). She may pick them up and hold them in her clasped hands when she kneels again to pray for him (138).

[8] Here it is important to remember the older and fuller sense of the word "kind," connoting naturalness; see note 7, Act I. She is trying to get him to be his natural and right self again.

cent; it smacks of the Polonian style. And the old politician's matrimonial scheming, banished from Hamlet's thoughts by preoccupation with his own "conscience" and then with Ophelia's "orisons," rushes back to his mind. For just a moment he fancies, mistakenly, that her father prompted the device of returning his gifts. And this bit of supposed disingenuousness on her part, so small in itself, is for him a climactic symptom and symbol of the great disease he is combating: the dishonesty that he has found more and more in Denmark and, finally, to some extent, in himself. She has mentioned the "noble mind." That is what he wishes to have and to promote, real nobility. But he is aware of things within him, as well as without, infecting the "noble substance" (I. iv. 37). Hence he is ready to cherish more than ever Ophelia's purity of soul, unique in Denmark. But now, after devout prayer, she can actually talk of the "noble mind" while carrying out Polonius's ignoble stratagem! Hamlet searches her face with deep dismay.

But she, too, is obviously and sincerely dismayed. "My lord! . . . What means your lordship?" Her words and, more, her looks, in response to his sudden question, make him certain that her device of returning the jewels is entirely her own, inspired only by her love of him. Therefore his tone becomes entirely gentle again. He contemplates her beauty. She is "honest and fair" (107), honest in herself, but now involved in a false situation. He warns her, indirectly but strongly: she must not let her "power of beauty" (111) be used by others any further as a decoy to him. For then it would become a "bawd," a sensual tool, and transform her beauty and virtue into its likeness. This means that she will become dishonest in spirit if she allows herself to believe that he can be induced to marry her. But he cannot state the point so crudely and cruelly as that; obviously, however, she understands him. She bends her head in deep sadness. Then, raising it slowly, she searches his face in great perplexity: he refuses marriage, but yet, she sees, he loves her still. He, anguished, reads in her eyes the query, How can you love me—and yet not love? Taking her hands he says brokenly, "I did love you once" (116). She weeps. "Indeed, my lord, you made me believe so." He suddenly puts his arms about her.

Then, quickly recovering his resolution, he holds her off, keeping her hands, however, and raising "a sigh . . . piteous and profound" (II. i. 94). Previously, in their dumb-show scene, he ought to have told her something of his awful mission but did not. Will he do so now, by way of explaining his unloving love? Our suspense here is keen because of the two hidden spies, Claudius and Polonius, of whom Hamlet is still unaware. But his proud vow of absolute secrecy holds. He must concentrate every thought and every feeling upon the great secret "enterprise" just ahead of him; its "current" must not be allowed to "turn awry" (87). Now, however, he must give Ophelia a true and plain reason for his refusal of marriage; and now he can do so. He is sinful and unworthy of her. In their dumb-show scene he had yearned to "speak of horrors" (II. i. 84) and did not; here he yearns to speak of his own "sins," and does. What follows is a central, crucial episode in the inward tragedy of Hamlet. The prince confesses himself, as plainly as his vow of secrecy and the limitations of his self-knowledge permit, to the woman he loves.

"You should not have believed me, for virtue cannot so inoculate our old stock but we shall relish of it: I loved you not." Whatever shoots of virtue a man may put forth are tainted with the old Adam. Hamlet's least questionable "virtue," he now feels, was his love for this girl; but it has brought misery to her. Therefore it could never have been *real* love, worthy of her. She should never have believed those wonderful vows which she has been inviting him to repeat. She must put out of her heart all love of him. She must find a higher kind of love, consonant with her purity and answering to her "orisons." "Get thee to a nunnery: why wouldst *thou* be a breeder of sinners?" Heavenly love and earthly love are imaged thus in vivid opposition to each other. The world is full of sinners. "I myself am indifferent honest"—he has come a long way since declaring, at the first, "I know not 'seems' " (I. ii. 76). No doubt he is as truthful and virtuous as the ordinary man; but then, he is not an ordinary man. Here he has in mind, as always, the fact that he is Prince of Denmark, "*born* to set it right" (I. v. 190); but at the present moment he could accuse himself of "such things that it were better" he had not been *born* at all (126). Like all great men who are great enough to find humility, he sees the difference between what he is and what he ought to be. And like all normal human persons he is deeply moved by the contrast between himself and the one who loves him best: love, above all, can "catch the conscience." The direct sequel of his opening words to her, "in thy orisons Be all my sins remembered," is the following: "I am very proud"—that is the most significant word—"revengeful, ambitious. . . . What should such fellows as I do crawling between earth and heaven?" Heaven and earth; the cosmic scene again. But here the swarm of dishonest creatures crawling the earth under the eye of heaven (II. ii. 176-182) includes himself. "We are arrant knaves all, believe none of us, go thy ways to a nunnery" (142). These words are spoken with tender, deeply mournful firmness.

But she does not move away. A woman is not repelled when the man she loves confesses guilt under the influence of her presence. Now more than ever he needs her help. Moreover Hamlet's sweeping, vague self-condemnation must seem to her, in her ignorance of his story, madly extreme. Those "offences at my beck" (127)—are they at all real? Are they not products of a deranged "imagination" (129), his own revealing word? Her eyes, fixed upon him, are full of prayer to heaven and of entreaty to him. And he knows that having told her much he ought to tell her more. But his lips are sealed by that very pride which he has just, for the first time, explicitly confessed; and his extremely conscious declaration of humility, as in the case of every man, re-arouses his pride. He hardens himself, shifting blame from himself to her. Her persistent devotion to him is making his renunciation of her bitterly difficult. Now he is ready to become self-protectingly angry at her—and just now his eye catches a movement of the arras.

"Where's your father?" he exclaims, seizing her wrist

"hard" and searching her face as in the dumb-show scene (II. i. 87), but this time very wrathfully. She is terrified, but not mainly for herself. She has just heard him say wildly that he is very "revengeful"; his madness is recurring. She must protect her father from her lover, and her lover from himself. To calm him she must keep calm herself. Mastering her fearful feelings she answers with quiet firmness, "At home, my lord." A lie, but at least as honest in purport as his lie to her above, "I loved you not." Her word "home," however, strikes a very sensitive nerve in his memory: it was at this "home" that the "tedious old fool" (II. ii. 223), now scheming behind the arras to marry his daughter to the prince, caused the prince to be shut out. So, "Let the doors be shut upon him that he may play the fool no where but in's own house—Farewell." Hamlet rushes off. She, unable to help him, kneels again and prays aloud, "O help him, you sweet heavens!" (138).

That prayer pierces him, more sharply than her initial, silent "orisons." He halts and turns about, swaying, with his hand to his head, utterly "distracted" (I. v. 97) by the conflict within. She, too, needs "help." But he must not let his conscience make a coward of him now: he clutches to his breast the manuscript that represents his enterprise "of great pitch and moment." He must crush his love for her absolutely, every jot and tittle of it. He will be cruel to be kind. For his own sake and hers—also, of course, to end the machinations of the listening old fool behind the arras—he will repulse her entirely and unmistakably. "If thou dost marry . . ." These cruel words, setting her instantly at a cold distance from himself, he utters with great difficulty. Then, hating the mental picture of her united to someone else, he goes on with a rush to give her a hateful "dowry" of fancied "calumny" (141), echoing unconsciously the apothegm of her brother, "Virtue itself scapes not calumnious strokes" (I. iii. 38). She would far better become a nun. But if she must needs marry, then let her "marry a fool," for "wise men" are wary of women: he is violently trying to objectify, ridicule, and dismiss the hateful idea of her marriage to someone else. She would best remain unmarried. He concludes, "To a nunnery[9] go, and quickly too. Farewell."

She repeats her preceding petition to heaven (138) in stronger form (147): "O heavenly powers, restore him!" He turns again quickly, her intensified prayer driving him to further desperation: he must repudiate that loving petition, a "heavenly" condemnation, as it is, of his own pride and uncharity.[10] He will thrust her utterly off his conscience, and into the category of "you" shallow court ladies—he had already shifted, above, from the personal "thou" to the impersonal "you" (144). "I have heard of your prattlings, too, well enough. God," to whom she is praying, "hath given you one pace and you make yourselves another: you jig, you amble, and you lisp. . . ."[11] The words are bizarrely inapplicable to Ophelia; they depict the very antithesis of her present words and posture. Now, certainly, Hamlet is putting an antic disposition on, but very feelingly, for to be wroth with one we love, when the fault is mainly our own, doth work like madness in the brain. She and her father and the court must be made to see that his love-madness, since they insist on regarding his state as such, has turned him entirely against women. "I say, we will have no more marriages. Those that are married already, all but one, shall live. . . ."

All but one! Of course he does not know that Claudius as well as Polonius is behind the arras. However, his violent determination to wrench Ophelia from his thoughts has led him into uttering a loud betraying threat against the king. This rank indiscretion sobers him. He grips himself quickly, as he did at the outset when he checked the excitement of his "enter-

---

[9] Here, but here only, Hamlet *may* be playing upon the Elizabethan sense of "nunnery" as a house of ill fame, in connection with the foregoing word "monsters," i.e., cuckolds. If so, the allusion is part of his violent effort, continued in the next scene, to stifle his craving for Ophelia by summoning up images of the most hateful possibilities of sexual passion.

[10] He must repudiate that prayer as Othello, more terribly, repudiates the sheltering forgiveness of the dying Desdemona—trying to hide his cruelty from himself (V. ii. 124-129).

[11] Instead of "prattlings" and "pace," Q1 and Q2 have "paintings" and "face." Probably Shakespeare used these more commonplace terms at first; the literature of the 1590's is full of them. Later he would reflect that the prattling, ambling court-coquette made a more pertinent and vivid contrast with the praying, kneeling Ophelia.

prise" (86) at the sight of the praying Ophelia; thus the Nunnery scene comes full circle. His wrath all gone, he contemplates for a moment the praying and loving girl with deep, quiet grief. Then, with a gesture of blessing over her, he says in a tone of mournful finality and farewell, "To a nunnery, go."

Ophelia alone, "most deject and wretched" (163), puts the tragedy of Hamlet and of Denmark (158) before her own:

> Oh what a noble mind is here o'erthrown!
> The courtier's, soldier's, scholar's, eye, tongue, sword,
> The expectancy and rose of the fair state. . . .

No one else has spoken in such high and discerning terms of him. Her brother was typical in talking smoothly of the "greatness" of the crown prince's *position*, its importance for the "sanctity and health of the whole state," while wondering covertly whether the wayward young prince would grow up into harmony with "the main voice of Denmark" (I. iii. 11-28). Shakespeare, however, has shown us from the beginning that the "main voice" needs to be swayed by Hamlet, not he by it: he alone could give this nation real "pith and marrow" (I. iv. 22). And this fact was and is apparent to the loving intuition of Ophelia. The "noble mind" in *her* (100) found the same in *him* (158). The "expectancy" of the state would be fulfilled by his becoming more and more "The glass of fashion and the mould of form, The observed of all observers," the right example for all, the "mould" of manners and morals, the shaper of the public judgment, of the "general censure" (I. iv. 35).[12] Hamlet had the beauty, the "rose," of true courtliness together with deep moral sanity. But now she sees "that noble and most sovereign reason Like sweet bells jangled, out of tune and harsh. . . ." Her soliloquy is designed by Shakespeare to establish our conviction that she, if rightly helped by him, would have been his right helpmate. He, largely because unfortunate, but ultimately because "very proud," has made a

---

[12] With Ophelia's "mould of form," compare Hamlet's "form of plausive manners" (I. iv. 30). In the Elizabethan philosophy of the gentleman, "form" was conceived as a determinant, as well as an expression, of right morals.

tragic failure in the duty of his love for her. She has indeed suffered, in a deeper sense than Laertes foreboded, a "Contagious blastment" (I. iii. 42). She seems to echo that phrase in mourning for Hamlet as "Blasted with ecstasy" (168).

We know that his "ecstasy" is transient. But we also see that he is now so "jangled" by inward conflict that his *complete* success in the public crisis just ahead of him is doubtful, despite the mien of quiet resolution that he has reassumed on quitting the stage. And very ominous for him is the new resolve of the king. Claudius re-enters with a sharply heightened sense of "danger" (4, 175). Hamlet's threat against "one" who is not to "live," mere madness to Ophelia's ears, was "not like madness" (172) in the ears of the guilty king. He is eager to have the prince sent away from Denmark at once. But he dares not override the different advice given by his chief councilor. Polonius, markedly curt to Ophelia here but otherwise dissembling his disappointed ambition, cherishes a final hope that the "queen mother" (190)—doubly authoritative as such—will secure a confession of "neglected love" (186) from Hamlet in his more complaisant mood "after the play." Thus the politic smoothness of Claudius and Polonius *towards each other* prepares their own ruin by occasioning the fateful Closet scene (III. iv). But the most significant point is that the king's secret remorse, above, has now been overtopped by his secret fear. Now he is preoccupied with his danger, not his sin. Therefore we perceive it is unlikely that the Play, no matter how successful, will succeed in making him proclaim his "malefaction" openly, to the whole court, as Hamlet hoped (II. ii. 621). In the present scene the king of the realm has confronted, and for the time being conquered, his conscience—just when the crown prince, in this and the preceding scene, has signally failed to come to clear terms with his. Claudius is readier for evil action than Hamlet for good.

III. ii. 1-281

But now we see Hamlet confronting masterfully his immediate task, the production of the Play. When he re-enters with manuscript in hand we perceive that the self-control gained in the last part of the "peasant slave" speech, shown in the "To

be" soliloquy, and regained in the finale of the Nunnery scene
has been fully established during the off-stage rehearsal of the
Play. His cue now is temperance and justness *in action*. He
talks upon that theme, first to the Players in prose, then to
Horatio in verse, with rising conviction and power. His style
is beautifully tuned to his theme because he himself is. He
has come to see (what Shakespeare sees) the world as a stage
whereon it is of main importance that each man act his current
part as best he can. Hamlet's world, termed by him at the
first an "unweeded garden" (I. ii. 135), became soon a thing
"out of joint" (I. v. 189), and finally a "sea of troubles" (III.
i. 59). This sea is more tumultuous just at present than ever;
but he is steadier than ever, though at the tragic expense of his
love. For he has now found a "good thing to be *done*" (I. i.
130): "the play's the thing" (II. ii. 634). And he is determined to play his present part effectually whatever may be the
outcome.

To do so he must have the right temper: he must control,
not chill, his feelings. He tells himself, as he tells the Players,
that "in the very torrent, tempest, and, as I may say, the whirlwind of passion, you must acquire and beget a temperance...."[13]
This virtue has to be *begotten* by the will within us even while
being *acquired*, learned, from dictate and example. One must
not be "robustious" and "tear a passion to tatters" (10); nor
on the other hand "too tame" (19). One must have "discretion" and keep to "the modesty of nature," i.e., the vital moderation evinced by human nature at its best. Nature at its
worst is often exhibited by the actors and by the audience (33
ff., 45). Pleasing a "whole theater" is no guarantee of real
success. Here Hamlet's thought connects with and goes beyond
what he said earlier about the "general censure" (I. iv. 35):
he repeats here the word "censure" (opinion or judgment) but
drops the adjective "general." Our aim must be to act justly,

---

[13] Q2 has "your passion." The omission of "your," in the folios, facilitates
our recollection of Hamlet's own capacity, as in the preceding scene, for a
"whirlwind of passion." We may note also that instead of "you must acquire
and beget a temperance," Q1 reads "give everything his [i.e., its] action with
temperance." This version, while omitting the admirable "acquire and beget,"
stresses the fact that Hamlet's present theme is temperance-in-action instead of
the easier and commoner temperance-in-theory.

on the stage, as on the stage of life. Therefore our criterion must be the "censure" of "the judicious" (31), never of "the groundlings" (12).

Suddenly and suggestively the "barren spectators" (46) Polonius, Rosencrantz, and Guildenstern reappear and are dismissed by Hamlet instantly. He now summons to his "service" (58), much to our relief and gratification, one who is eminently judicious and honest:

> Horatio, thou are e'en as just a man
> As e'er my conversation coped withal.

The word "conversation" intimates that the "love and friending" (I. v. 186) promised by Hamlet to Horatio has continued off stage. But the word "just" applied by the prince to his friend is new. This sudden encomium abashes the modest Horatio so much that he has to be reassured. He is informed that his justness was from the first perceived by Hamlet's "soul" (68), i.e., really but dimly. Now, however, it is clearly evaluated by Hamlet's mind and grasped by his "heart of heart" (78). Horatio himself has not changed: Hamlet has developed. With the new humility that we have been watching, above—a humility very far from saintly, liable to be overtopped at any moment by his pride, as in the Nunnery scene—he now sees in his friend the temperance that he himself needs most, and has in fact considerably gained through suffering and ill fortune.[14] For Horatio has been

> As one, in suffering all, that suffers nothing,
> A man that fortune's buffets and rewards
> Hath ta'en with equal thanks. And blest are those
> Whose blood and judgment are so well co-mingled
> That they are not a pipe for fortune's finger
> To sound what stop she please: give me that man
> That is not passion's slave, and I will wear him
> In my heart's core, ay in my heart of heart,
> As I do thee.

[14] With Horatio's relation to Hamlet compare that of the Palmer (Reason) to Sir Guyon in Book II of *The Faerie Queene*. Notice particularly the Palmer's absence from the scene through cantos vi and vii and his reappearance in canto viii for the crucial episode—like Horatio.

Horatio is at once the sign and the support of Hamlet's renewed temperance. In the first part of the "peasant slave" soliloquy the prince was certainly "passion's slave," and therefore felt himself the slave of circumstance, a "John-a-dreams" (II. ii. 595), a "pipe for fortune's finger." But now he is determined to master "outrageous fortune" (III. i. 58) in mastering his own passionateness. Since his nature is far more emotional than his friend's, he knows he has a far harder task in being one of "those"—the word looks beyond Horatio—who in crises of fortune maintain the right union of "blood and judgment." But he humbly appreciates the example, true though limited, afforded by his friend. And he desires the aid of his "judgment" in regard to the guilt of Claudius. In this matter Hamlet admits the possibility that his own "imaginations are"—the present tense of the verb is significant here as previously (II. ii. 632)—"foul as Vulcan's stithy." Therefore "we will both our judgments join In censure of his seeming."

It is Hamlet's new vein of humility, more than the practical need of a coadjutor in watching Claudius, that has caused him to infringe his fateful oath of absolute secrecy at the end of Act I. At long last he has confided to his friend the Ghost's communication regarding his "father's death" (82). He has not, however, informed Horatio of the queen's adultery, nor of his covert dilemma as to how he should proceed if the king's guilt is proved. Those two matters are closely interrelated; and the continued proud secrecy of Hamlet therein "cannot but make the judicious grieve" (31). His silence to his friend regarding Gertrude will be retrospectively emphasized by the fact that the *Murther of Gonzago* turns out to be largely an arraignment of her. Hamlet will "rivet" his "eyes" (90) to *her* face, not the king's, most of the time. We shall see that it is *her* conscience that her son is at heart most anxious to catch. He will not admit this fact to himself because it hurts his pride. He wishes to believe that his devotion to his great enterprise regarding the king has entirely submerged for the time being his feelings in regard to Gertrude as well as Ophelia. He reveals to us, however, his deep concern for both of them soon after the court has assembled to witness the Play.

The queen's mood, much to Hamlet's irritation, is here, unlike that of the now so tense and taciturn king, exceptionally smooth and cheerful. Her shallow soul has been certain from the first that what her son chiefly needs is cheering up (I. ii. 68 ff.; II. ii. 19 ff.; III. i. 10 ff.); and now comes her supreme opportunity. His mistress, Ophelia, having signally failed to charm his wildness, his mother will do her very best, adding her happy influence to the delights of the coming Play. Caressingly she urges her "good Hamlet" to sit by her (115). "No, good mother," he replies acidly, stressing her adjective,[15] "here's metal more attractive." He will puzzle and pierce the queen by showing her that the rejected Ophelia is still more congenial to him than his mother. Accordingly he reclines at the girl's knees, at first putting his head in her lap, cruel to himself and to her. In sequel to his last speeches in the Nunnery scene he talks court bawdry to her, extremely and factitiously, to stifle his real feelings. He crushes the pure passion aroused through contact with his "soul's idol" by determinedly keeping before his imagination the impurity and transiency of his mother's love for his father. This prattling queen made a monster of a noble king and now, more than ever, is covering her "wantonness" with "ignorance" (III. i. 152). Wrapped in wilful oblivion Gertrude is smiling cheerfully upon her gross husband and, alternately, upon her son. The bitter fancy strikes Hamlet that she is so adept in forgetfulness that she would thus demean herself even if her former husband had died "two hours" before this second ensemble of the court instead of "two months" (I. ii. 138) before the first ensemble: "look you, how cheerfully my mother looks, and my father died within's two hours" (135). The son of such a mother, surely, ought to wear no mourning: he should become, in addition to his assumed role of bawdy court-prattler, a merry "jig-maker" and a chanter of comic epitaphs (132-145). By thus parodying loudly his mother's levity, Hamlet tries to break it down so as to open her heart to the effect of the coming Play. But his efforts are totally unsuccessful.

[15] Hence the superiority of the "good Hamlet" of the folios to the "dear Hamlet" of Q2.

Nor does the ensuing *"Dumb-show"* have the slightest perceptible effect on her. This in spite of the fact that her double, the Player Queen, is the chief figure here, holding the stage unlike the others from first to last, except for a momentary absence at the middle when the murder is enacted. The murder is remarkably subordinated. The pouring of the poison by a nameless "fellow" into the Player King's ears, represented by a single sentence in the text, is a quick gesture, enigmatic to the court audience excepting Claudius, designed to soften him up in preparation for the frontal attack to be made upon his conscience later.[16] Hamlet's first target is not Claudius but Gertrude. The *"Dumb-show,"* so swift and spectral in its movement, is devoted to the equally rapid, strange, inhuman shift of the Player Queen's love from the Player King to his successor. Nevertheless Gertrude at the close is entirely and amazingly serene. Hamlet is nonplused. Intent upon further trial of her, he is impatient at the appearance of a "fellow" (151) to speak a prologue, which, however, turns out to be extremely brief—like "woman's love" (164). Thus the *short* Prologue symbolizes "what this show meant" (153) and what the immediately ensuing speeches of the Players are to mean: the preternatural *shortening* of Gertrude's love for Hamlet's father.

The Player Queen re-enters, hanging upon her husband "As if increase of appetite had grown By what it fed on" (I. ii. 143). Her clinging devotion to him sets the tune of the slow-chiming hexameters of the Play; and the images, like the rhythm, are consonant with her demeanor. At the outset the

---

[16] Surely the Dumb-show is designed to create the largest possible measure of dramatic suspense. The ambitious assumption of the throne by Claudius, which everybody knows about, is alluded to by the following: "Anon comes in a fellow [in Q2 'another man'], takes off his [the sleeping king's] crown, kisses it. . . ." Then, very abruptly, he "pours poison in the king's ears." This should be done on the stage with rapid, vague, puppet-like sweeps of the hand and without a vial (a "vial" is mentioned in Q1, not in Q2 and F1) so that the court audience will be entirely puzzled. They will thus be kept in the suspense of unsatisfied curiosity, while Claudius is thrown into the terrible suspense of guilty uncertainty. For he cannot yet be sure that the enigmatic gesture of the "fellow" indicates a complete discovery by Hamlet of his secret crime. There is no hint of the poisoning in the rest of the Dumb-show. The "poisoner," so termed in the script of the Play, which Claudius has not seen, does not of course appear as such when he re-enters to woo the Player Queen.

"most sacred bands" (170) of wedlock are emblemized by
sacred cosmic objects (164, 171):

> Full thirty times hath Phoebus' cart gone round
> Neptune's salt wash and Tellus' orbed ground. . . .
> So many journeys may the sun and moon
> Make us again count o'er ere love be done!

Her declared constancy is elaborately emphasized by all that
follows. Her love is so great that she is full of woe on account
of the Player King's declining health and, at the same time,
anxious that her sad fears shall not in the least add to his distress. When he declares that he must soon in the course of
nature die, she weeps and clings to him more fondly than ever.
In trying his best to comfort her he suggests that she may re-
marry with "one as kind" (186), i.e., as affectionate and congenial. But she cries out:

> In second husband let me be accurst,
> None wed the second but who killed the first. . . .
> A second time I kill my husband dead
> When second husband kisses me in bed.

Loud above those loud lines is Hamlet's interjected cry of
"Wormwood, wormwood" (191). For those lines, though they
refrain, like the Play as a whole, from directly touching upon
Gertrude's adultery, are designed to tell her conscience that
she has been *murderously* unfaithful. Surely, Hamlet thinks,
her cheerful composure will break here; but it does not. And
now the Player King utters a deal of gnomic breath upon the
fallibility of all human resolutions. The main purpose of this
lengthy speech (which later will be seen to have a general
bearing upon the second half of *Hamlet*) is obviously to lend
climactic force to the Player Queen's ensuing sacred oath. She,
returning upon the cosmic theme of the opening speeches—alluded to meanwhile by the Player King's "this fair world"
(185)—invokes (226) the hostility of the vital earth, the
radiant sky, the joyous day, and the reposeful night in case she
breaks her solemn word:

> Nor earth to me give food, nor heaven light,
> Sport and repose lock from me day and night![17]

Indeed, " 'Tis deeply sworn" (235).

In the terrific suspense of the ensuing pause in the action while the Player King sleeps, Hamlet, having failed to affect Gertrude with all his histrionic byplay, asks her now with quiet intensity: "Madam, how like you this play?" His tone is like that which we, controlling our temper, use to a child who has refused to confess a fault despite our most heated scoldings; and her six-word reply has in it something of the sweetly obstinate naughty child. More, this line of hers is the supreme instance of her gross equanimity; she nonchalantly criticizes her own fault in another: "The Lady protests too much, methinks" (240). Just that. And Hamlet is frustrated absolutely.

In perfect antithesis to that short, slow line comes now the rapid, crowded question of Claudius to Hamlet: "Have you heard the argument? Is there no offence in it?" (242). He knows that presently the fleet, murderous gesture at the center of the *"Dumb-show"* will be translated into plain words and actions. He cannot think that Hamlet could have discovered, by earthly means, the crime so completely hidden from human eyes and ears (I. v. 35-38). But he knows, as he will tell us later, that the crime was not hidden from "heaven" (III. iii. 36). And he feels that the punitive power of heaven is now at work mysteriously upon him. He felt it in the astounding, ghostly *"Dumb-show."* Previously it inspired "that speech" (III. i. 50) of Polonius which gave "so smart a lash" to his "conscience." And doubtless it will inspire the coming speech of the Player Murderer. So, in awful fear, Claudius betrays himself to Hamlet by his blurted query. The "argument" (the plot of the Play) has so far offered plenty of "offence" to Gertrude, which she has smilingly refused to accept. Therefore Claudius shows that he dreads "offence" *for himself* in the remainer of the Play.

---

[17] The second line means: May day and night lock from me sport and repose. The cosmic flavor of the couplet is strengthened in F1 by omission of the two following lines in the quartos which narrow the train of imagery:
> To desperation turn my trust and hope,
> And anchor's [i.e., anchorite's] cheer in prison be my scope.

Hamlet, thrilled by the king's betrayal of guilt but suppress-
ing his excitement with extraordinary self-control—begetting "a
temperance" in "the whirlwind of passion" (7-9)—replies in
a way that challenges and progressively undermines the self-
control of his enemy. Casually he introduces the dread word
hitherto not mentioned, "poison" (244). He suggests that the
next episode of the Play may be a "Mouse-trap" for a present
criminal; but instantly goes on to state that the sleeping Player
King is not really a king, in the original story, but a "duke," in
far off Vienna. Presently the word "wince" bears painfully
upon the present condition of Claudius and prepares him to do
much more than wince. Finally, as the nameless murderer
enters, Hamlet announces ringingly, "This is one Lucianus"—
not brother to the sleeping duke but—*"nephew* to the *king.*"[18]
Thus Claudius is informed that his own nephew, having in some
appallingly mysterious fashion discovered his crime, is about to
speak to him of it through the mouth of Lucianus.

The conduct of Lucianus at first is as silent as the *"Dumb-
show"* but, unlike that, not quick and transient. His gestures,
emphatic like those of "puppets" (257), together with his
"damnable faces" (263) represent the murderer's final struggle
with his conscience. The sleeping, helpless figure before him
has inspired white thoughts which have to be displaced by
"Thoughts black," his opening words. This and each succeeding phrase reconstruct the poisonous mood, rather than the
outer circumstances, in which Claudius "blasted" (269) his
brother's "wholesome" life (271, cf. I. v. 70). Claudius, at
first rigid, collapses more and more, slumping in his chair,
unnoticed, however, except by Hamlet, Horatio, and us.

For the eyes of the court are fastened intently upon Lucianus pouring the poison in the sleeper's ears, done this time,
as not in the *"Dumb-show,"* with an ostentatiously displayed
vial, the contents of which he has just been addressing. Hamlet, still admirably self-possessed, comments swiftly upon that
action and upon the original story written in "choice Italian"

---

[18] The words "king" and "duke" are often interchanged in Elizabethan
drama. But that fact only serves to facilitate Hamlet's sharp playing with
these two words in his present speech.

(274); then urges the Play forward to its proper close. There are more lines composed by him for Lucianus, climactic lines concerning his mother, giving voice to the finale of the *"Dumb-show."* Hence his impatient urging of the actor a moment ago (262 f.).[19] Hence his present adjuration to the court and, above all, Gertrude: "you shall see anon how the murderer gets the love of Gonzago's wife" (275).

But here Claudius struggles to his feet convulsively. And equally convulsive, in contrast with the even firmness of his preceding lines (272-275), is Hamlet's exclamation, "What, frighted with false fire?" The prince is far more disconcerted than triumphant. To be sure, the king, unable to endure the coming scene of the "murderer" and "Gonzago's wife," has proved himself guilty of seduction as well as murder. But also he has precluded Hamlet's final effort to catch the conscience of the queen. She, entirely oblivious now to all that the Play could mean for herself, is preoccupied with her husband: "How fares my lord?" As she supports her staggering "lord" off stage, Hamlet watches her with dumfounded fascination. He can utter not another word to her here. All the more is he determined, as we shall see presently, to visit her alone at once. But we of the audience are confronted by the question (to which I shall give an answer below): Why had not Hamlet anticipated the premature ending of his Play by Claudius's being "frighted" away too soon?

Polonius's injunction to "Give o'er the play" is engulfed by the king's great cry, a cry to heaven and earth as well as to the court, "Give me some light. Away!" (280). Instead of the "false fire" (277) that is burning him he wants "some light." This gives symbolic significance to the general outcry with which the great scene ends, while the amazed, endarkened courtiers crowd away pellmell: "Lights, lights, lights!"

---

[19] Hence, too, we may add, his initial urging of the Players to "Speak the speech . . . trippingly on the tongue" etc. He was anxious that the most melodramatic feature of the Play, the murder, should not be done so heavily as to detract from the ensuing catastrophe, the seduction.

(d) *my mystery*　　III. ii. 282—III. iii

III. ii. 282-417

Hamlet, too, needs light. The logic of stern justice demands that he dispose of the usurper, now proved a criminal, and take the throne that belongs to him. Only thus can he proceed, immediately and effectually, with his great task of setting Denmark right. And the time for the deed is precisely now when Claudius and his supine court—in direct contrast to their state at the close of the first ensemble (I. ii. 121 ff.) —are, for the moment, utterly disordered. Supernal justice demands also, however, that Hamlet shall execute Claudius *in the spirit of justice,* subduing his revengeful feelings on the one hand and, on the other, his unconfessed abhorrence of regicide. But this he is not yet ready to do. He is not yet rightly tempered for his task. He needs a fuller and clearer light of justice *within.*

That need was shown us in previous scenes. Nevertheless we are now in keen suspense. For during the Play Hamlet has borne himself with such self-mastery that we can hope for his maintaining it in the sequel. We hope he will at once consult Horatio, then take decisive action. But he does neither. For a moment he stands entranced, as stated above, his eyes following his mother. Then (so I believe) he moves galvanically, half drawing his sword and taking a few steps after the retreating crowd. A moment ago he adjured Lucianus in mockingly melodramatic tone, "Come, the croaking raven doth bellow for revenge" (265). That line mocks Hamlet himself now. Previously he himself bellowed for revenge on Claudius, before being sure of his guilt, in a moment of wild passion (II. ii. 610). But, as emphasized above (204),

> What to ourselves in passion we propose,
> The passion ending, doth the purpose lose.

Hamlet halts, sheathing his sword slowly. We sympathize with him fully because we know how hard it is for a thoroughly human person to slay an enemy who, conscience-struck and helpless, is also the sovereign of the land. But we also see that this prince is failing in a public duty. We perceive now the full significance of the fact that never once except *"in passion"* has Hamlet proposed actually to kill Claudius, nor ever faced frankly his inward reluctance to do so. We recall his evasiveness on this point after the subsidence of his passion in the "peasant slave" soliloquy. Now, therefore, he "doth the purpose lose." At the same time he is losing his new self-mastery, for the following reasons.

The enterprise of catching the king's conscience was, unlike the task of killing him, not proposed "in passion." It was undertaken after the checking of passion, upon true and reasonable grounds (II. ii. 617 ff.). Hence Hamlet was able to carry it through successfully, begetting a strong temperance in the midst of strong emotions. But at present that temperance is dissolving. Impatiently, irresolutely, he strides to the empty thrones, glances at the king's, then stares fixedly upon the queen's. In her case the Play, though most of it was aimed at her, has been a total failure. If only she could have witnessed the final, unacted scene, the murderer getting the love of Gonzago's wife, she might have succumbed! Hamlet longs, passionately and bitterly, to break down her defenses. He has taken the smile utterly from her wicked husband's face: not Claudius but "this pernicious woman" is the "smiling villain" (I. v. 105 f.) now. He yearns to catch her conscience as he has caught the king's. Right reason would tell him that this could best be done after the exposure and execution of her criminal husband; but at present Hamlet is not listening to right reason. In the ensuing episodes, culminating in his killing of Polonius, we see him becoming more and more "passion's slave" (77), involved indeed in a "whirlwind" (7) of conflicting emotions: revengeful wrath against Claudius; loathing of the necessary execution; dim impulses towards a just serenity; and, above all, the urgent desire to confront his mother alone.

Hence the flushed excitement with which, turning from her vacant seat, he hurries now to the patiently waiting Horatio. The ensuing dialogue between the prince and his friend is the antithesis of that which preceded the Play, and very reminiscent of that which followed the Ghost's departure in Act I. There

Hamlet begins with a falconer's call (I. v. 116); here, with a wildly chanted stanza, "Why, let the stricken deer go weep. . . ." Here, as there, he is covering up his inward confusion and steeling himself proudly against taking Horatio into further confidence. Here, far more than there, he needs to unbosom himself fully to this "just man" (59) now so close to his "heart's core" (78), his very "Damon dear" (292), ready to counsel and abet him. But Hamlet has reverted to his inhuman secrecy. And the prudent Horatio, rebuffed when he tried initially to draw from his prince a plain confession instead of "wild and whirling words" (I. v. 133-140), will not again obtrude. But his four short, dry speeches here say to Hamlet in effect: put off your theatricalism and face calmly the fact that this king is only too obviously a murderer.[20] All the more, however, Hamlet tries to outface his main failure with extravagant delight in his partial success. "I'll take the Ghost's word for a thousand pound," he cries, echoing his earlier assertion "It is an honest ghost, that let me tell you" (I. v. 138) and indicating, here as there, that his confession to his friend shall go no further. To celebrate the success of the Play and to end his embarrassing conference with the critical Horatio, Hamlet abruptly calls for "some music" (302, 306), i.e., from the Players, while uttering doggerel still more forced than his preceding stanzas.

But here Rosencrantz and Guildenstern enter in pompous haste. And they draw from Hamlet "a whole history" (309) indeed. Before the Play he exchanged them speedily for Horatio (55 ff.); now, the reverse occurs. The "good Horatio" (297), in effect dismissed—like the justness and temperance of Hamlet's own "soul" (68)—becomes a silent, deeply concerned onlooker. His face reflects *our* growing foreboding while we watch Hamlet give way more and more to his tangled emotions. The two newcomers, on the other hand, reflect the present attitude of the court. For the courtiers the Play scene has meant merely a crucial outbreak of Hamlet's initial "un-

[20] Note Horatio's iterated "very well." It both satisfies and irks Hamlet—satisfies him with the knowledge that Horatio is utterly convinced; irks him with the implication that he should take instant action against the guilty and dangerous Claudius.

mastered importunity" (I. iii. 32): his unbridled emotionalism, his bitter ambition for the throne accentuated by his idealistic dislike of the quick wedding, and, above all, his hatred of the accomplished and charming king. Here and later we gather that the court has seen, or has at least willed to see, nothing more in the poisoning episode of the Play than a melodramatic, threatening insult to Claudius, who, after much forbearance, is greatly, and naturally in the court's opinion, disturbed by the implacability of the mad crown prince. At the same time the persistent oiliness to the crown prince on the part of Rosencrantz and Guildenstern, and presently of Polonius—oddly mingled with their new tone of peremptoriness—makes evident that he would meet no insuperable opposition at the present moment if, with the help of Horatio, he would take sanely and justly strong action. We see that he could well master this weak and "out of joint" Denmark with its unnerved king if only he could master himself.

But even while the king of the realm is "marvellous distempered" (312) the prince of the realm is in "distemper" (351) too. Certainly his "wit's diseased" (333), as he himself puts it, though in a deeper sense than Rosencrantz and Guildenstern understand. A few moments ago, at the culmination of the action of the Play, his wit, along with his self-control, was at the height of its prowess. The rhythm of his sentences then, in spite of the terrific strain his emotions were undergoing, was measured and firm. Now his manner is full of fits and starts because he no longer knows his "course" (II. ii. 627). Witlessly, in the presence of the royal spies, he threatens the "purgation" (318) of the king and declares his desire for immediate "advancement" to the throne (354-359); thus doing in words what he ought to be doing in deeds, compensating himself emotionally at the expense of princely prudence. The dialogue with his schoolfellows here is the exact contrary of its predecessor (II. ii. 225 ff.). There he was their master because he was his own; his wit and prudence were superb. There his final thrust at this brace of tame hawks, turning upon the proverb of "hawk" and "handsaw," was triumphant (II. ii. 387-398). Here, his recourse to a "musty" proverb (358)—while indeed "the grass grows," as we of the audience see—is a lame conclusion. To better it he hastily seizes upon the "recorder" (360).

By means of this instrument he tries to recover his self-command and, also, to penetrate finally the conscience of his schoolfellows. They have killed his friendship for them. His Christian duty of loving them as neighbors remains, wearing a decidedly difficult and ironic air, as he had affirmed, above, "by these pickers and stealers" (349). He now takes Guildenstern apart, to deprive him of his fellow's support, and flatly accuses him of treachery (360-363), eliciting from him, however, only a more fulsome piece of falsity than ever, fulsome and also sophisticated. For the two new courtiers have by now well learned the "craft" (II. ii. 290) that came so hard to them at first, the art of lying easily. Well then, Hamlet urges, playing "upon this pipe" is "as easy as lying." Not so the art of playing on Hamlet. "Why, look you now, how unworthy a thing you make of me" (379). His appeal, plain, vivid, and at first gentle, is addressed to the most obvious kind of neighborly decency and fair play in his hearer. Guildenstern ought to be overcome with shame. But his face, like that of Rosencrantz in the offing, maintains its hard, unctuous dissimulation. Presently therefore the prince's tone, dropping its gentleness, becomes more and more severe and threatening till it culminates in " 'Sblood[21] . . . *you* cannot play upon *me*" (386-389). He implies that *he* can play upon *them*. His final effort to catch their conscience having failed, he justly asserts a mastery of them, on their own chosen ground; a mastery which, as the sequel will prove, he can maintain.

But that small triumph serves to throw into relief his larger failure. In this respect the "little organ" (385), the recorder—one of Shakespeare's most exquisite symbols—is charged with significance. Hamlet has declared, "you would seem to know my stops, you would pluck out the heart of my mystery, you would sound me. . . . do you think that I am easier to be played on than a *pipe?*" Alas he is, in the present crisis, "a

---

[21] Again the oath " 'Sblood" expresses Hamlet's sense of gross unnaturalness, as in II. ii. 383. See note 16, Act II.

pipe for fortune's finger To sound what stop she please" (75).
Of course he has baffled the spies' attempt to "pluck out" his
secret incentive, the Ghost's message, now proved valid.   It is
clear that Claudius, desperately wondering about Hamlet's
awareness of his crime, has instructed them to threaten, for
the first time, his "liberty" (352) so as to force him into revealing the cause of his employment of the *Murther of Gonzago*.
And we know that if, playing into the king's hands, he had told
the spies the least word about the Ghost, he would quickly have
been confined as hopelessly and dangerously insane with the
hearty consent, so Polonius intimated (III. i. 194), of court
and councilors.   For us and for Horatio, however, Hamlet's
allusion in the phrase "heart of my mystery" is not only to his
secret regarding his father's Spirit, which we already know, but
also to the present state of his own spirit.   Before the Play he
declared, and during it he demonstrated, that temperance and
justice were in his "heart of heart" (78).   So now the phrase
"heart of my mystery" means to us that his conduct, for the
time being, has deserted those two great virtues; that his purposes are confused, a "mystery" to himself; and that fortune,
accordingly, is playing upon him like a "pipe."

In particular, fortune is sounding fatefully one of his
"stops," his pressing desire to go to his mother before, instead
of after, executing Claudius.   The two spies were "playing"
him better than they knew when they told him, above, that the
queen "in most great affliction of spirit"—because of Claudius
ostensibly but perhaps, as Hamlet can imagine, because her conscience is at long last afflicting her—"desires to speak with you
in her closet ere you go to bed" (323-346).   The prince promised to "obey"; but of course he might visit her before going
to bed and yet seek the king first.   We hope he will.   But now
Polonius enters to cast his weighty straw in the balance; incidentally to doom himself, unwittingly.   Hamlet, more ironically than he knows, greets him for the first, and for the last,
time with a "God bless you, sir!"   For here the old man is
an instant relief from the schoolfellows, as they were formerly
a relief from him (II. ii. 220-230) before they became patently
despicable.   Hamlet's righteous wrath at them might well have

impelled him, in driving them off, to go straight to their master, the king, if Polonius had not come, declaring: "My lord,
the queen would speak with you, and presently." Not, this
time, "ere you go to bed" (344) but "presently" (392), i.e.,
at once.

That fateful word "presently," really at work in Hamlet's
mind since the end of the Play in relation to the alluring "matter" of "my mother" (336 f.), clutches now at his will. For
a minute he staves it off. Whimsically, cloudily—recalling to
us his "mystery"—he looks up at the sky: "Do you see that
cloud? that's almost like a camel."[22] In suspense we wonder
whether or not he will go directly to his mother. Polonius,
anxious that he should, tries to soothe the mad prince into filial
obedience by agreeing with his every cloudy fancy (395 ff.).
"Then will I come to my mother," Hamlet declares teasingly,
"by and by," using this phrase as an ambiguous equivalent for
"presently." As others "fool" him, he intimates aside, he will
fool them: "By and by is easily said." He dismisses them all,
"Leave me, friends"; pointedly including the lingering Horatio, who unlike the others does not fool Hamlet and could help
him, if only Hamlet willed, not to fool himself. The prince
had said to him before the Play, "we will both our judgments
join." But they are now disjoined. So are Hamlet's "blood
and judgment":

> 'Tis *now* the very witching time of night,
> When churchyards yawn, and hell itself breathes out
> Contagion to this world. *Now* could I drink hot blood,
> And do such bitter business as the day
> Would quake to look on—Soft, *now*, to my mother:
> O heart lose not thy nature. . . .

Obviously the last thing he can actually do just now is to "drink
hot blood": his melodramatic effort to whip up his revenge-
passion is an utter failure. His "heart," his blood, in defiance
of princely judgment, urges him to go to his mother at once.
It is indeed "the very witching time of night"—sequel to the

---

[22] Q2 reads: "Do you see yonder cloud that's almost in shape of a camel?"
The Folio reading, throwing emphasis on the word "cloud," brings out the
symbolic allusion to Hamlet's cloudy state of mind.

"mystery" and "cloud" above: Hamlet is as one bewitched. The first of the three "now's" in the passage quoted above is violent in tone; the second, wavering, followed by the conditional verbs "could" and "would"; the third, a complete, enchanted yielding: "Soft, now, to my mother."[23]   He has yielded to the lure of the fatal "presently."

All would have been different if the conscience of his mother had been caught by the Play. And this would doubtless have occurred if the final, omitted scene had been put on, showing, with the aid of Hamlet's pregnant comments, "how the murderer gets the love of Gonzago's wife" (275); for the substance of that scene, presently enacted for Gertrude alone by Hamlet in dramatic monologue (III. iv), has the desired effect. Why, then, did Hamlet not foresee that the final scene would be forbidden by the king, that the king's conscience would be so violently moved by the first part of the Play as to preclude the rest?   The answer is that the prince's constant hatred of his uncle—hatred bitter "while my father lived" (II. ii. 382), intensified tremendously by Claudius's crimes, and never mitigated in the whole course of the drama by a single touch of mercy—made him underestimate the force of conscience in the king. The prince expected that the king's guilt would "itself unkennel," during the "speech" (86) of Lucianus, to the "heedful . . . eyes" of himself and Horatio (89-91), *not* to the eyes of the court. Previously he had spoken of "guilty creatures," in general, being "struck so to the soul" that they "proclaimed their malefactions" (II. ii. 618-621), but he believed that Claudius might merely "blench" (II. ii. 626). He did not in the least expect that this extraordinarily crafty villain would allow himself to be so "frighted" (277), in public, as to rise and end the Play. He did not anticipate that the king's conscience would prevent the Play's catching the conscience of the queen. Thus hate, proud hate, close to the very "heart"

---

[23] Q2 has "soft, now to my mother." F1 has "Soft now, to my mother." This is the better punctuation because it stresses the climactic "now" in its relation to Hamlet's softening mood. In my text I have placed the wavering comma before as well as after "now" but with intent that the second pause should be the heavier. The passage echoes the close of the "To be" soliloquy where Hamlet's mind turned to another woman with "Soft you now, The fair Ophelia . . . ," thus punctuated in both Q2 and F1.

of his complex "mystery," blinds Hamlet (like Othello, Iago, Lear, and others) to something in the hated person that the protagonist's own welfare requires him to perceive. It is the cause of his being so astounded and unbalanced by the premature ending of the Play that he decides with fatal imprudence to complete the Play, so to speak, in his mother's closet before killing the king.

But on his way to her closet, ironic fortune, or Providence, brings his hate to a dreadful culmination by confronting him with the king kneeling and praying to heaven.

III. iii

Here, as never before, Claudius is shown alone with Rosencrantz and Guildenstern, now his close intimates. But despite the inward agony of his conscience, presently to be displayed in soliloquy, he utters to them not a single self-betraying syllable; he is as discreet with them as Hamlet, above, in certain passages, was the reverse. Off stage they have made their new report to the king: the prince has wildly threatened to take the throne (III. ii. 317 ff., 354 ff.) and has broken with them utterly. Claudius turns both these points to good account. The spies, no longer serviceable as such, shall be the prince's escorts, really his guards as the context shows, on the voyage to England. The danger, formerly alluded to by Claudius in general terms (III. i. 4, 175), is now very specific: "I like him not, nor stands it safe with us. . . ." The opening and closing pronouns of this line form, together with the central "nor," an effectual counterpoint. The "I" conveys initially a sharp personal fear which his listeners shall continue to hear distinctly when it is taken up into the concern for the royal "us," the head of the Danish government. Such "Hazard" (6) may not be endured by the "terms of our estate" (5). This handsome phrase denotes the safety of the realm while connoting, what his two friends know well, his vulnerability as a usurper hated by the heir apparent. The nervous uncertainty of Claudius's previous speeches to these two (II. ii. 1 ff., III. i. 1 ff.) is entirely gone. He has regained his initial accomplished imitation of innocent and pious majesty (I. ii. 1 ff.).

His bearing, along with the exultation of Rosencrantz and
Guildenstern upon the high success of their courtly ambition,
gives the cue for their ensuing grandiloquence. Their praise of
Claudius's "fear" (8) as animated solely by his royal care of
his subjects is conventionally fulsome. Not so, however, is the
striking picture that Rosencrantz—exceptionally inspired for
the nonce as if by the overruling spirit of justice and order—
proceeds to give of "majesty" as a "massy wheel" fixed precari-
ously upon "the summit of the highest mount" with "ten
thousand lesser things . . . mortized and adjoined," ever in
danger of "boistrous ruin."[24] This passage, prepared for by
the words "holy and religious" (8), reminds the audience that
the "sanctity and health of the whole state" (I. iii. 21) is a
main theme of this drama, and makes us realize that the
"strange eruption" boded at the outset to "our state" (I. i. 69)
is now in crucial process. We know that the "spirit upon whose
weal depends and rests The lives of many" (14), and which
demands "all the strength and armour of the mind" (12), is
in imminent danger from the two opposed heads of the state:
a king prudent but criminal, a crown prince noble but now
tragically imprudent.

In that passage, however, Claudius hears merely a testimony
to his own supremacy and to that general fear of change and
disturbance which is the chief asset of a settled usurper. He
declares, with hardened resolve and fine tactic, "we will fetters
put upon this fear" (25, 8). Smoothly, too, he hearkens to
the elder statesman Polonius, who enters as the two younger
courtiers depart and who, despite the Play scene, is not yet
ready for the banishment of the crown prince. Blissfully ignorant of the instant "commission" (3) of the two new favorites
the old man chatters confidently of his own plan (III. i. 184 ff.),
still formally approved and backed by his politic sovereign
(30 ff.).

Now come two extraordinary and parallel soliloquies by
king and prince, sudden, startling outbursts, yet all along carefully prepared for by the dramatist. Here the two men who

---

[24] The passage recalls many others in Elizabethan literature in praise of
order, in the universe and in the state, e.g., *Troilus and Cressida* I. iii. 75-137.

are the heads of the realm are heedless of that realm's fate and fortune.[25] They are morbidly concerned, each in his own way, with their private problems. And their self-centered emotions, though for the moment sincere, are strikingly unveracious. The two are not true to themselves and it follows "as the night the day" (I. iii. 79) that they are false to the interests of every man, of "those many many" (9) dependent upon them. The public spirit nobly shown by the prince in the first act, and by no means entirely lacking in the king, is here totally absent from both. The remorsefulness in which Claudius indulges is self-centered, irrelevant, and ineffectual. So is the revengefulness of Hamlet. The two protagonists are here swept by opposite waves of passionate feeling, which the poet makes us understand fully and sympathize with—and condemn.

Claudius's preliminary fit of remorse (III. i. 49 ff.) gave way quickly to his new sense of danger. His second and shattering fit, at the close of the Play, has suffered much the same fate; so we have gathered from his words to Rosencrantz and Guildenstern above. Nevertheless, his present confession is very moving and, at first, promising. In revulsion from his hypocritic mien to the devoted Polonius, "dear my lord" (35), who had unwittingly lashed his conscience in III. i, he cries out suddenly, as soon as alone:

> Oh my offence is rank, it smells to heaven,
> It hath the primal eldest curse upon't,
> A brother's murther.

His "rank" sin, pervading with its stench the "undiscovered country," the invisible realm of the spirit, has risen to "men's eyes" (I. ii. 258) in the Play scene just because—the awed sinner seeks now no further explanation of Hamlet's discovery —it is known to and cursed by the "heaven" above, like Cain's unconcealable crime. It is primarily a "fault to heaven" (I. ii. 101), not to man, as Claudius has inwardly felt from the first. He admits that fact plainly and fully now, laying aside

---

[25] The "massy wheel" above (17) would at once suggest to the Elizabethan audience the well-known Wheel of Fortune; and that audience would be keenly conscious of the king's and the prince's selfish disregard of the fortune of the kingdom, now in danger of "ruin" (22).

for the time being all his accomplished hypocrisy. Prayer, therefore, is his "sharp" and "strong" need (38-40). His guilt, however, is stronger. But it can be overcome by the divine mercy. "Is there not rain enough in the sweet heavens To wash it white as snow?[26] . . . Then I'll look up, my fault is past."

But he knows he can have neither mercy nor any reality of prayer unless he is willing to proceed from remorse to "repentance" (65).[27]   Repentance means an entire turning away of his soul from his sin, and therefore involves penance and restitution, a giving up of the "effects" (54) for which he did the murder, "My crown, mine own ambition, and my queen." Here his already determined banishment of Hamlet recurs to us pointedly. The present safety of Claudius requires it; but his soul's salvation, on his own showing, requires the rescinding of it. He does not mention it, but it is certainly in the uneasy background of his mind while he ponders, "May one be pardoned and retain th' offence?" (56). Here the word "offence," finely prepared for in his opening line (36), comprises both the sin and its "effects," notably the throne, kept from Hamlet by "the wicked prize itself," i.e., by the very power which the throne has conferred on Claudius:

> In the corrupted currents of this world
> Offence's gilded hand may shove by justice,
> And oft 'tis seen the wicked prize itself
> Buys out the law; but 'tis not so above:
> There is no shuffling, there the action lies
> In his true nature, and we ourselves compelled
> Even to the teeth and forehead of our faults
> To give-in evidence.

That keen image of the heavenly, above the earthly, justice is central in *The Tragedy of Hamlet, Prince of Denmark*. The speaker uses the present tense: Judgment Day is here and now,

[26] Mercy "droppeth as the gentle rain from heaven" (*Merchant of Venice* IV. i. 185). Claudius's words reflect two passages in the Bible concerning "rain" and "snow," Matthew 5:45 and Psalms 51:7.

[27] A very sharp distinction between remorse and repentance, as in orthodox Christian thought, is prominent in Shakespeare's work from *Hamlet* on. The theme culminates in the deadly remorse of Macbeth and his Lady, devoid of any touch of real repentance. For a vivid allegorical treatment of the subject, see *The Faerie Queene* I. x. 23-29.

taken in the near future, a revenge *completely* out of keeping
with his proper character and "course of thought" (83). Here,
and here only, Hamlet is an absolute idealist, and a very bad
one: his ideal, unlike himself, is blatantly trite, immoral, and
unchristian. Yet he can throw his emotion into it fully, for the
time being, because of his personal hatred of Claudius. Previously Shakespeare has shown us how natural, though bad,
that hate was; here he shows us how extremely stultifying it
can be. Hamlet has no jot of that charitable understanding
of the wicked Claudius which Shakespeare has just given us
so fully in the king's soliloquy. Accordingly the prince can
make himself feel sincerely hesitant (85)

> To take him in the purging of his soul
> When he is fit and seasoned for his passage.

That time, in common charity, is exactly the right time for
executing a criminal. But Hamlet's Christian humanity, as
well as his sense of public justice, is overtopped by his personal
hatred of the criminal. This hate bolsters emotionally his
excuse for procrastination.

The gross outburst of that hate in the "bloody villain" passage (II. ii. 605-610), though quickly displaced by the just and
temperate project of the Play, was, as we saw, not viewed by
Hamlet in its "true nature" (62). He rebuked but did not
uproot his primitive revengefulness. Therefore the gross passion remained latent in him. A few minutes ago it stirred in
the "hot blood" verses (III. ii. 406-410); weakly, to be sure,
but sufficiently to remind us of its existence. And now Hamlet
can whip it up in support of an image more "horrid" (88) than
the "horridly tricked" Pyrrhus (II. ii. 478) whom his soul
abhorred. His imagination pictures Claudius taken in some act
devoid of any "relish" of salvation (92):

> *Then* trip him, that his heels may kick at heaven,
> And that his soul may be as damned and black
> As hell, whereto it goes.

This vision is as "rank and gross in nature" (I. ii. 136) as
Claudius's own crime; it "smells to heaven" (36). Of course

it is factitious, a rationalization of the prince's present delay. But the pride that set him upon this invention and, more, the hate that inspires it are tragically real. Actually, then, it is Hamlet's absolute lack of charity for the man Claudius that prevents his timely execution of the criminal king.

In this scene, as a whole, Shakespeare displays the fact that true justice is charitable; that, in divine reality, "mercy seasons justice" (*Merchant of Venice* IV. i. 197)—tempers it and preserves its true quality. Both the protagonists manage to "shove by justice" (58), when it confronts them, by divorcing it from charity and mercy. Claudius, praying for mercy, is not taught by "that same prayer" to render to Hamlet a "deed of mercy"[28] which would also be a deed of plain justice. And Hamlet's conduct is as unjust as it is unmerciful. The ideal revenge which he proposes is not only blackly primitive but pettily domestic, irrelevant to his Denmark's needs: it is a substitute for just and timely action. The execution of Claudius here would have been at once just and merciful: it would have prevented his doing "further evil" (V. i. 70) to the commonweal and to his own soul. In short, this scene shows prince and king offending against "heaven"—against the spirit of just charity, of charitable justice.[29]

The close of the scene leaves us with acute premonitions as to what "heaven" and the two protagonists will do next. We perceive that the king is now ready to do a greater wrong than merely banishing Hamlet; for the contrite benevolence which he had previously maintained, though dwindlingly, for the prince is now, in effect, ended. And on the other hand the prince is prepared to perpetrate something violently rash. If he had deferred his regicide in that spirit of honest humility which he achieved before the Play, acutely aware of his own

[28] *Merchant of Venice* IV. i. 201 f. Portia demonstrates that Shylock's procedure is equally unmerciful and unjust, but her legal details are unconvincing. In the present scene the principle is applied convincingly to the hero as well as to the villain of the piece. Shakespeare treats Hamlet with unswerving justice, consequently with a firmer and richer charity than appeared in the earlier play.

[29] Brutus, contrariwise, offends "heaven" by a theoretic imitation of charitable justice in killing Caesar. Brutus and Hamlet do not think too much: they think wrongly, each in his own way, each misled by unconfessed pride.

shortcomings and his need of patient temperance, he would not have thrust his sword blindly through the arras in the next scene. At present he is indeed, this time without confessing it, in a mood that is "very proud, revengeful, ambitious, with more offences at my beck than I have thoughts to put them in" (III. i. 126 ff.). Now he is indeed, what he previously condemned, "passion's slave" (III. ii. 77). At this moment he can do a deed ruinously rash and wrong.

(e) *this picture ... and ... this*   III. iv—IV. iii

III. iv. 1-102

That fact, known to us, is unknown to the optimistic Polonius. He is buoyed high in mood by his success in persuading the prince to "come straight" (1) to "his mother's closet" (III. iii. 27), to be spied on by himself. His policy of "indirections" (II. i. 66) is here in its zenith. Confident of his ability to find "Where truth is hid, though it were hid indeed Within the Center" (II. ii. 158), he has found no mystery at all in Hamlet's "mystery." He is certain that the young man's madness, though of course aggravated by several well-known political and domestic circumstances, had its "origin" in "neglected love" (III. i. 184-187). This will surely be confessed by Hamlet when his devoted mother breaks him down by scolding him for his outrageous "pranks" (2) while touching his heart by telling him how much she has "screened" him. The scolding is of first importance. She must "be round with him" (5, III. i. 191), severely plain in speech instead of maternally "partial" (III. iii. 32). That, we know, is precisely the opposite of the right advice for the present occasion: it will make the queen exacerbate the prince's bad mood. In short, the Polonian psychoanalysis of Hamlet, though carefully thought out and in its way acute, is based on imperfect premises and is fatally irrelevant to the patient's present state of mind.

Hamlet, to be sure, had suddenly checked his internal "hell," but without at all discarding it: "My mother stays" (III. iii. 95). The image of her awaiting him swings him, quickly and transiently, from primitive revengefulness to primitive filial yearning. His call, outside, as he approaches her closet has a piercing, rising pathos: "Mother, mother, *mother*" (6). Even now, if only she would be her natural yielding self, the hovering disaster could be escaped. But, stiffened by the advice and by the concealed presence of the old councilor, she confronts her son with a dark frown, to which he responds sharply, repressing his filial yearning: "Now, mother, what's the matter?" And she declaims the very thing which he cannot now bear: "thou hast thy father," Claudius, "much offended." He has just been seeing, in ghostly vision, "my father" (III. iii. 76, 80) killed and sent to his account, with soul unpurged, by the black incestuous villain whom his mother, now for the first time in the drama, brazenly terms "thy father." His wrath rises hotly against this "husband's brother's wife" who is also "my mother" (15 f.).

She retreats from him—unlike the quiet, firm Ophelia under similar circumstances (III. i. 133 ff.)—while weakly trying to reinforce her own authority with the vague threat of summoning "those that can speak" (17), not naming Polonius. So that when, seized by Hamlet and forced into a chair, she screams for help and a muffled voice answers her cry, he at once, and naturally, assumes that the near-by Claudius has, characteristically, exchanged praying for prying, an act that has in it "no relish of salvation" (III. iii. 92). All of Hamlet's accumulated revengefulness, so fully indulged in his soliloquy a few moments ago, overflows now. And it concentrates in an overwhelming impulse to end the "rat" (23) who has secretly gnawed the bond between him and his mother.[30] He had wished to convert her and get her on his side before doing the deed. But now he finds the poisonous king lurking *in spirit* between him and his mother's "inmost part" (20), turning her soul against him, and also lurking in body, so he thinks, behind the arras. Swiftly the prince draws his sword and kills the "rat."

Also, he believes, he has killed the king of Denmark. And now that he has managed to do this deed, he is overcome by

---

[30] My allusion is to Kent's description of Oswald (*Lear* II. ii. 80). Hamlet's allusion is to the Elizabethan sport of rat-hunting; but doubtless he has the other and deeper meaning in mind.

his (and the Elizabethan) innate horror of regicide. Standing fixed he listens to the dying groan behind the arras, the muffled "I am slain," and to the queen's piercingly sincere cry, "Oh me, what hast thou done?" He would fain not be aware of his deed. "Nay, I know not," he says in a low tone, breathing hard; "is it—the *king?*"[31] That last word, elsewhere applied by Hamlet to Claudius rarely, reluctantly, and bitterly, is uttered here with fear and awe. He will not yet lift the arras and face his deed. He turns to his mother. Her demeanor, different from that of a wife who has just lost her husband, must seem to him to mean that her personal grief is submerged in her horror at her son's murder of the anointed sovereign. He shares, for the moment, her horror. But when she cries out upon his "rash and bloody deed," condemning him entirely, not herself at all, he rouses himself at once. Admitting his own misdeed he points to a worse one on her part, a worse kind of regicide:

> A bloody deed, almost as bad, good mother,
> As kill a king and marry with his brother.

By wedding the regicidal brother, by becoming sacramentally one with him, she, though unaware of his crime, has incurred its guilt while adding that of incest. Preparation for this point was the "wormwood" line in the Play, "None wed the second but who killed the first" (III. ii. 190). And now her horrified exclamation "As kill a king?" (30) serves simply to establish his regained firmness. The thought of all the criminality of Claudius, criminality shared by his wife, enables Hamlet to face the horrid fact that he himself has now killed a king. Resolutely he declares, "Ay, lady, 'twas my word." Then he lifts the curtain from his deed: he thrusts aside the arras—and discovers the body of Polonius.

Hamlet staggers back in dismay and grief too deep for

[31] Compare Macbeth's use of "know" at the close of II. ii—"To know my deed, 'twere best not know myself"—in revulsion from his destruction of the king, who is presently termed by Macduff the "Lord's anointed temple" (II. iii. 73). In the quartos and folios Hamlet's line reads: "Nay I know not, is it the King?" This, I think, is a pentameter verse (like the three verses that follow) but with one foot represented by a pause, or pauses, and consequently with cumulative emphasis on the word "King." Hence my insertion of a dash.

words. Certainly "a rash and bloody deed is this": his mother's pronouncement, now understood, is dreadfully true. For a moment he stands in deathly silence, transfixed by conscience. All the criminal folly of his conduct since the Play scene (as he will later confess aloud) rushes upon him. And, unlike Claudius in the preceding scene, he begins a real repentance. Therefore, unlike Claudius, he will not indulge in elaborate remorse for the past to the exclusion of his present, pressing duty: he must convert his mother. He checks her lamenting, and postpones his own, by quick, severe words to the dead spy:

> Thou wretched, rash, intruding fool, farewell,
> I took thee for thy Better, take thy fortune,
> Thou findst to be too busy is some danger.

Justice, though not charity, is in those lines. The "intruding fool" intruded mainly, as we have seen, by assuming the role of his "Better," the king, in secretly promoting the queen's minatory bearing towards her son. Incidentally the word "rash" echoes her use of it, above, in application to Hamlet. The prudent old councilor, such is the sharp irony here, has in the end surpassed the young prince in rashness.

Finely prudent is the prince, however, in his ensuing procedure with his mother. He turns her roused emotions to account in breaking down her guard of bad habit. "Leave wringing of your hands. . . ." He will now wring her heart if, as appears just now, it is "made of penetrable stuff," and if it be not too much overlaid with the brass of "damned custom" (37). Her sin is Denmark's sin. The "weary, stale, flat, and unprofitable . . . uses of this world" (I. ii. 133) are now condensed by the tragically experienced prince into the short, smiting phrase "damned custom." This it is which has enabled the realm and its queen to accept, smoothly, heartlessly, unnaturally (II. ii. 380-385), a base sovereign as the fully satisfactory sequel of a noble one. Hamlet is thinking of his dead father; but Shakespeare, here more than ever, makes us think of the prince himself and of all the great values connoted by him which low social "custom" rejects. It is significant that Gertrude's adultery is not named by her son in this very inti-

mate scene. He regards that crime as entirely subordinate to
her main sin, emphasized in the Play, her facile turning to a low
love when she had known and vowed herself to a high one.
This tragic "falling off," so distressing to Hamlet and to the
world of the spirit (I. v. 47-57), is unrecognized by his mother
in her world of "damned custom." Of this world she becomes
now a vivid symbol. Hence the climactic and representative
quality of the Closet scene. In this closet is the world that
Hamlet is trying to set right.

"You are the queen," he said to her above (15); and now
he tells her that by reason of her authoritative role in society
her "act" (40) has distorted, throughout her realm, the true
quality of love—and of all that depends upon love, from natural "modesty" (41) to supernatural "religion" (47). Her
"act" affronts beauty and goodness equally. It "blurs the
grace," hollows the "virtue," "takes off the rose." It puts
"marriage-vows" on a level with the proverbially false, impious,
and ugly "dicers' oaths." It "plucks" from the holy sacrament
of marriage

> The very soul, and sweet religion makes
> A rhapsody of words. Heaven's face doth glow;
> Yea, this solidity and compound mass,
> With tristful visage as against the doom,
> Is thought-sick at the act.

"Heaven's face" (48) harboring, so to speak, the "blush" (41)
that the queen and realm have lost "doth glow" with shame
and indignation at the "act." The impassive earth itself, "this
solidity and compound mass," sensing an air of doomsday, is
sick with the thought of the "act." Thus again, but more
spiritually than in the opening scene of the drama, do "heaven
and earth together" demonstrate (I. i. 124).

The wretched queen, already badly shaken by the fate of
Polonius, is cowed by the cosmic "thunder" (52) in her son's
words, so different from the "earthly thunder" of Claudius's
false majesty (I. ii. 128). "Ay me, what act ... ?" She senses
its import, though distantly and vaguely. Swiftly her son brings
it home to her. "Look here upon this picture, and on this. . . ."

Bending, he has caught up from her bosom the miniature of Claudius attached to a chain about her neck, placing it alongside the one he wears of his father. But as he proceeds he drops the miniatures and sketches the two pictures, effectually, upon the vacant air—the vacant, but (in preparation for the coming again of the Ghost) the more and more ghostly, air. The Play had given, without perceptible effect upon the queen, a "counterfeit presentment" of the "two brothers" (54). Now Hamlet gives it unescapably, and with that cosmic and mythical note which, though not absent from the Play, was far more emphatic in the two opening scenes of Act I. "So excellent a king, that was, to this, Hyperion to a satyr" (I. ii. 139) is echoed now in the following:

> See what a grace was seated on his brow,
> Hyperion's curls, the front of Jove himself,
> An eye like Mars to threaten and command,
> A station like the herald Mercury
> New lighted on a heaven-kissing hill:
> A combination and a form indeed
> Where every god did seem to set his seal
> To give the world assurance of a man.

That "heaven-kissing hill" recalls the "high eastern hill" of dawn at the outset (I. i. 167); while the "herald Mercury" alludes not only to the late king's manly "grace" but (by Shakespeare's fine art) to the fact that his spirit, presently to appear again, is a messenger from the unseen world. The dominant idea of the passage, however, is that a great ruler has always a Divine Right. Here Hamlet's father is more than a "goodly king" and a distinguished "man" (I. ii. 186-188): he is the representative of divinity on earth.

Hamlet strives with beautiful power to reach his mother's "brazed" conscience through her imagination, through her senses (71 ff.), and through her sense of "shame" (82). His words come full circle when he summons to her face a true "blush" (82), the "grace and blush of modesty" (41) which she as queen has blurred for her subjects. He had said that her conduct "Calls virtue hypocrite" (42); now he declares that "virtue" can melt like "Wax" for "flaming youth" with "no shame" since age, in the person of the queen and "matron," has yielded to "Rebellious hell" (82-87). It is this idea that finally breaks Gertrude down. Like Claudius, she is naturally a kindly person. Having helped to deprive her son of his throne, she has ever been anxious to do no further harm to him and no harm at all to anyone else. Therefore her son's terrific picture of the evil effect which her example must eventually have upon "youth" makes all her shame overflow, the shame which she has hitherto managed to keep hidden from herself. Now her eyes are turned perforce into "my very soul" (89). She had all along told herself that her sin of the flesh was ephemeral. Now she finds, beyond the flesh, "black spots" too deeply ingrained in her "soul" to lose "their tinct": they have tragically impregnated her spirit and the spirit of her kingdom, particularly the spirit of her own son's contemporaries, "flaming youth."

But while converting his mother Hamlet is unconsciously displaying the conversion of a more important prince, himself. Shakespeare, by means of an intensely dramatic juxtaposition of two opposite pictures, Hamlet in III. iii and Hamlet in III. iv, forces us to compare the present prince with him of the preceding scene. There he was given over to an idealistic, selfish, unveracious, and ineffectual passion of revenge. Here, penitent for the "bloody deed" to which that passion led him and moved by love now instead of hate—love for his mother, his father, and his country—he can rise, though not without lapses, to an extraordinary height of charitable justness. When he tells his mother that properly at her age "the blood is tame, it's humble, And waits upon the judgment" (69) we are made to feel that this is true of the prince himself at present. Here again, as during the Play scene, his feelings, though at white heat, are swayed by his judgment. In the preceding scene "reason panders will" (88), producing a false rationalism to satisfy wilful desire. Not so here. True to his present unselfish purpose he even refrains from confronting his mother with her sins against himself; his allusions to these are distant. He wants the queen to be moved by issues larger than her son's unhappiness. And in striking contrast with his inhuman view of Claudius he shows a penetrating human understanding of his mother. He is justly severe to her; but he admits with a touch of humane humor that she has been "cozened at hoodman-blind" (77). He is restrained and merciful as well as just—so far.

Again, however, he loses his temperance when he comes to think of her present sexual relations with Claudius (91). The Ghost's final pronouncement on that matter (I. v. 82) was dignified and public-spirited:

> Let not the royal bed of Denmark be
> A couch for luxury and damned incest.

But the very opposite of that "royal" style is Hamlet's now:

> Nay, but to live
> In the rank sweat of an enseamed bed,
> Stewed in corruption, honeying and making love
> Over the nasty sty—

Again he is carried away by his personal hate of Claudius, accentuated here by his crucial failure, a few minutes ago, to end that criminal: he is trying to compensate that failure with violent words. He exaggerates grossly the element of mere and sheer lust in the love (as Shakespeare has shown it to us) of Gertrude and her second husband. And thence he works himself up wildly to a new and blind misappraisal of Claudius. This astute hypocrite becomes in Hamlet's distempered fancy a motley court fool, "A king of shreds and patches" (102)—

III. iv. 103-217

Instantly, here, the raving prince becomes aware of a monitory presence:

> Save me;[32] and hover o'er me with your wings,
> You heavenly guards! What would you, gracious figure?

As at the very first, but here far more poignantly, the ghostly father has responded to the son's state of mind. This time the

---

[32] The semicolon of F1 (comma in Q1, no punctuation in Q2) suggests that the "Save me" is addressed primarily to the Ghost himself. The context makes perfectly clear that the Ghost, this time, is a *saving* presence. Instead of the steel armor of Act I he now wears domestic attire; according to Q1 a "night gown," i.e., dressing gown.

"figure" is unquestionably a "spirit of health" (I. iv. 40), a "gracious" being invoked by the kneeling prince as belonging with, not over against, the "Angels and ministers of grace" (I. iv. 39).   Indeed the Ghost, we soon perceive, has been much "purged" (I. v. 13); this spirit itself is really now a "minister of grace."   Before It speaks Hamlet knows Its message *in his own spirit* and puts it into vivid words (106-108).   He declares that since the Play scene he has been a "tardy son"; he has let "go by" the great opportunity for the "important acting of your dread command."[33]   And at this very moment he is "lapsed in time and passion," i.e., absorbed in time-wasting, intemperate emotion: he is substituting blatant *revengefulness,* precisely as in the Prayer scene (III. iii), for just and timely *vengeance.*

The Ghost's ensuing speech echoes Hamlet's but stresses the idea of "purpose" (111).   Obviously the prince's purpose regarding his mother as well as Claudius is at the moment "almost blunted."   By tainting his mind (I. v. 85) with unreason, in his passionate outburst, he has been driving her into a delirium (94 f.) that can spoil her repentance.   And now the "amazement" (112) of her weak nature (114) is terrific at seeing and hearing him converse, as she says, with the "incorporal air" (118).   For to *her* the Ghost is invisible.   That fact is at first startling to us because we see him, and we remember that Horatio and the soldiers saw him.   But despite all of the Ghost's present mercifulness to her in word and mien, overlooking her sin against his love and self-esteem (I. v. 48 ff.) and reviving his marital tenderness for her (I. ii. 140-142) in spiritual form, she cannot see him.   In spite of Hamlet's incredulous urgency and his aid (125 ff.)—prepared for above by his spiritual picture of her first husband (55 ff.)—she sees absolutely nothing: "Nothing at all, yet all that is I see" (132).   We are made to understand that her spirit, having given itself to a lower love, is now blind to the spirit of him whom once "she would hang on" (I. ii. 143).   Hence the present "piteous action" (128) of the Ghost.   Silently and longingly, "in his

---

[33] The word "dread" connotes the deep repugnance of Hamlet for the required regicide.

habit as he lived" (135), he waits in vain for a sign from Gertrude, then "steals away." His visit has no beneficent result
for his former wife except through the medium of his and her
son. The result for Hamlet is that, having swung from mad
cursing of Claudius to intensely emotional pity for his father,
he regains in the end his equilibrium, and resumes his "purpose."

After a moment of silent effort he is able to say to his
mother, "My pulse as yours doth temperately keep time"
(140). And throughout the rest of the scene he keeps his
feelings, however powerful and diverse, under superb control,
as in the Play scene, but more admirably since now his problems
are more complex and difficult. Firmly, effectually, he proceeds
with his double task, the conversion of his mother and the preparation of counter measures against Claudius. Above all he
evinces a new religious attitude and a touch of supernal peace.

He knows clearly now (144) that only divine "grace" and
"unction" can really convert Gertrude:

> Mother, for love of Grace,
> Lay not a flattering Unction to your soul
> That not your trespass but my madness speaks. . . .[34]

The "rank corruption" (148) which, just before the Ghost
entered, Hamlet had ranted about in sheerly physical terms
(92 f.) he now describes as a spiritual sin that, "mining all
within, Infects unseen." Therefore he urges, "Confess yourself to Heaven, Repent what's past, avoid what is to come."
Winningly he adds, putting his arms about her, "forgive me
this my virtue. . . ." He is a son, a far from saintly one, preach-
ing to his mother! In a gently satiric tone he adds that, in such
an extremely oily court, even "Virtue itself," let alone Hamlet,
"must" (would have to) bow low before "Vice" and "woo for
leave to do him good." He kisses her. His speech has been
penetrating, just, and tender, like the "Heaven" to which he
has referred her. So all her defenses go down. She clings to

---

[34] Here I have retained from F1 two capital letters, those of "Grace" and
"Unction," to bring out the Christian significance that these words had for
seventeenth-century readers. Of course in F1 many words are capitalized for
emphasis, e.g., the following in the present speech: Pulse, Musick, Test, Grace,
Unction, Ulcerous, Corruption, Heaven, Compost, Weeds, Virtue, Vice.

him, weeping loudly: "O Hamlet, thou has cleft my heart in twain." He responds with deep intensity:

> Oh throw away the worser part of it
> And live the purer with the other half.
> Good night—

But just here, holding her face between his hands, studying it with loving intentness, he feels fully what a hard task she has before her in breaking the grip of "damned custom" (37). With fine spiritual strategy he urges her to employ in the service of virtue that very "monster, custom" (160) which has hitherto consumed her "sense" (71, 161): that "devil" can also be an "angel," the angel of good habit. It will enable her to accomplish the first duty which true repentance requires, the giving up of some plain "effect" (III. iii. 54) for which the sin was done. "Good night—but go not to mine uncle's bed":

> Assume a virtue, if you have it not. . . .
> For use can almost change the stamp of nature
> And either throne the devil, or throw him out,
> With wondrous potency. Once more, good night;
> And when you are desirous to be blessed,
> I'll blessing beg of you.[35]

She had lifted her hands to bless him, after the good custom of a mother parting from her child at night: she is very "desirous" to do so. But he clasps her lifted hands between his with a smile. She has not yet really removed the barrier between herself and him and, far more importantly, between herself and heaven. With loving tact he reminds her that in forming her new good habit of life she needs the divine help which she has not yet sought: she needs to become "desirous to be blessed" by heaven. Implicitly his words and gestures iterate here his chief entreaty above (144-150): "Mother, for love of grace. . . . Confess yourself to heaven, Repent. . . ." At the same time,

---

[35] The twofold nature of custom has all along been known to Hamlet. But at the first, like most young persons, he was acutely conscious of the *evil* potentialities of custom (I. ii. 78), use (I. ii. 134), and habit (I. iv. 29). Now, more experienced and patient, he stresses the value of *good* custom, use, and habit. For the word "throne," see the Furness Variorum Edition of this play, I, 303 f.

however, he confesses implicitly his own sin and need. When his mother obtains the divine blessing he will "beg" *it*, along with her maternal blessing, for himself.

Dropping her hands he points solemnly to the arras: the body of "this same lord," whom he shrinks from naming, has been present all along in the rear of the scene and of Hamlet's consciousness. He bows his head now in grief, then contritely crosses himself:

> I do repent; but heaven hath pleased it so
> To punish me with this, and this with me,
> That I must be their scourge and minister.

Those lines, condensing the tragic theme of the whole drama, summing up the action so far and preparing for what remains, are profoundly true of the methods of "heaven." The divine merciful justice turns men's sins and errors to its own account. Hamlet with his limited designs and dubious passions has been, and will further be, its twofold agent, its "scourge and minister."

He planned to catch, not to cure, the conscience of the king; and thereafter he planned to "trip him that his heels may kick at heaven" (III. iii. 93). But heaven's plan was larger. Hamlet, beyond his will, was the means of bringing Claudius into a deep remorse and then of prolonging his life, to repentance—this prospect is not yet utterly closed—or else to filling the cup of his wickedness to overflowing. That situation is clear to us, not to Hamlet. But he now senses the fact that his blind murder of Polonius has served, by humbling his own proud self, to render him both more charitable and more effective in his treatment of his mother. What he sees most clearly, however, is the point of chief urgency. The three lines quoted above, taken together with his confession to the Ghost (106-109), show that he regards the slaying of Polonius as the direct consequence of his *revengeful* postponement (III. iii. 88 ff.) of the execution of Claudius; heaven has made the second sin the punishment of the first. At the same time heaven has punished "this with me." The "this," accompanied (I think) by an inclusive gesture, denotes Polonius's spying while connoting the general dishonesty of the time, of which Polonius became in Act II the main emblem. Hamlet does not in the least justify his crime *against the person* of the comparatively innocent old councilor, the tool of his "Better" (32). He implicitly admits his own crucial dishonesty. Having slaughtered Polonius instead of the king on crooked grounds, he cannot at present term himself even "indifferent honest" (III. i. 123).

The elaborate, self-centered histrionism of his confession to Ophelia in III. i is entirely gone. A simple religious humility, prepared for in the scenes preceding the Play, has come upon him now. He who was "born to set it right" is religiously aware of his tragic need of being set right himself: "I do repent." The heavens are scourging, and ministering to, the guilty prince himself along with his guilty kingdom.

His repentance entails the utter abandonment of his black ideal of killing the "soul" (III. iii. 94) as well as the body of Claudius; no touch of it recurs in the remainder of the drama. All the more realistically he faces now the immediate situation in regard to his enemy. He reckons—though not sufficiently—with that "witchcraft" of the king's "wit" (I. v. 43) which he has hitherto ignored in its bearing on his own fate. Claudius, who could seduce Gertrude from Hamlet's father, may succeed in seducing her, at least partially, from her new allegiance to her son. She may let out the fact that he is only "mad in craft" (188). Hence the prince shrewdly supplements his moral and religious urgencies by appealing to her feminine delicacy, her queenly pride, and her maternal fears for her son in order to keep her from further intimacy with Claudius. "One word more, good lady" (179). Taking her hands again and speaking, not with the bitter violence that frightened her above (91 ff.), but with vivid satiric humor, he makes a repellent picture of the endearments of the "blunt king" (182)—blunt, i.e., crudely obtuse, in spite of all his cleverness, to the finer quality of love. This king, Hamlet intimates, is not a truly human lover: he's a toad, a bat, a tomcat (190). Should his low arts be able to deceive a lady who *can* be what her son will love admiringly, "a queen, fair, sober, wise?" (189). He attributes to her with religious art the character he wants her to have. Will she, like the "ape" in the story, be easily fooled into ruining the realm, including her son and also herself (196) since her new and better life depends on him? Thus Hamlet forestalls the gross wheedlings of Claudius with fine cajolements of his own. Lovingly skilful as never before, he wins from the soft queen a firm vow of secrecy, which, in the sequel, she keeps.

His stress upon this vow, however, makes us perfectly certain of what we had already felt: he will not again try to kill the king *tonight*. Above, for a moment, perhaps, he pondered doing so while declaring "I must be cruel, only to be kind . . . worse remains behind" (178). But he quickly set that purpose aside; and we do not blame him, considering all that has happened this night. From what ensues here, however, it is evident that he is not yet facing fully his natural reluctance for the hateful deed. He snatches at the opportunity of making "my two schoolfellows . . . sweep my way and marshal me to knavery" (202 ff.), i.e., to the deed of regicide; he will not make his meaning explicit for the queen. In the rash excitement of his recent encounter with Rosencrantz and Guildenstern he told them, and through them Claudius, that he wanted the throne at once (III. ii. 354 ff.). Now, by way of counterstroke, they have the royal "mandate" to conduct him to England. They have been promoted from spying snakes to "adders fanged" (203), empowered, he knows, by the "serpent" that "did sting" secretly his "father's life" (I. v. 39). Hamlet's own life is now in secret danger—as he divines, actually with keen relief. For his task will no longer be that of killing, at bedtime prayers or otherwise, a king who has hitherto spared and cultivated him. From now on he has to *defend* himself and his succession to the throne.[36] To that point the plotting of Claudius will doubtless develop; Hamlet hopes so, with firm courage. He is confident, far more than we are, that he can outwit his clever uncle. His zest as a youthful soldier and

---

[36] Christian casuists of the time, while condemning revenge on behalf of oneself or another, permitted killing in defense of one's own life—though not the killing of a king. But Shakespeare's audience would fully approve Hamlet's defense of the life of the future king, viz. himself; and in V. ii, for reasons that will be made clear in my text, they would approve the killing of Claudius for the sake also of the kingdom.

tactician adds itself to his relief at being able to regard his coming regicide in "one line" with his enemy's "craft" against himself:

> For 'tis sport to have the enginer
> Hoist with his own petar; and 't shall go hard
> But I will delve one yard below their mines,
> And blow them at the moon: oh 'tis most sweet
> When in one line two crafts directly meet—
> This man shall set me packing. . . .

"This man," Polonius, still unnamed by Hamlet, was a counter in the king's game when alive, and will continue to be so though now a casualty of war, mere "guts" (212). With rough satiric tongue, as in the case of his words to Ophelia at the Play, Hamlet eases the heaviness of his crime against her father. For the first time he calls him a "knave" (215), signalizing him as partaker and symbol of all the court "knavery" (205) that is now gathering to a head against the prince. Well, "*this* counsellor," at least, is now silent. Hamlet, departing and "*tugging in Polonius,*" is drawing all the old fellow's circumlocution and machination "toward an end."

But at the door he pauses. Longingly and lovingly he looks back from the body, and from his own dark deed, to his mother. And his parting words have a fuller poignancy than his "Mother, mother, *mother*" (6) at the outset of the scene. Yearning anguish, recalling his penitence over the body (174), appears on his face now, and is heard in the tone of his final "Good night, *mother.*"[37]

IV. i

The sequel of that anguished parting is the queen's "profound" sighing (1) and, finally, her lovely verses in telling the king where her son has gone (24):

> To draw apart the body he hath killed,
> O'er whom his very madness, like some ore

---

[37] His previous "good night's" to her (159, 170, 177, 213), each uttered in a different tone, are summed up in, and transcended by, the charged emotion of this finale. Shakespeare has here repeated on a higher level the technique of Juliet's iterated "good night" to her lover (*Romeo and Juliet* II. ii. 120-186).

> Among a mineral of metals base,
> Shows itself pure. He weeps for what is done.

She knows that now, alone with the "unseen good old man" (12) and with his own sin, Hamlet is showing to heaven a penitence entirely "pure"—"unmixed" (as he himself would put it) "with baser matter" (I. v. 104). In contrast, the king's regret for his most faithful servant, Polonius, is quickly submerged in the baser matter of self-concern: "Oh heavy deed! It had been so with us had we been there"—the last thought which the queen's skilfully euphemistic account of the deed (7-11) would have suggested had Claudius not been guilty and selfish. The repentance of the prince is proceeding while the king's "thoughts remain below" (III. iii. 97).

Claudius hastily covers his egoistic outbreak with altruistic regards for the safety of "all . . . everyone" (14 f.), even adducing his "love" (19) for Hamlet himself. But his dominant thought is that of getting the prince shipped away at dawn (29) and of alleviating the blame (17), bound to be accentuated by rumor (41), that the violent death of his chief councilor at the hands of the crown prince must bring upon himself as king. To meet the situation he sets himself to employ all his "majesty and skill" (31). But at the last he declares, half aside, "My soul is full of discord and dismay." The discord is essentially that conflict between remorse and self-interest evinced by his "soul" in the Prayer scene.[1] The call of self-interest, now, is sharply imperative; but remorse, too, is sharpened, for the moment, by the new and startling crime resultant from his own: certainly his "offence is rank" (III. iii. 36). Hence his "dismay. . . ." We wonder if the prince will benefit, in one way or another, from the king's inward "discord and dismay."

IV. ii

Hamlet, in accordance with his new decision, is awaiting a counterstroke from his uncle. He has put away his tears for Polonius along with the "stowed" (1) body, but is musing heavily. He starts—"What noise?"—at the multitudinous cry

---

[1] Of course, as he will later tell Laertes, his heightening designs against Hamlet are in "discord" also with his love for Hamlet's mother.

of his name by *"Gentlemen within,"* his uncle's courtiers in pursuit of him. Eager for direct conflict, he puts his hand to his sword and demands loudly, "Who calls on Hamlet?" But he adds a disgusted "Oh, here they come" when only Rosencrantz and Guildenstern enter. They, obeying intelligently the hasty command of the king, have left their "further aid" outside and will "speak fair" to the prince (IV. i. 32-37), avoiding the appearance of forcible arrest. But, in marked contrast with even the heightened boldness of their approach to him after the Play, their tone is now proudly peremptory: "What have you done? . . . Tell us. . . ." (5-7).

Hamlet, knowing their "counsel" (11), makes a final effort to force them into the open, and out of their present employment, by deliberately shocking, insulting, and scaring them. Returning upon his last words to Rosencrantz at their previous meeting (III. ii. 379 ff.) he again gives the fellow a plain hint of his own quick-coming "advancement" to the throne (III. ii. 354). He is the "son of a king" (14), i.e., the right heir of a great sovereign, whereas his schoolfellow is the "sponge" of another sort of king, "a sponge . . . that soaks up the king's countenance, his rewards, his authorities . . ." in the end, to be squeezed "dry again." Discarded by this dissimulating king, and also by the king to be, Hamlet himself, the sponge will indeed be dry; such is the suggestion. But Rosencrantz, though perceiving it well enough, declines to "understand" (24). Therefore Hamlet, shrugging his shoulders with an air of finality, passes off his adjuration as "a knavish speech" for a "foolish ear" (25). Henceforth the two schoolfellows whom he once loved shall be for him merely "adders fanged" (III. iv. 203).

And now Rosencrantz, after a reinforcing exchange of glances with Guildenstern, uses his first "must" to Hamlet: "My lord, you must tell us where the body is, and go with us to the king." Hamlet responds, "The body is with the king, but the king is not with the body": the king is artfully staving off his share of guilt for the death of Polonius.

HAMLET	The king is a thing—
GUILDENSTERN	A thing, my lord?
HAMLET	Of nothing: bring me to him, hide Fox, and all after.

The "thing" that the two schoolfellows have chosen to worship and serve is a worthless person and also, as suggested above (14), not their rightful king: he is a king, as well as a thing, of nothing. He's a pretender, a Fox—let's go find him. Hamlet hopes to find him in a particular way: he hopes the perturbed Fox will betray himself by making an overt move to destroy the crown prince.

IV. iii

But Claudius, having subdued the "discord and dismay" shown during his previous appearance, is again completely master of himself, and of others. His "wisest friends" (IV. i. 38), the councilors closest to him after Polonius, are made to feel how "dangerous" to them *all* is Hamlet—"this man" (2), as the king terms him, not now "chiefest courtier, cousin, and our son" (I. ii. 117)—so long as he "goes loose." He has killed the chief councilor; he may well proceed to kill the others; such is the artful intimation.

> Yet must not we put the strong law on him:
> He's loved of the distracted multitude,
> Who like not in their judgment, but their eyes. . . .

The inference is that Hamlet, despite his supposed lunacy, here not mentioned, is an entirely responsible "offender" (6), deserving capital punishment, but able to evade it by an appeal to the people. Clearly the effectual course is to exile him at once and without public advertisement, but not as if in precipitate fear on the part of the councilors for their own safety: the deed "must seem" the result of "Deliberate" (9) weighing of public interests. A difficult situation, this; like a "desperate" disease demanding a "desperate" remedy. Obviously the silent councilors agree entirely with the remedy proposed by Claudius. Hence the clever king is now ready to face the prince serenely in full concourse of the courtiers.[2]

[2] Q2 has *"Enter King, and two or three"* at the beginning of this scene and, at the close of Claudius's opening speech, *"Enter Rosencrantz and all the rest."*

Hamlet enters, "guarded" (14), but only in honorable fashion—attended by armed courtiers, not deprived of his sword. By quick action he could now—so he will afterwards confess to us—kill the king. But now he will do so only when Claudius palpably endangers *him*. Repentant for the dreadful result of his own revengeful plotting he will attend that of Claudius, alert to meet stroke with stroke. But Claudius knows his man. He knows Hamlet's "sweet and commendable" sensibility (I. ii. 87); he knows his deep grief for "the body he hath killed" (IV. i. 24). At once, therefore, he plies that theme, rubbing it in: "Now, Hamlet, where's Polonius?" (17). And indeed the prince's imagination is still heavily obsessed with the poor body that he has consigned to the "dust" (IV. ii. 6), to be the prey of "worms" (21). But with swift satire he turns the theme against Claudius. Those worms are "politic," like the old councilor and like his master. A "king" who has fattened his fortunes upon his subordinates will be an imperial "diet" for those same worms; and on these a fish may feed. Hence it is clear that a "king," no matter how triumphant, may in the form of fish-flesh "go a progress through the guts of a beggar" (33)—when the king is dead! Here the prince's tone is threatening, eager to provoke an answering threat from Claudius. He, however, continues to "bear all smooth and even" (7). He refuses, like his two underlings in the preceding scene, to be drawn from cover. With assumed obtuseness, he, like them, holds the theme off from himself, then swings it back to the prince's crime: "Where is Polonius?" (34).

"In heaven," Hamlet rejoins with sudden tragic gravity, glancing up at the "heaven" that is punishing him (III. iv. 173). Then his look fastens darkly upon the king, who belongs to "the other place" (37). Thus the prince under cover of his antic disposition threatens his enemy with imminent death and judgment, hoping to elicit from him some hostile gesture.[3]

[3] Hamlet's hiding of Polonius's body has three motives: remorse, simulation of madness, and desire to gain time for provoking Claudius into overt hostility. The third point shows the bearing of Hamlet's line, above, "This man [i.e., the dead Polonius] shall set me packing" (III. iv. 211), "packing" in the double sense of hasty departure and plotting, plotting to unveil the coming plot of Claudius.

But the subtle "engiuer" conceals his "line" (III. iv. 206, 210) while fully discerning Hamlet's. So far from revealing the least design against the person of the crown prince, the king declares that the voyage to England, officially for the purpose of demanding "neglected tribute" (III. i. 178), is really on behalf of the prince's "especial safety," which the king tenders as "dearly" as he grieves for "that which thou hast done" (44) —a masterly finale. Hamlet parodies it: "Farewell, dear mother" (52); his mother's incestuous mate has exhibited an ultra-motherly care for his safety! "My mother: father and mother is man and wife, man and wife is one flesh; and so, my mother." This parting thrust is a bitter return upon the theme of Hamlet's first soliloquy, the hasty, incestuous marriage. And here too, as in that initial court scene, the prince has been utterly baffled by the king's smooth, triumphant hypocrisy.

The action of the central phase of the drama has roused the conscience of the king and the conscience of the prince: this, to be painfully developed towards the spirit of true justice; that, to be suppressed. The ensuing soliloquy of Claudius (60 ff.) is the sequel of his central and crucial one (III. iii. 36 ff.). There, his rich remorse fell short of repentance because he would not surrender the crown. Heaven gave him another chance when the prince's killing of Polonius instead of himself filled his "soul" with "discord and dismay" (IV. i. 45). But now all his remorse has been nullified by "the hectic in my blood" (68)—a phrase that suddenly opens all the selfishness beneath his altruistic claim that Hamlet was a "disease" endangering the public weal (9, IV. i. 21). A diseased, feverish fear of the loss of his *own* worldly "joys" (70)—"My crown, mine own ambition, and my queen" (III. iii. 55)—obsesses him completely. At the same time he has benefited from Hamlet's less elaborate but far more fruitful remorse.[4] The prince's re-

---

[4] This fact, pointing up the truth that real repentance normally runs counter to one's *worldly* interests, is a keen stroke of tragic irony. Shakespeare has prepared for it by emphasizing the difference between Hamlet's remorse for killing Polonius and Claudius's remorse for killing his own brother. The king, like the sentimental, murderous Macbeth (I. vii. 21), works his remorse up to the image of a "new-born babe" (III. iii. 71), smothering in thick emotion the will to repent. Hamlet, on the contrary, simply "weeps for what

pentance for his own crime has had the effect—very natural
though by no means necessary—of postponing a further attempt
to end his uncle; whereas that uncle, in lieu of repentance, proceeds to attempt the quick ending of his nephew. The secret
letters of Claudius to England import, he now tells us, "The
present [i. e., immediate] death of Hamlet" (67).

---

is done" (IV. i. 27) and evinces repentance by change of conduct; but the
change does much to bring about his *worldly* downfall by providing Claudius
with time to develop his secret plots against the prince.

Heaven Ordinant

(a) *my dull revenge*   IV. iv

"Go, CAPTAIN," says Fortinbras at the head of his marching army, "from me greet the Danish king . . ." (1), whom we have just seen plotting the murder of the Danish prince as insidiously as he effected the murder of the prince's father. The elder Hamlet defeated the elder "ambitious" Fortinbras; moreover he "smote" the "Polacks" (I. i. 60 ff.) against whom (23) young Fortinbras is now proceeding. The elder Hamlet made Denmark a "great power" that wrung from England "homage" (IV. iii. 60-64). But England's "tribute" has recently been "neglected" (III. i. 178). Times have changed. As we were shown in the first two scenes of this drama and have since been made to feel often, Denmark, though still possessed of martial power, is no longer a martial state. An inevitable reaction from the "emulate pride" of militaristic adventurousness (I. i. 83 ff.) towards the opposite extreme of national softness was exploited by Claudius. He has made the state astutely and comfortably selfish. And he has now schemed to end the only Danish leader, Hamlet, who is capable of establishing the true temper of the state: strength with justice; power in the service, not of militarism, but of militant virtue.

Hamlet, the "expectancy" of the "fair state," possessing the "courtier's, soldier's, scholar's eye, tongue, sword" (III. i. 159 f.), wears at present a sleeping sword; but in this scene, as so often, he evinces the soldier's eye and tongue. He watches with keen appraisal the passing army; inquires of the captain its purpose and the name of its commander; estimates the coming battle's cost in lives and money (25); and is surprised that

Poland has decided to defend the "straw" in question. There-upon the statesman in him speaks:

> This is th' impostume of much wealth and peace,
> That inward breaks, and shows no cause without
> Why the man dies.

This useless conflict—the word "Fortinbras" means brazen bravery[5]—is a symptom, not a cause, of social decay. Peace based on wealth and ease is smooth without, diseased within; the abscess gathers and breaks "inward." Unlike Hamlet a superficial observer would blame the restless energy of Fortin-bras while not perceiving the real and mortal malady of the body politic, "much wealth and peace." That malady, such is the intimation here, is at its height, not in Norway or Poland, but in Denmark. The "impostume" is Hamlet's new, intenser image for his "unweeded garden" (I. ii. 135) and "time . . . out of joint" (I. v. 189). As a soldier who is also prince and thinker he hears anew the call for militant virtue in his *own* conduct regarding the kingdom he was born to set right. The march-time of the soldiery, now passing into the distance, is heard, transfigured, in the movement of his superb soliloquy (31 ff.):

> How all occasions do inform against me,
> And spur my dull revenge! . . .

There he utters the word "revenge" for the very last time. The idea of vengeance, to be sure, will be with him to the end. But he now feels acutely, what Shakespeare has made us see from the beginning, that sheer revengefulness as the main in-centive of regicide, in the case of such a nature as his, must be ineffectual. At the first we saw him delay "my revenge" as soon as he learned that the criminal, however "foul, strange, and unnatural" his crime, was king of Denmark, and though the Ghost adjured him not to be "duller . . . than the fat weed . . ." (I. v. 25-40). Now, he appropriates that very word dull. He confesses that his revenge is, not merely "tardy" (III. iv. 106), but "dull" as a jaded horse unresponsive to the "spur" (33). And with clearer self-knowledge he real-

[5] Compare Sir Huddibras (hue of brass) in *The Faerie Queene* II. ii. 17.

izes that in this matter he has been guilty both of wrong thought and of thoughtlessness.

His thoughtlessness he will call nothing less than "Bestial oblivion" (40). And this heavily self-accusing term has in it a certain rightness despite the fact that Hamlet is the last man of whom we would say (34 ff.) that the "chief good and market of his time" is "but to sleep and feed":

> Sure, he that made us with such large discourse
> Looking before and after, gave us not
> That capability and godlike reason
> To fust in us unused. . . .

He has always known this; and in many matters he has shown himself "noble in reason . . . in apprehension how like a god" (II. ii. 317-320). But in the particular matter of revenge, all the more strikingly because of his inclusive "capability" as thinker, he has been almost void of thought. He has had several outbreaks of revengeful passion, primitive emotion closely akin to animal unreflectiveness: revenge has been in his feelings, not in his "philosophy" (I. v. 167). On the rare occasions when he *has* tried to think upon it, he has thought poorly: his thoughtlessness gave place to wrong thinking. The ideal revenge that he thought-up in the Prayer scene was as crude as his general thinking is fine. Much better was his thought at the close of the Closet scene. There—freed from the gross and for him incongruous notion of taking Claudius "drunk asleep, or in his rage, Or in the incestuous pleasure of his bed, At gaming, swearing," or some similar act (III. iii. 89 ff.)—he foresaw the imminent possibility of catching the king plotting against him, thus making "sweet" (III. iv. 209) the bitter task of regicide. But this idea, too, was obscurantist; for Claudius, if deserving of death, had deserved it on prior and larger grounds.

So that Hamlet, as he is now sharply aware, has never really meditated the actual, particular nature of his prime task. That fact is glaringly apparent to us after watching the noble and religious meditation that he brought to bear upon another duty, that of converting his mother. Immediately before (III. iii.

73 ff.) and immediately after (III. iv. 202 ff.) his great performance of that duty we were shown, in vivid contrast, his thoughts upon his other, uncongenial task, that of killing Claudius. In both cases his "godlike reason" was unused; in each case he took refuge in a "craven scruple Of thinking too precisely," i.e., with spiritually timid, evasive scrupulosity, "on the event" (41).

That word "event" is a euphemism for the necessary regicide. Even here he evades naming the thing; just as he has refrained, and will refrain to the end, from uttering the name of the murdered Polonius when the context calls for it. His terrible error regarding Polonius has increased, as we have seen, his hesitation in killing the king. But he does not face that fact here; nor does he face the deeper reasons for his hesitation, the "heart" of his "mystery." He does, however, confess the weight of that mystery with a new simple frankness. Formerly he declared, regarding the essential cause of his melancholy, "I know not" (II. ii. 307). And now he has reached the point of making the same admission regarding, specifically, "the event":

> Now, whether it be
> Bestial oblivion, or some craven scruple
> Of thinking too precisely on the event,
> A thought which quartered hath but one part wisdom
> And ever three parts coward, I do not know
> Why yet I live to say this thing's to do,
> Sith I have cause, and will, and strength, and means
> To do it.

"I do not know. . . ." Here we of the audience are given in a high degree the dramatic satisfaction of knowing, or feeling that we know, the hero's mystery better than he himself does. And now, immediately after the passage quoted above, the speech shifts from thought to emotion, but without the violent shift of tone and rhythm that occurred several times in the course of the "peasant slave" soliloquy (II. ii. 575 ff.). For the present speech, like the "dram of eale" monologue (I. iv. 13 ff.) and like the lines to Horatio before the Play (III. ii.

61 ff.), has in it a pervasive, governing spirit of temperance. A single tune marches on while the speaker passes from impassioned thought to thoughtful passion, and from self-scrutiny to outward facts (46 ff.).

Having done the best he can at present in self-scrutiny, Hamlet, like every normal person, looks again outward. Dropping the inward problem of revenge, he turns to something palpable, the question of "honour." In this sphere, like every gentleman of his time, he can find "Examples gross as earth" (46), gross as the "solidity and compound mass" that he invoked as witness of his mother's shame (III. iv. 49). Wisely he began the conversion of her by appealing to obvious honor; now he appeals to it, less wisely but effectively, to point the conversion of himself. Above, the excursion of Fortinbras was for Hamlet, from the standpoint of practical statesmanship, a symptom of a mortal disease in society (27-29); now it becomes, from the ideal standpoint of "honour," an instance of "divine ambition" in a "delicate and tender" (48), i.e., ingenious and finely nurtured, "prince." Fortinbras's "spirit" (49), not his actual conduct, is lauded by this fellow-prince[6]—the spirit that

> Makes mouths at the invisible event,
> Exposing what is mortal and unsure
> To all that fortune, death, and danger dare,
> Even for an egg-shell. Rightly to be great
> Is, not to stir without great argument,
> But greatly to find quarrel in a straw
> When honour's at the stake. . . .

Greatness of "spirit" is evidenced by refusing to "stir,"[7] i.e., to resort to violence, "without great argument," a great motive; but such a motive may be found, sincerely if irrationally, in a "straw" (55, 26) *if* one's "spirit" believes "greatly" that "honour" so demands. "How stand I, then . . . ?" (56). Hamlet's cause, so far from being a "straw" or "egg-shell" like that of Fortinbras, is in itself, not merely in the motive it affords, un-

---

[6] Compare Hector's praise of the chivalrous *spirit* of Troilus, succeeding his statesmanlike condemnation of that young warrior's irrational and costly *conduct*, in *Troilus and Cressida* II. ii. 188 ff.

[7] The word "stir," like "dull" above (33), echoes the Ghost's initial admonition to Hamlet (I. v. 32-34).

questionably great. It appeals to his "reason" (58, 38) equally
with his "blood." And so, to his "shame" (59) he sees the
"imminent death" of thousands of men for a mere "fantasy and
trick of fame" while he himself, in a truly great cause, hesitates
to slay—such is the unspoken conclusion—merely one man.[8]

That unspoken conclusion evades, as Hamlet consistently
does, the fact that for him a king of Denmark, no matter how
wicked, is not to be ended so easily as an ordinary person. "Oh,
from this time forth," he concludes abruptly, "My thoughts
be bloody, or be nothing worth." These words are spoken
with painful but firm and simple resolution. The prince has
now left far behind him his violent, wordy outbreak against
the "bloody . . . villain" (II. ii. 607-610) and his artificial
thirst for "hot blood" (III. ii. 408); nor, on the other hand,
will he again soothe his conscience with "some craven scruple
Of thinking too precisely." He has finished with thoughtless
bloodiness and with bloodless thoughts: his very "thoughts,"
if pertinent and effectual, must be "bloody." He will concentrate his mind on the plain doing of his hateful job, the shed-
ding of royal blood, in whatever form that job may assume—
"the event" (41), "the invisible event" (50).

No longer is he confusedly "prompted to my revenge by
heaven and hell" (II. ii. 613). These two regions, these two
states of mind, have become for him distinct. The "black as
hell" revenge (III. iii. 94) which he once planned for Claudius
led directly to his hellish killing of Polonius. In that sequence
of cause and effect he perceived the hand of "heaven" (III. iv.
173). And he will perceive it increasingly (as will be shown
below) during the rest of his career. We may see it already in
his growing union of temperance and humility. His self-
humiliation in the "peasant slave" soliloquy was violent and
morbid; his ensuing confession to Ophelia of his sins (III. i.
119 ff.) was, though truthful, emotionally extreme and there-

---

[8] Hamlet is trying to minimize his coming regicide, the killing of Claudius,
by picturing a vast heap of the corpses of *ordinary* men; for this reason the
previous "Two thousand souls" (25) becomes eventually, in his fancy, "twenty
thousand" (60). Behind those unhidden slain, heaped upon their little piece
of ground (62), the prince tries to hide from himself the obnoxious deed of
the destruction of the king of Denmark.

fore not effectual. In the Play scene he achieved extraordinary temperance in *action;* but at the close of that scene his pride at catching the king's conscience, together with his bitterness at missing his mother's, betrayed him to confused passions and false moves. His repentance for the killing of Polonius brought him a firmer humility. *And in the present soliloquy he is temperately humble and humbly temperate.* He does not spur his "dull revenge" with dubious heavenly and hellish promptings. His blood and judgment are well commingled in the dedication of his sword—firmly grasped, I think, as the soliloquy closes—to a princely "honour" which, as he says, is "rightly," though not supremely, "great." His state of mind is far from supreme justice; but he has progressed remarkably in practical justness.

(b) *be patient*   IV. v—IV. vii

IV. v

However, Hamlet's conversion has been achieved at dreadful cost. Ophelia's madness is closely related, actually and symbolically, to the diseased confusion now rising in his nation. The "unweeded garden" is coming "to seed" (I. ii. 135 f.). The "Something . . . rotten in the state of Denmark," which the prince should have excided, is having its natural "issue" under the rule of the unseen powers: "Heaven will direct it," said Horatio prophetically (I. iv. 89-91). He, significantly, is now companion and adviser to the queen in her son's absence. She enters the scene in still greater perturbation than when we last saw her, refusing, despite her native kindheartedness, to speak with the "importunate," utterly "distract" girl outside, whom no one, as Horatio urges, can help pitying (2 f.). He himself is exceptionally disturbed beneath his calm surface. But, unable to help Ophelia personally, he represses his emotion of pity and tries to ward off a danger to Hamlet's kingdom. He urges the point that the people, by reason of Ophelia's wild conduct, are getting into that worst of all moods, brooding uncertainty. This, as the queen of the realm knows and admits, may produce "Dangerous conjectures in ill-breeding minds"

(15). She rouses herself therefore to speak with and control the distracted girl. But, alone for a moment, she reveals to us her deepest trouble. Convicted of guilt in the Closet scene, she is still far from having made her peace with heaven. Therefore she is weak within and full of dark forebodings; every trifling mishap, let alone disasters such as Ophelia's madness, wears an accusing and ominous air:

> To my sick soul, as sin's true nature is,
> Each toy seems prologue to some great amiss,[9]
> So full of artless jealousy is guilt,
> It spills itself in fearing to be spilt.

This aphoristic passage serves as "prologue" to the remainder of the scene and, indeed, of the drama: Denmark, like its queen, has a "sick soul" premonitory of retribution.

"Where is the beauteous majesty of Denmark?" (21). That yearning line of wild, piercing beauty does indeed "move The hearers to collection" (9). So do the girl's ensuing ejaculations and songs. She extends and answers Gertrude's question "How now, Ophelia?" by chanting

> How should I your true love know from another one?
> By his cockle hat and staff, and his sandal shoon.

She knows, as ever, that Hamlet loves her, though he is now far off like a pilgrim. But when pressed for the import of "this song" (27) her note drops to elegy: "He is dead and gone, Lady, he is dead and gone. . . ." Hamlet's absence, and his mortal danger which we know and which her soul divines, are running in her mind along with her father's obscure death and burial. In her next stanza the "true-love" tears (39), sequel of the previous phrase "true love" (23), are shed for both her father and her lover. When Claudius, now entering, attributes her state of mind entirely to grief for "her father" (45) she pointedly adverts to her lover in a rollicking ballad of "Saint Valentine's day." It is a fantastic echo of Hamlet's

---

[9] I have retained the comma after "amiss" in Q2 and F1, instead of replacing it with a colon or semicolon, because the ensuing line may have had for Shakespeare a floating denotation, referring to what precedes as well as to what follows.

outburst against marriage in the Nunnery scene and of the gross
jocosity with which he tried to stifle his love for her while
reclining close to her at the Play. He madly parodied their
love then; she does so now, but with extreme poignancy, singing
a light song of love and desertion with an excruciating mien of
loneliness. The floodtide of events that has swept him away
from the thought of their love has left her alone with it, and
with death.

But she concludes, "I hope all will be well, we must be
patient . . ." (68). She knows that wrong has been done and
that suffering must follow; but she wishes to alleviate, not increase, all the sin and misery. The impact of grief and dread
has unsettled her mind, but not her character. She has put
away self-pity and resentment. Religious patience is hers, more
than ever, with increase of "Saint Charity" (59).[10] Her madness is "sweet bells jangled out of tune," but not "harsh" (III.
i. 166). Grace, wild yet heavenly, was in her initial greeting
to the queen; and it is in her closing, lingering "good night,
good night."[11]

The patience of Claudius, the very antithesis of Ophelia's,
is also reaching its acme. As artful as hers is artless, it has a
fascinating evil beauty. With his conscience smothered under,
and with Hamlet proceeding to a seemingly certain death, the
king is alert to save his "joys" (IV. iii. 70) by bending to his
own advantage every new event; first, Ophelia's madness.

Gertrude is weeping for it: she, now aloof to her husband
in private, is overwhelmed, he sees, by remorse for the past.
Gradually and patiently he focuses her mind upon the present,
the present danger threatening himself and her as sovereigns.
This danger is due to nothing in the past, he insinuates, except
Hamlet's "violent" deed (80). Ophelia's malady, so far from
having anything to do with her hapless love for the prince, is

[10] Compare the sequence of patience and charity in the case of King Lear,
II. iv. 274, III. ii. 37, 72 f., III. iv. 26 ff. Patience prepares for Charity in
The Faerie Queene, Book I, canto x.

[11] We recall Hamlet's different, yet not wholly different, "good night" in
the close of the Closet scene. And Ophelia's "good night, sweet ladies," ignoring the king's presence, has a thematic relation to the prince's "Farewell,
dear mother" when parting from and slurring the king (IV. iii. 51). This
play is a great word-symphony with intricate and cumulative counterpoint.

entirely owing, so Claudius insists from the first, to grief for "her father" (45): "her father slain" (79) . . . "good Polonius' death" (83) . . . Laertes' "father's death" (91). By dwelling upon Hamlet's crime, without so terming it, Claudius seeks to prepare the queen, indirectly, for the coming death of her son in sequence to his "just remove" (81); directly, for the rising trouble in the kingdom, which, he concedes with fine art, he himself fomented "greenly" (83) by interring Polonius secretly in an affectionate endeavor to shield the prince (IV. i. 30-32). Thus Hamlet's deed, according to the king, is the source of all that has brought the regime to a desperate pass: "the people muddied, Thick and unwholesome in their thoughts and whispers," (81) and "poor Ophelia," as symbol of the present condition of the realm,

> Divided from herself and her fair judgment,
> Without the which we are pictures, or mere beasts. . . .

and finally Laertes, maddened too in his way by "his father's death," ready to arraign "our persons" (93). The plural here insists that the queen shares the king's danger. But underlying the whole adroit, feelingful speech is Claudius's concern for himself. It leaps to the forefront when he exclaims at the close that the situation is charged abundantly with "death" for "me" —"Like to a murdering-piece" (95 f.).

That image reminds us sharply that he himself is a murderer,[12] and that his present desperate plight goes back mainly, not to Hamlet's deed, but to his own deed of regicide. Immediately "*A noise within*" is heard, confused and tumultuous. Claudius demands the protection of his bodyguard, "Switzers" or mercenaries, in suggestive contrast with the initial guard, "liegemen to the Dane" (I. i. 15). Our rising sense of diseased disorder in the state overflows with the Messenger's rushing words:

> The ocean, overpeering of his list,
> Eats not the flats with more impiteous haste[13]

[12] A "murdering-piece," a small cannon or mortar loaded with many projectiles, was often called a "murderer."

[13] I have used "impiteous" for the "impitious" of Q2 and "impittious" of F1, usually regarded as misprints of impetuous. It denotes the pitiless, re-

> Than young Laertes, in a riotous head,
> O'erbears your officers: the rabble call him Lord,
> And as the world were now but to begin,
> Antiquity forgot, custom not known,
> The ratifiers and props of every word,
> They cry, "Choose we! Laertes shall be king"—
> Caps, hands, and tongues applaud it to the clouds—
> "Laertes shall be king, Laertes king!"

That soft name "Laertes," iterated by Claudius so caressingly when he was new on the throne (I. ii. 42 ff.), seems likely now to push him from the throne. He attained it by violating "Antiquity" and "custom"—the "ratifiers and props" of every "word" by which society lives, particularly the word "king"— far more evilly than the people know. But they know he is a usurper. And therefore they are ready to blame him entirely, as he has shown himself well aware, for the chief councilor's obscure death. Thus an "even-handed justice" (*Macbeth* I. vii. 10) is confronting the subtle courtly usurper with a blatantly popular counterpart, a potential usurper in the person of the dead councilor's son.[14]

"Laertes shall be king." That cry, following upon Claudius's winning speech to her, rouses the soft queen to extraordinary resolution:

> How cheerfully on the false trail they cry!
> Oh, this is counter, you false Danish dogs.

Her own son is the true successor to the throne; and her husband, no matter how guilty, is still, so he has persuaded her, the prince's sponsor. When Laertes enters with drawn sword demanding, "O thou vild[15] king, give me my father," she clasps him and tries to calm him. But Claudius, knowing his man, encourages him to work off his wrath in words (129) while staying him from violent deeds by making him feel the

---

lentless retribution of which Laertes and his followers are here the instruments. The idea of impetuosity, also present, is sufficiently conveyed in the context.

[14] Criticism has urged the contrast of Hamlet and Laertes at this juncture instead of that which is urged by the dramatist, the ironic contrast between Laertes and Claudius.

[15] Q2 has "vile." The *d* of "vild," clashing upon the first consonant of "king," lends the line additional force.

hellish wickedness of "rebellion" (121) and "treason" against
the Lord's anointed:

> There's such Divinity doth hedge a king,
> That Treason can but peep to what it would,
> Acts little of his will.

The patience of this "vild king," the opposite of Ophelia's
supernal patience, is now so consummate that without the slightest visible tremor he can warn the young man eloquently against
the very sin which he himself hiddenly, and so horribly, committed at the first.   Laertes is deeply struck; for a moment,
between awe and anger, he cannot speak (127).   Then, with
a sudden sense that he is being "juggled with" (130), he bursts
forth:

> To hell, allegiance! vows, to the blackest devil!
> Conscience and grace, to the profoundest pit!
> I dare damnation: to this point I stand
> That both the worlds I give to negligence,
> Let come what comes, only I'll be revenged
> Most throughly for my father.

Those lines are, for us, an extreme parody of the revengefulness of Hamlet at its very worst (III. iii. 88 ff.).   The prince
never consigned "Conscience and grace" to hell.   The anti-hero,
Laertes, has taken his stand at a "point" lower than the lowest
which the hero reached and which he has now left far behind.[16]
Instantly Claudius begins (136) to cherish the young man's
evil passion, turning it to his own purposes.   Drawing Laertes
aside he offers to inform him of his father's real "enemies,"
encouraging him to be a dutiful son and a "true gentleman"
(148), who in the service of revenge will employ—in accordance with low genteel convention—his "judgment" (151) as
well as rage.

Into that guilty atmosphere comes Ophelia with her innocent flowers, and with mood more peaceful than before.   Her

---

[16] Perhaps some of the Elizabethan "groundlings" (III. ii. 12), like many
modern critics, felt that Laertes was here exhibiting, in contrast to Hamlet,
a vital vigor.   But most of the contemporary audience would respond to
Shakespeare's intention of making Laertes, in contrast to Hamlet, guilty of
an utterly nihilistic impiety, political and religious.

heart is sane. But insane, really, is the turmoil of hellish revengefulness mixed with grieving love that now overcomes her
brother; searing "heat" firing sevenfold bitter "tears" (154).
Grossly he vows a revenge that shall pay for her madness "by
weight"—then, on the contrary, feels the immeasurably "pre-
cious" (162) beauty of her love and kindness. He *feels* it,
because of his sincere affection for her, but does not really *see*
it; such insight is beyond his vulgar and sentimental nature.
At the first he failed lightly (I. iii), now he fails tragically, to
understand how "fine in love" (161) her nature is. He can
actually image her, her the unrevengeful, as tacitly urging
"revenge" (168). Here he speaks with mad fixation. She,
however, tries to share with him her peace. After slowly approaching him she suddenly (175) gives him recognizing, lingering words of love together with speaking flowers: "There's
rosemary, that's for remembrance. Pray, love, remember; and
there's pansies, that's for thoughts," thoughts of love instead
of thoughts of revenge.[17] Rapidly she hands Claudius the
opposite emblems, fennel and columbine for flattery and in-
gratitude.[18] Her significant looks, too, caution her brother to
beware of this king.

Discerning the queen's "sick soul" (17) Ophelia shares with
her the "rue" (181) of sorrow. This flower can mean for Gertrude not merely grief but also grace and repentance if worn
with the right "difference" (183); but she lacks constancy and
so a single monitory "daisy," emblemizing faithlessness, goes
to her, in lieu of faithful violets: "I would give you some violets, but they withered all when my father died." Such is his
daughter's right and poignant epitaph for Polonius; the old
councilor, whatever else may be said of him, was faithful according to his lights unto the "end" (186). So will his daugh-

[17] The pansy, emblemizing thought, meant also love and courtship. Here
as in I. iii Ophelia's love for her brother blends in her pure spirit with her
love for Hamlet.

[18] This is the sequel of her words to the king above (41 ff.). There she
intimated that he had refused to entertain divine grace, recalling to him the
story of the "baker's daughter" transformed into an "owl" for refusing bread
to Christ. But she concluded: "Lord, we know what we are, but not what
we may be. God be at your table." Now, feeling that God is definitively
excluded from that table, i.e., from the fellowship of Claudius, she is warning
her brother, strongly, against that fellowship.

ter be to her lover: "For bonny sweet Robin is all my joy"—
She breaks off, inhibited from singing, in the presence of the
king and Laertes, a sequel to the "true love" stanza (23-26)
which she sang in allusion to Hamlet when alone with his
mother and his friend Horatio.[19]   But here, as there, the
thought of her absent lover merges into that of her dead father:

> And will he not come again,
> And will he not come again?
> No, no, he is dead, go to thy death-bed,
> He never will come again.

Her last words (199 f.) before actually going to her death are
a prayer—and we recall her devotions on behalf of Hamlet
(III. i. 89, 138, 147)—that God will have mercy on the soul
of her father, "And of *all* Christian souls, I pray God.   God be
wi' ye."[20]

Different is her brother's ensuing appeal to "you gods"
(201).   It is as bitter as his preceding speech (188) was prettily
sentimental:

> Thought and affliction, passion, hell itself,
> She turns to favour and to prettiness.

"Prettiness!"   He is obtuse to that "Conscience and grace" in
her which he discarded a few minutes ago for *himself* (132).
He unwittingly echoes the "pretty" (40, 56) applied to her by
Claudius.[21]   The "hell" in Laertes (131, 188) has been flow-
ered over, not in the least cured, by his emotion for Ophelia.
And now, much more than beforehand, he is malleable, as the
watchful Claudius perceives.   Quick to "commune" with his
"grief" (202) the king flatters him with equality: Laertes shall
have the "crown" if the king is in the least guilty regarding
Polonius; otherwise the king will "jointly labor" to satisfy

---

[19] In the previous song her lover was a pilgrim; now, significantly, he
seems to be an outlawed wanderer.   Her line is apparently taken from a lost
ballad of Robin Hood.

[20] This simple "good-bye" with its depth of Christian peace is intended to
contrast with her previous, courtly, elaborate "Good night" (73); which,
however, had a sweetness of patience preparatory for the present peace.

[21] My point is not affected by the fact that the word "pretty" had often
a finer sense in Shakespeare's time than in ours.   For he, unlike Laertes and
Claudius, thinks of "Charity" (59) and Christian "grace" (182) in connection with Ophelia, and he does not let the queen or Horatio call her "pretty."

Laertes' soul if only—this important point is nicely implanted—
he will "lend" the king his "patience" (210). Laertes does so;
and he will do so far more fully in the sequel. Claudius's
spirit, not Ophelia's, determines the quality of her brother's
"patience" in the concourse of dark events ahead.

IV. vi

The patient Horatio, on the contrary, is now to be, more
than ever before, the confidant of Hamlet.[22] His patience is
analogous to Ophelia's, as we were made to feel in the preceding
scene when he stood watching her with silent sympathy. His
silences in the course of the drama are, like hers, intensely
expressive: both of them show in their quiet looks and gestures
deep emotion under control. Both, along with their selflessness,
have firmness of character. Ophelia's brain has given way for
the time being under terrific blows of fate; but not her very
self. Her madness, as Shakespeare depicts it, is due, not to any
native weakness, but to strong repressed love and sorrow finding relief in mental aberration, which, however, is overtopped
by her Christian charity. She too is "As one, in suffering all,
that suffers nothing" (III. ii. 71). Horatio with less to suffer
has a patience less sublime than hers but essentially the same.
It is not mere passivity. Outward inactivity has been forced by
fate and by Hamlet's proud aloofness upon his friend and upon
his loved one. But these two are inwardly capable of beneficent
action because their patience has the religious and moral quality
of the truest gentility. And it centers in an utter, unswerving
devotion to Hamlet as man and as crown prince.

Hamlet's failure to make due use of that devotion has had
tragic consequences which are now being fully displayed. His
pride of mission withdrew him from his friend and from his
loved one after his initial encounter with the Ghost. His great
plan for catching the conscience of the king was instrumental in
completing his breach with Ophelia. At the Play he employed
Horatio in a minimum degree and then dismissed him. Thus

[22] The modern location of scene vi in *"Horatio's lodging"* or *"Another
room in the castle"* violates Shakespeare's design. On the same spot, in the
same decadent court, where Laertes is drawn into the king's service Horatio
is drawn fully into the service of the prince.

Hamlet came to the central crisis of his life divided from the two persons, the only persons, close to him in spirit. They were designed by "heaven" to companion him in his utmost need, one on either side of him, Ophelia with her Christian humility and love, Horatio with his philosophic temperance and plain honesty.[23] They would have helped him to face with charitable justness, and with a mind fixed upon the "good" (I. i. 130; I. ii. 158) of "the fair state" (III. i. 160), his hard task of punishing and supplanting the guilty king of Denmark. Instead, he confronted that task alone, alone with his pride and confused passions, which, morbidly active as a result of the Play scene, blinded him to the essential nature of his duty and to the nature of his inward obstacles. The mad mood of vengefulness which brought about his killing of Polonius, with all its dire consequences, could master his soul only in isolation from Ophelia and Horatio—from divine grace and humane self-control.

But in the present scene, with soul converted after his killing of Polonius, and now with his life preserved as by a miracle from the machinations of Claudius, Hamlet evinces in his letter to Horatio a new intimacy of spirit with this friend. Horatio has plenty of emotion but refuses to emotionalize. So it was when he listened to Hamlet's great praise of him (III. ii. 61 ff.); and when he saw the king terrifically convicted by the Play, he declared laconically, "I did very well note him" (III. ii. 301). And that sentence, his last before a long silence, is our cue to his subsequent bearing. He "did very well note," with deeply grieving concern, the ensuing mad procedure of his beloved prince and, in the upshot, the madness of Ophelia. His sole speech regarding her, as remarked above, was characteristically percipient, objective, and practical. And now the Servant's surprising news that there are "letters" for him (2) causes him to remark merely:

> I do not know from what part of the world
> I should be greeted, if not from Lord Hamlet.

[23] A prominent theme in political treatises (e.g., Erasmus's *Education of a Christian Prince*) from ancient times down to the seventeenth century was the prince's need of the right kind of friends and advisers before, as well as after, he became head of the state. This subject was continually in the mind of Shakespeare and his audience.

These lines are a quiet dramatic sequel of the utter loneliness of Ophelia in the preceding scene. Horatio, too, is solitary in the "world," apart from his relation to Hamlet. He reads the prince's amazing letter aloud, without comment, in a tone of ever intensifying but subjugated emotion.

The pirate ship "of very warlike appointment" (16) recalls the adventurous marching army of Fortinbras which, while a deadly symptom of too much "wealth and peace" (IV. iv. 27), chimed with Hamlet's fresh resolve for militant honor. The great "valour" with which he boarded the attacking vessel "alone" is veiled by his soldierly, humorous understatement (18-20). Intriguingly nonchalant is the first two-thirds of the missive. Then comes this: "Let the king have the letters I have sent, and repair thou to me with as much haste as thou wouldst fly death. I have words to speak in thine ear which will make thee dumb. . . ." The words "king" and "death" symphonize darkly. And the note of intimate appeal to Horatio running through the whole letter rings full in the warm subscription: "He that thou knowest thine, Hamlet." That he knew Horatio to be *his*, the prince had declared earlier (III. ii. 68-70). His present declaration is the sequel and complement of that statement, after a tragic interval. Hamlet, sorely tried and humbled, will now take his friend completely, for the first time, into confidence and counsel (as will appear in Act V). Horatio, who was always Hamlet's, knows from the letter that Hamlet is now his. He lifts the letter (I think) to his lips, silently, devotedly, and proceeds to obey with utmost speed.

IV. vii

Meanwhile the king and Laertes, like the prince and Horatio, have entered into a new and close association. Claudius has become the intimate "friend" of Laertes and director of his "conscience" (1 f.). We hear no more of the "wisest friends" (IV. v. 204) who, if consulted, could conceivably have put the young man on his guard. Claudius has obviated that possibility by flattering Laertes' "knowing ear," particularly with the significant, confidential information that "he which hath your noble father slain Pursued my life" (3 f.). This

fact, perceived and blurted out by Claudius to Gertrude immediately after the event (IV. i. 13), has since been carefully
submerged by him because it raises the very embarrassing question of Hamlet's motives. This question is surely close to
Laertes' tongue when he now inquires why the king has not
"proceeded," i.e., openly and directly, "against these feats, So
crimeful and so capital" (6 f.), murder of the chief councilor
and attempted regicide. Claudius evades the main point, as to
Hamlet's incentives, with a speech that poetically elaborates
undeniable facts: the queen's devotion to her son, the king's to
her, and the "great love" of the people for the crown prince—
an emotional congeries designed to captivate the sentimental
Laertes. He, however, still evinces dissatisfaction. He broods
on his injuries; as above (IV. v. 156) he weighs them quanti-
tatively: the loss of a "noble father" and the madness of a
"sister"

> Whose worth, if praises may go back again,
> Stood challenger on mount of all the age
> For her perfection. But my revenge will come.

That encomium on Ophelia, though true in fact, is strikingly
cheap in word and tone. Cheap in quality is Laertes' passion
of "revenge," which he now resumes.

Immediately Claudius tunes in on the word "revenge,"
simulating what he does not feel but wishes to foster in Laertes,
the blatant sense of honor that belongs to conventional gallantry
(30 ff.). He repudiates the unspoken opinion which the impetuous youngster has every reason to hold in regard to his
smooth sovereign: "That we are made of stuff so flat and dull
That we can let our beard be shook. . . ." He hints at the
coming death of Hamlet in England. "I loved your father,
and we love our self"—as Laertes loved his father and is now
more and more loving his own conceited self under the king's
tutelage; "And that I hope will teach you to imagine"—

Here the inbreaking "news" (36) from Hamlet, brought
by a messenger, teaches the king, Laertes, and above all us to
"imagine" very much. The prince's curt missive to the king,
the antithesis in every respect of his letter to Horatio, is de-

signed, successfully, to throw Claudius into wondering fear
and confusion. The king is addressed with crying sarcasm as
"High and mighty," mocking, for us, the ruffling tone of his
interrupted speech above. The writer is "set naked on your kingdom," the kingdom properly belonging to the destitute prince,
who tomorrow, with abject apologies in the presence of those
"kingly eyes" which are so unkingly, will "recount the occasions[24] of my sudden and more strange return. . . ." The baffling
strangeness of this return is stressed in a postscript by the stabbing word "alone" (53). Claudius cannot see how his latest plot
could possibly have been discovered by Hamlet; and yet, the
prince's solitary, safe return—like his discovery of the murder in
the Play scene, apparently the work of offended "heaven" (III.
iii. 36)—wears a preternatural air. Is it "some abuse" (51),
some weird illusion?[25] Reason says it cannot have happened.
It cannot "be so" (58)—but, with the letter for evidence, cannot be "otherwise"! The guilty king is again "marvellous
distempered" (III. ii. 312), brooding upon the "occasions" of
Hamlet's mysterious, accusing "return" and upon the quick-
coming results of it.

To us the prince's full intention is evident. His laconic
letter tells us that he is now set for final action. Beforehand we
were convinced that he would take the king's life when he
caught him plotting against his own (III. iv. 205 ff.; IV. iv.
66). Proof of this plot he has now, in some manner, obtained,
as indicated by his letter to Horatio; and his mind and will
have completely risen to the occasion. So far from being passionate, embarrassed, and confused, as he was after the Play,
his two letters, capping the climax of that spiritual reconstruc-
tion begun in the Closet scene, show him at once very militant
and very temperate, in full control of himself and of the situation. A previous assertion uttered unconvincingly in words is
now uttered by his whole bent and bearing, "I know my course"

---

[24] Q2 has "occasion" instead of "occasions." The plural is necessary to
forestall an assumption on the part of Claudius that the only reason for
Hamlet's return is the sea-fight, of which the king will presently learn.

[25] Compare Macbeth's "strange and self-abuse" (III. iv. 142). His earlier
words, "function Is smothered in surmise, and nothing is But what is not"
(I. iii. 140), give an intensification of the present condition of Claudius.

(II. ii. 627). His coming course is plain. With Horatio's aid Hamlet will confront the king in public with the proof of his having planned the death of the heir to the throne, as secretly as he achieved the death of the heir's father. The Play scene's evidence of the *old* murder will be confirmed by the proof of the attempted *new* murder. That proof, withheld from us until we shall hear it confided by Hamlet to Horatio (V. ii. 1-26) in immediate preparation for its being made public, will be irrefragable and conclusive. The people, so ready to support the doubtful cause of Laertes (IV. v. 98-110), will certainly support their beloved prince (18-21, IV. iii. 4) against the usurping king who has tried to destroy him. And (as will be actually shown on the stage, V. ii. 333 ff., when the king's final plot against Hamlet is divulged) the court's opposition to Hamlet will be reduced to the minimum. The prince will execute Claudius and take the throne that belongs to him. It is thus that Hamlet plans to "recount" to the "High and mighty" the "occasions" of his "sudden and more strange return." Such is what Shakespeare induces us to "imagine" (35) by means of Hamlet's summary letter to the king, considered in its full context.[26]

The imagination of Laertes also is fired (54 ff.). Deeply dissatisfied with the distant and vicarious revenge promised him by the king, he is rapt by the news of Hamlet's coming:

> It warms the very sickness in my heart
> That I shall live and tell him to his teeth,
> "Thus didest thou."

In this case, we hope, explanations between the two young men will ensue and Laertes, very impressible and essentially good-hearted, will soon be won to make common cause with the crown prince. That probability is apparent to Claudius. He rouses

---

[26] Here, as ever, we must remember that the most *dramatic* possibility is likely to be the truest to Shakespeare's intention. Having begun the very dramatic plot of Claudius for employing Laertes, the author now proceeds to cross it with an action still more intensely dramatic because more deeply tragic. In terms of melodrama: the hero has fully determined to kill the villain just when the villain is finding a way of killing *him*. To fancy, as closet critics have done, that Hamlet's determination here is not veritable is to go counter to Shakespeare's plain design of constructing a catastrophe that shall have the maximum of theatric effect.

himself from his broodings with galvanic efforts (58 ff.) that reveal a quick, hard inner struggle with old and new remorse. A new crime, fatal for Hamlet's life and for Laertes' character, has already seeded itself in his mind; and the seed rapidly grows, as he regains his evil self-control, into "an exploit now ripe in my device" (65). If successful it will obviate two open challenges, Laertes' to Hamlet and Hamlet's to Claudius: the prince will not confront the king with those words uttered by Laertes which the king dreads to hear again, "Thus didest thou." But how can Laertes be persuaded to be content with a demise of Hamlet that shall appear mere "accident" (69)? With patient, utmost skill Claudius works upon his young friend's imagination, gradually blotting from it the idea of an open, honest combat by substituting the picture of a darkly fascinating and advantageous intrigue.

At the outset Laertes unwarily consents to be "ruled" even while averring hotly that[27] the king shall not "o'errule" him "to a peace" (60 f.). Claudius rejoins firmly and significantly, "To thine own peace"; then pauses a moment to let the words sink in. His appeal, veiled and effectual, is to the flattered youngster's inclination to proceed in harmony with his sovereign's interests and, accordingly, with his own. Laertes' worldly fortunes, dependent upon those of Claudius from the first (I. ii. 42 ff.), are now by means of the king's art becoming inextricably intertwined with them. And those joint fortunes would be fatally crossed by Laertes' *open* killing of the prince, sole heir to the throne, beloved by the people (16-24) and by the "queen his mother" (11, 68). That event would close the career of the young courtier. It would bring execration upon him, also upon his friend the king. Claudius, whose status, dubious from the start, has of late suffered heavily, would not be able or willing to continue sponsoring Laertes: such is the fine implication of his present speech and its context. The worldly interests of both men require that for Hamlet's death

[27] The hot tone of this line is carried over from Laertes' preceding speech. This great temptation scene is the forerunner of still greater ones, *Othello* III. iii and *Macbeth* I. vii, where the tempted person—there the hero instead of the anti-hero of the play—seems at first, like Laertes, entirely averse to the sort of crime that he will eventually undertake.

"no wind of blame shall breathe . . ." (67); the predicate is artfully left incomplete. It is obvious that "so loud a wind" (22) of blame as would be excited by open action would frustrate not only the purposes of Claudius, as he declared above, but also the career of Laertes. The young man is thus faced with a sharp dilemma. His *inward* "peace," in conflict with his outward fortune, calls for an open and honest quarrel with the prince. But after a moment of painful hesitation he consents to a fatal, and so far entirely undefined, "accident" (69) for Hamlet; thus he assures his own *external* peace, peace with Denmark, the queen, and the king. "My lord, I will be ruled," he says weakly, adding quickly, in a futile attempt to salve his honor, words that bring him still further into the king's toils, "The rather if you could devise it so That I might be the organ."

"It falls right," says Claudius in smooth, trap-like triumph. Then he begins to advance slowly towards the foul heart of his scheme, camouflaging the approach with elaborate and charming speeches. He flatters his young friend's "sum of parts" (74) while suggesting that his own "settled age" can contribute to their joint procedure a complementary "health and graveness" (82). Speciously full of health is his appreciation of youthful pursuits, warfare (84), riding, and fencing. We admire the "witchcraft of his wit" (I. v. 43) when he cleverly describes the "witchcraft" (86) of the horsemanship of Lamond, friend of Laertes, who deems him "the brooch indeed And gem" (94) of the French nation. This very Lamond gave a "masterly report" of Laertes' skill with the rapier. It did "envenom" (104) Hamlet with envy: that verb, we know, is exactly wrong for the prince's character but exactly right for what the king is now doing to Laertes. He inoculates this courtier with an intense ambition, apparently healthy but in the sequel poisonous, to outshine the prince of Denmark, as well as the leading "scrimers" of France (101), at the prime art of fencing. An open mortal duel with Hamlet, as Claudius has antecedently made evident, would result in public infamy for the successful Laertes; but a public conquest of the prince at a friendly "play" (106) of foils would be a great and fruitful honor.

Laertes, full of delighted excitement in that prospect, has for the moment forgotten his dark cause, revenge for his father's death.

Instantly, therefore, the tempter suggests to him that perhaps his grief for his father was unreal, insincere, "A face without a heart?" (110).

> Not that I think you did not love your father,
> But that I know love is begun by time
> And that I see, in passages of proof,
> Time qualifies the spark and fire of it:
> There lives within the very flame of love
> A kind of wick or snuff that will abate it. . . .

Nothing is more perturbing to generous youth than that line of thought. And Claudius utters it with the conviction of personal experience; he has seen the queen's love decay, first for her great former husband, recently for himself. When he proceeds to urge lengthily that we ought to act when heart and will are still warm and strong, without "abatements and delays" (121), Laertes' swift remorse mounts to passionate impatience. Certainly he will show his filial loyalty "in deed More than in words" (126). Strong words of revenge for his father he uttered when he first broke into the royal presence. Then he was ready to kill *the king*, despite "Conscience and grace" (IV. v. 132). Now, turning that impious passion, revived, against *the prince*, Laertes declares himself willing "To cut his throat i' the church."

"No place, indeed, should murder sanctuarize, Revenge should have no bounds," says Claudius. Thus culminates, with deadly irony, the hypocrisy of this king who had yearned, in his own sanctuary, to pray sincerely, "Forgive me my foul murder" (III. iii. 52). The "heaven" that he then feared and entreated he is now outraging. He goes on with spidery smoothness to weave together the two opposed strands of Laertes' mood: desperate revengefulness, and craving for public honor. The latter is drawn to the fore again by a broad hint of tremendous "fame" (133) for Laertes when he wins a royal "wager" (135) in a fencing-match with the prince. And in the very flush of that triumph the other passion, revenge, can be satiated without tarnish of "fame" and without infraction of worldly "peace" (62). A devilish "peace" governs the climactic words of Claudius (135 ff.). Hamlet, "being remiss,"

> Most generous, and free from all contriving,
> Will not peruse the foils; so that with ease,
> Or with a little shuffling, you may choose
> A sword unbated, and in a pass of practice
> Requite him for your father.

That initial praise of the prince is a bold, necessary, and effectual stroke. The implied point is that Hamlet deserves death in spite of his two enemies' "generous" recognition of his generous, free, and open nature; thoughts of which are bound to assail Laertes—as they did formerly under Ophelia's influence (I. iii. 14-16)—in the coming final scene. Then and there Hamlet, prevented from having speech with Laertes beforehand, will no doubt declare himself (as indeed he actually does, V. ii. 237 ff.) "free from all contriving" in regard to Polonius's death. Therein, nevertheless, he was fatally "remiss," heedless; and—this is the thought that the prescient tempter wishes to keep uppermost in Laertes' confused mind—will be so again, this time fatally for *himself,* in regard to the foils. *His seemingly accidental death will be a fair requital for his allegedly undesigned killing of "your father."* If it be true that "revenge should have no bounds," as Laertes' pious sovereign and sober mentor has declared, then surely the proposed stratagem is a very natural, as well as brilliant and profitable, way to "Requite" Hamlet. Thus the foul heart of the scheme, the project of the "sword unbated," is made to slide with ease into the tumid heart of Laertes.

"I will do't," he declares, breathing hard, then overwhelms the quick protest of his conscience with rushing evil imagination, "And for that purpose I'll anoint my sword. . . ."[28] He will

---

[28] This device, proposed by Claudius, evidently, in the old *Hamlet* play, was transferred by Shakespeare to Laertes. With the present speech compare Macbeth's lines immediately before his murder of Duncan (II. i. 49 ff.). There, too, conscience is muffled by melodramatic play of fancy upon the coming evil deed. In the present scene the Elizabethan audience would think of the Italianate practice of poisoning a person who stood in one's way. They

hide from his inner eye the dishonorable point of that sword
by dipping it in an "unction" marvelously "mortal" (142 f.)—
he will not term it plainly a foul, murderous poison—which
once in a fanciful moment he had bought from a mountebank.
He describes its magical power in elaborate terms. Finally,
"I'll touch my point With this contagion, that if I gall him
slightly, It may be death." Thus he muffles and conciliates
his conscience: he will not need to run that "point" through
Hamlet's heart as the king's plan required.

Claudius is deeply disturbed. He perceives that under the
new scheme Laertes may, at the crisis, shrink from hitting
Hamlet at all since the slightest wound will be fatal. So may
"our drift look through our bad performance" (152). In other
words, as he and we know, the two young men may come to
explanations that will unmask him. For a moment he harbors
the hope of persuading Laertes through "further" (149) conference to rescind his new notion; then, swiftly pondering, he
decides otherwise. He reappeals to Laertes' desire for fame
by reminding him of the coming "wager" (135), now termed
more elaborately "a solemn wager on your cunnings" (156),
and urges him to make the contest "violent" (159). There is
good hope, Claudius thinks within himself, that in the heat of
rivalry Laertes will thrust vehemently. But if not, the king
will have ready a "drink" for Hamlet. Since Laertes has proposed to employ a "venomed stuck"—Claudius, unlike Laertes,
gives it a brutally plain name—his conscience cannot well object
to the king's proposed "chalice": Claudius speaks as euphemis-
tically of his poisoned wine as Laertes had spoken of his poisoned sword. The king *alone*, so he intimates, will carry out
"*Our* purpose" (163) in case of the failure of his accomplice,
who will thus be deprived of the glory of vanquishing the
crown prince of Denmark at swordplay. In short, Claudius
with patient subtlety has given his young friend the strongest

---

would think also of that brutal assassination of one's enemies which, still common in England in the fifteenth century, had gradually yielded to the honorable
duello. Of perennial interest, however, is the point noted above: Laertes, like
Macbeth, overwhelming the protests of his conscience by means of concentrated, murderous imagination.

possible incentives to subdue his conscience and fulfil his announced determination of slaying the prince by sleight.

The final form of Claudius's plot against Hamlet—an envenomed sharp rapier in Laertes' hands seconded by an envenomed cup in his own—recalls a crucial line in the Play scene: "Thoughts black, hands apt, drugs fit, and time agreeing" (III. ii. 266). That verse at the center of *The Tragedy of Hamlet, Prince of Denmark* is now seen to be prophetic as well as retrospective. The next line, "Confederate season, else no creature seeing," points back to the "secure hour" (I. v. 61) of Claudius's first crime and stresses its complete concealment from all human eyes. Throughout this drama, as in its successors, *Othello, Lear, Macbeth*, and others, Shakespeare iterates and reiterates the fact that concealed, specious evil, not plain wickedness however great, is the chief cause of ruin for persons and for societies. Claudius's ability to make "foul" seem "fair" (*Macbeth* I. i. 9) attains its apogee in the present scene. But it appeared in his very first speech on the stage, addressed to the whole court. The first individual singled out by his politic smile was Laertes (I. ii. 42 ff.). From then on, as we now realize, every word uttered by or concerning this young gentleman was preparing him to become the dupe of Claudius in the end. Laertes, like his king, is essentially vulgar, devoted to cheap sorts of pleasure and success, of custom, kindness, and piety. And now the underlying egoism of his showy piety regarding his father and sister has betrayed him into partaking what would ordinarily repel him, murderous hypocrisy. Laertes is degenerately the son of his father. The good Polonius, who would never have assented to the assassination of the crown prince, let alone the secret poisoning of him, shared the king's dishonesty lightly: his son has learned to share it heavily.

In that way and in many other ways we are made to feel the decay of the "sanctity and health of the whole state" (I. iii. 21). The poisonous spirit of Claudius has permeated the "wholesome blood" (I. v. 70) of Denmark: it is now "Thick and unwholesome" (IV. v. 82). Hamlet, who alone discerned the deadly disease of "Seems" (I. ii. 76) in its very beginnings, has let it grow and spread because he himself became infected with it, owing, originally, to the absolute secrecy of the murder. The prince would have struck down openly and quickly an open killer of his father.   As it was, his high sense of justice, conflicting with and presently overtopping his hatred of Claudius, compelled him to seek indubitable proof of the hidden crime. Normally a man of quick action, "free from all contriving" (136), he was forced to delay and to contrive.   And his forced dissembling, while bringing to the fore an entirely subordinate though fascinating side of his nature, his histrionic ability, clogged his central instinct for direct, open, honest procedure. Tragically he allowed his outward dissembling to penetrate inward: he would not face honestly his aversion for regicide.   In the central scene (III. iii) he was as histrionic, spiritually, as his praying enemy.   From that central dissimulation the prince has now been freed by tragic agony and providence, but too late, probably, for the remedying of his country.   Unless heaven and his own converted wit prevent—such is the situation in the close of Act IV—he will be ended by the secret disease of Denmark, dire "contagion" (148), before he can expose it and institute justice.

Our premonitions for Denmark are deepened by the death of Ophelia, the sole member of the ruling caste of "the fair state" (III. i. 160) whose heart has stayed entirely untainted by the spreading dishonesty.   Far beyond the poisonous scene we have just been watching, her sorrowful purity gleams in a landscape of the spirit where grief inclines to peace—like this leaning tree:

> There is a willow grows aslant a brook,
> That shows his hoar leaves in the glassy stream.

The willow is for lonely, sorrowing love.   But she comes to *crown* it, with "garlands" (169) that her fancy has made of common flowers in the open fields.   Her love and pain are now wide-reaching and impersonal.   She has left behind the herbs of personal implication that she gave to her brother and her two sovereigns.[29]   And very far behind her now is the "violet in the youth of primy nature" that was once hers (I. iii.

---

[29] She still has "daisies" (170) but not "a daisy" (IV. v. 184), which she gave with pointed singleness to the queen.

7); but so also is the rank growth that smothered her hopes, the time's "unweeded garden" (I. ii. 135). *Her* weeds are different; she wears them with a difference: "her *coronet* weeds . . . her weedy *trophies*" (173-175). She, rather than the queen, who speaks her elegy, is queen. Gentle triumph is in her ending. Common things, touching her, are no longer ordinary. The "weeping brook" belongs forever to her whose weeping has ceased, has been transmuted into song:

> Her clothes spread wide,
> And mermaid-like, a while they bore her up,
> Which time she chanted snatches of old tunes,
> As one incapable of her own distress,
> Or like a creature native and indued
> Unto that element. . . .[30]

Her "melodious lay" (183) lingers above, in our spirit's hearing, when her body is "Pulled . . . to muddy death." The body belongs to "muddied" Denmark (IV. v. 81). The un-soiled soul, speaking through the lovely words and motions of this great passage of poetry, is released now into full peace.

Religious peace, crowning her religious patience. Peace far above Laertes, whom the king has overruled to his "own peace" (62). The sorrow of her brother here (184-192) as previously (IV. v. 154 ff.) is, unlike Ophelia's *common* things, her "weedy trophies," painfully *vulgar:* "Too much of water hast thou. . . . I have a speech of fire that fain would blaze. . . ." His tearful, revengeful "rage" (193), violating even more than in scene v his sister's spirit, has to be calmed, as the closing lines of the present scene intimate, by the evil patience of Claudius.

---

[30] Q1 has "there she sat smiling, Even mermaid-like, twixt heaven and earth"—as though enthroned cosmically. Q2 has "she chaunted snatches of old lauds," reflecting her Christianity. But "lauds" with its ecclesiastic flavor is too narrow for the present context. Incidentally that word is surpassed in tone and assonance by "tunes" (Q1, F1), which rhymes vocally with "indued" two lines below.

(c) *my sum*   V. i

V. i. 1-240

While the king and his two dupes, Gertrude and Laertes, retire, two grave-diggers enter who are determined not to be duped by anyone. The elder of them, the "sexton" (176), is, like Ophelia and unlike Laertes, close to common veracity. His first words raise in us an honest and relieving yet strange, choked laughter: "Is *she* to be buried in Christian burial that *wilfully* seeks her *own* salvation?" That is exactly what Ophelia did not do: hence her salvation. But the ever unnamed "she" of these clowns is not Ophelia but merely a corpse found in the muddy bed of a brook. "She" obviously went to the water; it did not "come to" her (20): clearly, therefore, "she" did not drown herself "in her own defence" (6). "She" is a suicide, excluded from the churchyard by Christian law, admitted, however, by reason of rank favoritism. The verdict of the coroner, the "crowner" (3-5, 24), was swayed by high society. The plain "truth," uttered by the Second Clown in a sudden outburst of righteous indignation, is "If this had not been a gentlewoman, she should have been buried *out of* Christian burial" (26-28). That is an indictment, quite Hamletian in nature, of Denmark's dishonesty. In "this world," whose hypocritic "uses" (I. ii. 134) and "corrupted currents" (III. iii. 57) have been displayed throughout, the sad fact is that "great folk . . . have countenance . . . to drown or hang themselves more than their even-Christian" (29-32). We, unlike the speaker, know how little of a *grande dame*, how much of an "even-Christian," i.e., fellow-Christian, was Ophelia. The two Clowns' lucubrations upon "her" are a wonderful, relieving parody of Ophelia's Christian gentility.

The First Clown has a proletarian snobbery of his own, a grand class consciousness. He believes that the only true "ancient gentlemen," lineal sons of Adam, are those who dig the earth (34). And the very greatest of all these is he who, builder as well as digger, "builds stronger" (46) than any other. The grave-maker builds "houses"—here this word com-

prises all the dwellings, noble and simple, of all the world;
and the "houses that *he* makes last till doomsday" (66).

That tremendous dictum rings out while Hamlet approaches
—on his way to doomsday. Such is our feeling, not his. From
first to last of the ensuing episode *his spirit* has not the least
touch of deathliness.[1] No graveyard emotion but merely
chance, providential and dramatic chance, has brought him to
this place. He has entered "*afar off*," attired as a traveler, in
earnest conversation with Horatio, discussing what has happened and what he has to do. His mood, as when we last saw
him (IV. iv) and more especially in his subsequent two letters
(IV. vi. 12 ff.; IV. vii. 42 ff.), is one of quiet firmness and of
readiness for climactic deeds. He is about to pass by. But he
draws near, suddenly fascinated, when the First Clown sings.
The fellow chants folk-verses[2] of youth and love, age and
death, as lately Ophelia did. Building a "house" for the unknown one, he digs and heaves, grunts and sings:

> In youth when I did love, did love,
>   methought it was very sweet. . . .

Hamlet's and Ophelia's young joy in love was "sweet, not last-
ing" (I. iii. 8). But if that recollection touches the prince now,
it is instantly banished as out of keeping with his present affairs
of state. So fully and gravely are his feelings dedicated to the
great business he has in hand that he is startled, for a moment,
by the Clown's opposite attitude: "Has this fellow no feeling
of *his* business that he sings at grave-making?" But he quickly
and humorously admits the naturalness of the effect of "Custom" (76 f.), his own old friend and enemy (III. iv. 161 ff.).
Thus Hamlet's opening lines give the keynote of his bearing
throughout the ensuing episode: his mood is objective and
realistic, sardonical while humorously sympathetic.

"That skull" (83), thrown up by the Clown as he digs

---

[1] The so-called "graveyard imagination" of the Romantics, by saturating
Hamlet in this scene with self-centered gloom, spoiled the chief dramatic
contrast: the opposition of the hero's light mood to the deathliness of his
environment.

[2] Shakespeare puts into the Clown's mouth, with suggestive alterations,
the most vivid stanzas of Thomas Vaux's racy elegy, "The Aged Lover Re-
nounceth Love."

deeper. . . . "It might be the pate of a politician, which this ass now o'er-offices; one that could circumvent God. . . ." That officious "pate," supposedly the high opposite of an ass's, is now jowled up and down by a high-officed ass. Or the skull might be that of a flattering "courtier" (90). We have watched in the course of this drama a smooth court surrounding a royal "politician" who has tried, and is still trying, to "circumvent God." Now we are made to feel that all are being drawn by the laws of Providence "toward an end'" (III. iv. 216), along with the prince himself.[3] In fact in this amazing scene, as a whole, Shakespeare sums up in weird semi-allegory the whole thematic pattern of *The Tragedy of Hamlet, Prince of Denmark.*

Hamlet broods satirically, but not bitterly as in earlier scenes, on courtiers and politicians. They are his fellow human beings, moving like himself from birth through life to death: "Did these bones cost no more the breeding but to play at loggats with 'em? Mine ache to think on't" (99). A painful mortal sympathy, won from dire experience! He can feel now in his very *bones,* as not previously (IV. iii. 20 ff.), how "common"—communal, one might say—is the mortal process of "Passing through nature to eternity" (I. ii. 72 f.).

But that gamesome phrase "play at loggats," capping all of the stranger's irreverent remarks, offends the important grave-digger. He himself can joke at his profession, but with a difference. It is no mere macabre game, has nothing in common with loggats. Therefore his final stanza, sung while he completes his digging—the "pick-axe" and "spade" cutting into bottom "clay" (104)—celebrates resoundingly the dignity of his labor. He is preparing a "meet" reception for one who is not yet turned to bones, let alone loggat-bones; a decent, solemn "shrouding-sheet" shall drape the coming "guest."[4] However,

---

[3] The jaw of the skull of Claudius, after a time, will be jowled about appropriately "as if it were Cain's jawbone, that did the first murther" (85; cf. III. iii. 37 f.).

[4] In the original poem the stanza runs:

> A pickaxe and a spade
> And eke a shrowding shete,
> A house of clay for to be made,
> For such a gest most mete.

The dramatist gives "pit" instead of "house" because he has used the latter

when the Clown tosses up another skull, Hamlet expatiates
upon it, "the skull of a lawyer" (107) this time, more quizzically than ever and at greater length. So that when the prince
puts the, for us, shivering question, "Whose grave is this, sir?"
(127) the sexton is fully in the mood to reply curtly, "Mine,
sir." So indeed it is; he will not have it expropriated by the
idle, mocking wit of a strolling gentleman. Presently he will
consign this grave to "such a guest" (105, 130), he insists, as
will be worthy of it. Consequently he no longer envisages the
corpse as a mere "she" who drowned herself "se offendendo"
(9) and deserves no "Christian burial" (28). *Now* the corpse
must be reverenced along with the good grave which he has so
expertly built for it. It is no longer a pampered "gentlewoman"
but a real "woman," an "even-Christian" (32): it is "One that
was a woman, sir, but"—he may sign the Cross over himself
and the grave—"rest her soul, she's dead" (146).

The prince, provoked and delighted by this self-honoring
rustic, confers with him now man to man—as previously with
players, soldiers, and pirates—while always and easily keeping
his "own honour and dignity" (II. ii. 557). He is interested
in this fellow's vocation as he is in all crafts. "How long hast
thou been a grave-maker?" (154).

The Clown's reply brings the calendar of the play full
circle: "Of all the days i' th' year, I came to't that day that
our last king Hamlet o'ercame Fortinbras."[5] That day, for
this yokel, as for the scholar and soldiers in the opening scene,
is the nation's great day. The present king, his court, and his
doings are entirely out of the picture; in the foreground, still,
is "Our last king" (I. i. 80). His conquering "day" is known
to all, is in the reckoning of even "every fool" (159), because
it was a day of national promise as well as national power: on
that day an heir to the throne appeared, bearing the king's great
name. "It was the very day that young Hamlet was born."

Here the "young Hamlet" is named as suddenly and naturally, after his father, as he was at the first (I. i. 170) after

---

word above in an unforgettable picture (66), to which the present "pit" adds
depth and room.

   [5] The "came" and the "o'ercame" chime beautifully: the sexton's work is
for him equally important with the monarch's.

the appearance of his father's spirit. (It has reappeared here through the grave-builder's historic memory.) But there his name is ushered by poetry of the "God of day," "our Saviour's birth," and hopeful "morn" (I. i. 150 ff.); here, by prose, sardonic and beautiful, racy and mystic, concerning Christian burial, clay, skulls, and a new grave for one unnamed. This grave-digger is earthy-real; all the more our thoughtful fancies are set aswim by the allegory that looms continually in the air about him; looms, fades, and looms for a moment again. Maybe he is Death? At any rate his work for Death began with the beginning of Hamlet's life. And it matters little to him that this once so hopeful prince has been "sent" (163) away to England to consort with other madmen. And "it's no great matter" whether he recovers his wits nor "Upon what ground" (175) he lost them. The important "ground" for this impassive builder in clay is "here in Denmark: I have been sexton here, man and boy, thirty years"—one full human generation, comprising the prince's birth and probably, as we now expect, his death.

That is our thought, not Hamlet's; the more we harbor it, the more we are struck by the fact that he does not. Here, close to death, his attitude towards it is extraordinarily impersonal. In the "To be" soliloquy he mused upon his own ending, indirectly but elaborately; then, sweeping the "pale" question aside, he plunged into the "current" of his great "enterprise" (III. i. 84-88). This, after turning much "awry," is now setting strongly towards its goal; and the prince is determined to divert none of its force into personal considerations. He will utter not the slightest melancholy allusion to his own fate even when instigated to do so by the sexton's animadversions upon public affairs. Bent upon decisive action in the near future, he can bandy light words with his new friend upon the very ineffectuality of the great King Hamlet's son. Then, still more humorously, he brings the subject back to the sexton's profession, drawing from him grotesque observations upon the tempo of decay in corpses. In short, while *our* mortal premonition rises, so does Hamlet's impersonal jocosity.

But suddenly that attitude is dispelled for a minute by the

skull of the late king's jester. This "mad rogue" (196),[6] while
too remote from Hamlet's supreme enterprise to impinge upon
his resolution, is too close to his heart for trifling recognition.
For the jester's sake the prince ceases jesting (202): "Let me
see. . . . Alas, poor Yorick!" He peers into the vanished face,
as at the first, with more awful intentness, he peered into that
of a greater spirit: "Alas, poor Ghost!" (I. v. 4). Revering
and sharing the majesty of his royal father, Hamlet has also
a side akin to the royal jester. The prince, too, when so dis-
posed and when time permits, can be "a fellow of infinite jest,
of most excellent fancy."[7] Again he sees, beneath this skull,
the "back" he rode "a thousand times" in fun. He will *not*
see the eyes; they, too poignant, are unmentioned. But he sees
the mocking, changeful mouth that dropped words of affection
for a congenial child: "Here hung those lips that I have kissed
I know not how oft"[8]—

Abruptly Hamlet checks his elegiac emotion. He resumes
his macabre, satiric jesting with the aid of the now "jeering"
(212) skull. And presently his imagination flashes up from the
Danish king's jester to the greatest of all kings, Alexander,
whose remains, however, are now in a condition far more "base"
(223). For his reeking skull (221), unlike the jester's, has
long ago vanished; his "noble dust" (225) is all dispersed. At
present it is used, perchance, to stop the "bung-hole" (226) of
a "barrel" to keep the good beer in, or a "hole" (237) in a cot-
tage "wall" to keep the ill wind out: the vulgarest pleasures
and needs of *the world* may be served by "that earth which
kept *the world* in awe." Here we remember "how a king may

[6] The lifted *dry* skull makes the sexton think of his own *wet* "head," drip-
ping with the wine poured thereon by the skull's former owner. No doubt he
grasps his "stoup of liquor" (68), with dramatic suggestiveness, after handing
the empty skull-vessel to Hamlet.

[7] This trait, along with Hamlet's other and various capabilities, is comprised in the sixteenth-century conception of the Complete Gentleman.

[8] The second verb "have kissed"—instead of the past tense "kissed" or
"did kiss"—completes the moving beauty of the first verb "hung." The
mercurial lips that once "hung" there belong entirely to the past; but the
kisses, in Hamlet's affectionate memory, are close to the present. This effect
is intensified by the tonal and rhythmic loveliness of the sentence as a whole.
The alliterative "h" points up the vocalic variety in the following sequence:
"Here hung . . . have kissed . . . how oft."

go a progress through the guts of a beggar" (IV. iii. 32). That
was Hamlet's acrid way of expressing the same idea when he
was last in the presence of Claudius. There he was threatening
his enemy, bitterly but uncertainly. Here, completely sure of
his ground, he is threatening him with clear certainty, in casual
and impersonal terms. The fate of "Imperial Caesar" (236)
obviously comprises that of all lesser kings, including the present decadent king of Denmark. The prince gestures lightly, I
think, in the general direction of the royal palace of Elsinore
while chanting his stanza (236-239) with loud jocularity—and
then, suddenly, this king who is in his thoughts appears. "But
soft, but soft, aside: here *comes* the king"—

V. i. 241-322

Instantly Hamlet is tense and alert; concentrated upon his
"business" (73) as when he entered the scene, and, as throughout the scene (excepting the brief lament for Yorick), extraordinarily objective and impersonal. He is fully ready now to
do justice upon the royal criminal. But he himself has done
injustice to others, above all to Ophelia; and "heaven" will
"punish" him for this, and "with this" (III. iv. 173 f.):

> The queen, the courtiers. Who is it they *follow*,
> And with such maimed rites? This doth betoken
> The corse they *follow* did with desperate hand
> Fordo it own life.

He repeats the word "follow" while his eyes follow intensely
the unknown corpse, the hapless "it." Once more, this time
involuntarily and with piercing pathetic irony, Hamlet does
injustice to that peaceful "hand." Not that hand but the hands
of others, including his own, fordid that "life"; those hands,
not hers, have been "desperate," and can again be so. In a
few moments Hamlet's "love" (II. i. 102-104) and "imagination" will again wax "desperate" (I. iv. 87).

Desperate just now, however, is the showy shallowness of
Laertes. "What ceremony else?" he exclaims wildly. His
soul loves "ceremony." This "very noble youth" (247), thus
generously termed, aside, by his prince, is bent to assassinate
that prince with poisonous secrecy under the protection of a

royal "solemn wager" (IV. vii. 156) at a court ceremony.
"What ceremony else?" he cries again, more loudly.   From
the very first, when he showed his "duty" at Claudius's "coronation" (I. ii. 53), he has lived and breathed in an atmosphere
of right ceremony, not right honesty.   That is his misfortune;
it has kept our sympathy for him warm.   But now he revolts us;
while also the face of the listening prince (retired from the
view of those on the stage) shows surprise and rising disgust.
Here Laertes succumbs to the hypocrisy, not of the consummate
Claudius, but of his own consummate vanity.   The egoistic
sentimentality of his laments for Ophelia in the preceding act
was natural enough to be pardonable.   But his present outbreak
appears repellently unnatural.   It defies the very dictates of his
own external gentility: *right* ceremony forbids a rude outcry
for *more* ceremony *here*.

Far more natural are the quiet words of the Priest, who is
sincerely observing the proprieties taught by his church.   To
this grave he brings "charitable prayer" (253).   And a lovely
thing that he is forbidden by his vows to "sing" (260) for one
"whose death was doubtful" (250) sounds nevertheless in his
and our hearts: "a requiem and such rest to her As to peace-
parted souls."   But Laertes grossly violates her peace.   Here
and now, if nowhere and no time else, he should be quiet.   His
vain anger pollutes his appropriate "violets" (263); and his
raging image of a "churlish priest" lying "howling" in hell is
viciously wrong at the grave of her whose last words asked
mercy for "all Christian souls" (IV. v. 199).   With an effort
we detach from his wrong mood his right epitaph for her: "A
ministering angel shall my sister be. . . ."

"What, the fair Ophelia!" (265).[9]   Hamlet's cry is swift,
low, stricken.   It comes like a white flash of lightning over
against the background of his elaborate, impersonal jestings
upon death above.   "Where be your gibes now? (208). . . .
Now get you to my lady's chamber . . ." (212).   His Yorick-

---

[9] The word "fair" echoes of course Laertes' use of it in the preceding
speech, where it introduces two cognate adjectives, "unpolluted" and "ministering."   Earlier Hamlet used the word in an image for his father, "this fair
mountain" (III. iv. 66).   There, too, its connotation was remarkably en-
riched by its context.

volubility is all gone.[10] After the word "Ophelia," the name
hitherto unnamed in this scene and uttered now by only him,
he has no more words. Elsewhere he gives such full and wonderful expression to many strong feelings that his present silence is deeply charged. Conceivably he might have said for
her something surpassing the image that he hung so vividly in
our minds a few minutes ago, "Here hung those lips." For
that early friend Yorick he had piercing words of mourning;
for Ophelia's father, a speech of deep repentance (III. iv. 172-
175). But now his mingled grief and remorse are too awful
to be told. He is as dumb as at his *first* parting with her (II.
i. 92-100); but his despairing gestures are equally revealing;
his sigh is far more "piteous and profound." The Priest committing her body to the grave is praying silently for her, as
she did for Hamlet in the scene of his *second* parting from her
(III. i). At the outset of that episode (in direct antithesis
to his initial mood in the Graveyard scene) he meditated lyr-
ically upon the "sleep of death" and the "undiscovered country." When he perceived her kneeling in devout stillness he
exclaimed with still awe, "The fair Ophelia . . . in thy orisons
Be all my sins remembered" (III. i. 89). That was the last
time, until now, that she was for him "fair Ophelia." Soon
came his rejection of her offered love and his violent tirade
against marriage, then, in the close of the Play scene, the sin-
fully cruel words of his *third*, and last, dismissal of her (III. ii.
256-262); and all this while he banished from his lips her very
name. But now, at the final parting, she is again "Ophelia"
and "fair." His love and his sin whelm him as he utters his
agonized cry of last greeting and last farewell: the rest is
silence.

"In youth when I did love. . . .it was very sweet . . ." (69).
The digging of the nameless grave began with that old song.
And now that song is echoed for us by the "sweet" (266)
verses of the queen, scattering flowers upon the "maid" whom
her son "did love" and (unheard by the queen and her company) has just named:

[10] Similarly Romeo when he learns of Juliet's death utters no direct word
of grief, despite his lyrical fluency, so strikingly shown in his preceding speech
(V. i. 1-30).

Sweets to the sweet, farewell.
I hoped thou shouldst have been my Hamlet's wife;
I thought thy bride-bed to have decked, sweet maid,
And not to have strewed thy grave.

A despairing gesture by the prince confesses (as his tongue will confess presently) that his mother in this matter, as in the matter of his grief for Polonius (IV. i. 24-27), had rightly read his heart beneath his obscurant words. He had never really given up the hope that Ophelia would some day be his wife. That hope's subconscious hold upon him was evinced by the very violence with which he thrust it from his conscious mind in the Nunnery and Play scenes; just as his very violence in the ensuing Prayer scene (III. iii) showed that his truest feelings were contrary to his loud words. His tragic uncertainty, proudly concealed from himself, regarding his just course with Claudius made him repudiate with ever-increasing vehemence the betrothal to Ophelia (betrothal in spirit, not in form) which seemed to him a clog upon his great political enterprise. But the recent clearing of his resolution regarding the king cleared away the barrier between him and his betrothed—too late. The "bride-bed" that would have followed upon the prince's assumption of the throne has become a "grave." The queen's lament also tells us what the prince's "holy vows of heaven" (I. iii. 114) told us at the beginning, and what Ophelia's firm charity made increasingly certain: she was designed by grace and nature to be "Hamlet's wife."[11]

Those two words sting Laertes into a quick passion of blent grief and rage intensified by hidden pangs of conscience. And we realize, with reviving sympathy for him, that his conscience underneath his vanity was a main cause of his gross anger at the clergyman. He is desperately disquieted by his coming murder of one who, as well as being his lawful prince, was beloved by his "fair and unpolluted" (262) sister: she is, in spirit, "Hamlet's wife." At this point, therefore, he suddenly loses all self-control. Oblivious of the presence of Hamlet's

---

[11] It is significant that Hamlet's last word to the living Ophelia was "husbands" (III. ii. 262), by way of bitter climax to the theme of "marriages" (III. i. 154) which his subconscious yearning for her forced his thoughts to run upon when in her presence.

mother he converts his self-relieving cursing of the Priest into
a terrific cursing of Hamlet (269 ff.), then *"Leaps in the
grave,"* and embraces the shrouded corpse:

> Hold off the earth awhile
> Till I have caught her once more in mine arms:
> Now pile your dust upon the quick and dead
> Till of this flat a mountain you have made
> To o'ertop old Pelion, or the skyish head
> Of blue Olympus.

That final image, touching the cosmic theme of the play and
followed by a moment of dead silence, is a serene peak of poetry
rising above the miry chaos of Laertes' heart. Here he is sincere. The wretched youth longs indeed for burial deep with
the dead. His spirit is lifted towards pure "skyish" peace as
by heavenly influence of the soul whose earthly form he clasps
"once more," his "ministering angel" (264). And she, in this
moment, we perceive breathlessly, may become the angelic minister of reconciliation between the two young men who love her
best with what is best in themselves. Their enmity can be
buried with her "earth." If only her brother's momentary
yearning for her peace will be met by words of peace from her
lover!

But Hamlet, ignorant of the coming crime that is on Laertes' conscience, sees only his showiness; and this the prince's
pride seizes upon to relieve his own far profounder sense of
guilt. He could bear the other's accusation against himself,
the "ten times treble" curse upon his head, and even the impu-
tation that Ophelia's fate was entirely due to his "wicked deed"
(269-272). But his bowed head rises and his face flushes at
what ensues. Already this princely upholder of good custom
had been disgusted by Laertes' rantings at the Priest. And now
the same righteous, grieving anger that was roused by Gertrude's hypocritic "tears" at his father's funeral (I. ii. 149)
rises against Laertes' hypocritic conduct in the grave of his
betrothed. Righteous, grieving anger; but, this time, exacer-
bated by bitter consciousness of his own guilt. All the more
significant, then, is Hamlet's control, not perfect but extraor-

dinary, of his present "towering passion" (V. ii. 80). He will
not let it put him beside himself as it did on earlier occasions.[12]
Here he maintains much of the self-mastery which we have
seen deepening in him, more and more, since his last outburst
of ecstatic rage, that against the "king of shreds and patches"
(III. iv. 102). And he does so despite strong incentives to
accept Laertes' "cue for passion" (II. ii. 587) as he formerly
accepted that given him by the actor. Here more than there,
surely, he is tempted to outdo his exemplar in histrionic conduct. Actually he outdoes him in self-restraint. Laertes is in
the madly emotional state, due to the inner conflict of conscience
and revengefulness, that Hamlet has left behind. The prince
advances to the grave with firm dignity: "What is he whose
grief Bears such an emphasis?" To be sure he proceeds to
utter words of satiric censure: he finds it too hard to subdue
his pride entirely along with his rage. But notice that he refrains from returning the other's curses and from accusing him
—as he once accused even Ophelia (III. i. 103)—of dishonesty.
His bearing invites Laertes to moderate his "phrase of sorrow"
(277), after the example of his prince, presently to be his king.
Here for the first time Hamlet assumes the sovereign appella-
tion of "the Dane," so suitable for that "royal Dane" (I. iv.
45) his father, so unsuitable for Claudius, who usurped it
in his initial speech to Laertes (I. ii. 44). "This is I," says the
prince to Laertes now, "Hamlet the Dane."

That is an invitation to Laertes to repeat in the crown
prince's presence, with frank and full explication, the horrid
charge proclaimed a moment ago in his supposed absence. And
all might yet be well if Laertes with bold sincerity would "tell
him to his teeth, 'Thus didest thou'" (IV. vii. 57). But
Laertes does not. The vanity of the young courtier, flattered
to the limit by Claudius, cannot bear the prince's superior air;

---

[12] Missing this point critics have missed the significant contrast here between the prince and Laertes. Most editors have accepted Q1's stage-direction
that Hamlet leaps into the grave after Laertes, though it was dropped in the
subsequent quartos and in the folios. The intention of the dramatist himself,
surely, was that Hamlet should not do so (albeit the earliest actors of the part
may well have insisted upon this melodramatic feat) and that Laertes should
leap out of the grave, when he grapples Hamlet, just as violently as he had
leapt into it. (For the famous verses on Burbage leaping into a grave, see
Edwin Nungezer's *Dictionary of Actors*, p. 74.)

at the same time his conscience prevents him, when so honestly challenged, from uttering the equivocations required by his secret plot. Therefore he is dumb, for a moment. He lets the clasped body decline from his arms and stands stupefied, swaying. Then, with all the violence of one who hears and repudiates the call of grace, he leaps from the grave and grapples at Hamlet's throat, crying, "The devil take thy soul!" Formerly the prince himself applied to the "soul" of the praying Claudius the same imprecation in far more violent form (III. iii. 94). Now, he rejoins simply, "Thou pray'st not well." Mastering with a supreme effort his old temptation to be "spleenative and rash" (284) he tries to bring Laertes to his senses by firm words of warning and command:

> Yet have I in me something dangerous
> Which let thy wiseness fear. Away thy hand!

Others sunder the two. Laertes' confused passions have choked him into silence. But Hamlet, as his mien shows, is about to utter something far more disturbing than hitherto. Therefore his mother pleads, "Hamlet, Hamlet!" and the gentle Horatio is peremptory as never before: "Good my lord, be quiet." But Hamlet cries, "Why, I will *fight* with him upon this theme. . . ." All present are electrified. Apparently the crown prince is accepting a subject's challenge: he will submit to trial by combat Laertes' accusation of the "wicked deed" (271), the killing of Polonius. That, seemingly, is what Hamlet means by "this theme." But the queen discerns in his face something different: "O my son, what theme?" And these words, from her who has mourned with simple sincerity for the one who should be "Hamlet's wife," loosen his pent-up feelings for Ophelia. In the Play scene, in the presence of the two sovereigns and their court, he had disavowed his love for her with wild, elaborate dishonesty. Now, in the same public presence, but at her grave, he makes restitution with honest tears and simplest words: "I loved Ophelia"—In penitent humility he confesses to all what he had tried proudly to hide from all, particularly himself. In his shattering first scene with her alone, his eyes, as she afterwards told her father, "to

the last, bended their light on me" (II. i. 100). Now, at the
very last, they bend their light, full of tears, on the grave where
she lies, while he confesses brokenly, "I loved Ophelia"—

It were well if he had stopped there. But his new meekness
in regard to Ophelia does not yet extend (as it will extend,
fully, in the next scene) to her brother. For Laertes' histrionic
emotionalism is reminiscent for Hamlet, excruciatingly so, of
his own former treatment of her. Therefore conscience, pride,
and despair combine in impelling the prince to repudiate the
other as fellow-mourner:

> forty thousand brothers
> Could not, with all their quantity of love,
> Make up my sum. What wilt thou do for her?

That question, particularly the word "do," stings Laertes to the
quick. The prince's confession of constant love instead of
"trifling," transient fancy (I. iii. 5, 14) for his sister had deeply
moved him. But now in swift revulsion from soft emotions he
recalls the vengeance he has undertaken to "do for her." Drawing his sword, this time, he struggles to reach the prince, while
the queen entreats, "For love of God forbear him" (296), and
the king exclaims, effectually, "Oh he is *mad*, Laertes" (295).
Claudius thus reminds his accomplice of the role of madman
which Hamlet played when he killed Polonius and which he
is now, so the king hints, on the point of reassuming. His conduct, unlike that of Laertes, will be excusable in the public eye
on the ground of his lunacy. Therefore to attack him openly
will bring opprobrium upon the rising young courtier, who accordingly must await the fencing-match, as planned. Laertes
relapses into acquiescent but sullen, restless silence.

And thereby Hamlet's anger at him is greatly intensified.
For a fateful minute the prince becomes indeed—once more, for
the last time—"mad" (297-307), though with an obvious
method in his madness. Formerly he tried to taunt Polonius
into an "honest" expression of emotion and purpose regarding
the silenced Ophelia (II. ii. 176 ff.); now he is doing likewise,
more tragically, with Polonius' son. Laertes' utter silence and
inertness, following hard upon his melodramatic violence, must

seem to Hamlet (unaware of the plot against himself) a crowning sign of gross insincerity. So he cries, " 'Swounds, show me what thou'lt do. . . ." Does Laertes wish both to "weep" and to "fight" (298, 289)? Is he sincerely mourning for his sister? If so, does he really desire a sword-combat with her declared and mourning lover beside her very grave?

Here is Laertes' chance to assert that the prince's grief makes no real amends and that they two, after removing from this sacred ground, should meet in a mortal duel. But Laertes keeps silent. Too obviously, in Hamlet's view, his loud vengeful curses were mere rant. At Ophelia's open grave, where if nowhere else simple truth should prevail, her brother has exhibited that prevalent disease of dishonesty which Hamlet has set himself, from the beginning, to cure. Once he strove in vain to persuade two foolish courtiers to be "even and direct" with him (II. ii. 298). His aim is the same with the present courtier; but his method, now that his long struggle against courtly crookedness is close upon its finale, is climactically strenuous. His declaration of the "sum" of his love is followed at once by a demonstration of the sum of his hate, his hate of dishonesty. He lashes Laertes with a series of taunting queries rising to this: "Dost thou come here to whine? To outface me with leaping in her grave?" No answer. Therefore Hamlet flings out finally a "burning" (305) caricature of the other's image of a heaped "mountain" (275) of earth. By outranting Laertes he tries to break through his evasive, dishonest silence —and fails.

Normally Laertes upon the capping jeer, "Make Ossa like a wart," would have been stung by rage into veracity; but his specious self-control is reinforced telepathically by the watchful Claudius. If the prince had urged quietly, like the subtle king earlier, "Laertes, I must commune with your grief" (IV. v. 202), the enmity between the two young men beside Ophelia's grave might have been "buried quick with her" (302). Hamlet has used a potent but, in this case, ineffective method in his madness. This fact he himself now perceives, silently; and his mother, seizing the moment, helps to deflect him towards the right course. She knows that beneath his brilliant, desperate taunting is the bitter "eisel" (299) of his repentance, as after the death of Ophelia's father; and so she declares:

> This is mere madness;
> And thus awhile the fit will work on him:
> Anon as patient as the female dove,
> When that her golden couplets are disclosed,
> His silence will sit drooping.[13]

Exquisitely these words indicate the "golden" charity which the white peace of Ophelia can incubate in the heart of Hamlet. We see his head "drooping" more and more as he hearkens. Then, approaching her brother with outstretched hand, he says firmly and quietly:

> Hear you, sir:
> What is the reason that you use me thus?
> I loved you ever—

And here for a moment the fate of Hamlet the Dane, of Laertes and Claudius, and of the whole kingdom sways in the balance.

The prince who had publicly declared his love for Ophelia has now done likewise, meekly, for her brother; at the same time confronting him in simple sincerity with a question which, unlike the series of insulting queries above, cannot justifiably be evaded. In effect Laertes is invited to state whether he soberly believes what he had loudly asserted in his grief and rage; namely, that the prince, despite his generally known "madness" just alluded to by the queen, is to be held entirely and solely responsible for the tragedy of Polonius and Ophelia. And we know that any reasonable response of Laertes to that reasonable invitation can be fruitful of peace and concord. Whether he answers yes, or no, or doubtfully, Hamlet can take

---

[13] In her previous speech on the same theme, Hamlet's penitence, Gertrude said that his "very madness" had in it a pure and true feeling "like some ore Among a mineral [i.e., a mine] of metals base" (IV. i. 25-27). Thus the image emphasized the persistence of his "madness." Now, however, it is "mere" instead of "very" madness, and the thought of it is dispelled by the ensuing image of the patient dove in place of the dark chaos of the mine. Such is one of the many ways in which Shakespeare makes us realize that Hamlet's self-command is now far deeper and saner than before, though his trouble is greater.

occasion to invite him to a private conference (as the king did, successfully, in IV. v. 202 ff.) concerning responsibilities and amends. But Laertes makes no reply at all. Upon his prince's avowal of affection for him he fixes his eyes on the ground, speechless from his inward conflict of conscience and pride. And Hamlet, aware of the other's pride but not of the burden on his conscience, allows his own pride to flare up once more. For Laertes' refusal to give a single word of "reason," or even the faintest sign of reciprocated esteem, is a superlative public insult to the crown prince.

But Hamlet, as he will admit in the next scene, ought to have borne even that insult patiently. He had done much to bring it upon himself. Superior to the other's showy vanity, he should have tried from the outset to mollify it; instead he intensified it. Therefore, at the last, he could have overcome it only by a public declaration of sorrow (actually to be made by him in the next scene) for the killing of Polonius. But to do this without the exonerating explanation, impossible just now,[14] of his mistaking the old councilor for Claudius demanded a degree of meekness beyond the reach of Hamlet in his present mood. Formally, of course, he has right on his side. All who are present must perceive that every precept of ordinary gentility requires Laertes to speak now. Nor, of course, can we be sure that if Hamlet had gone further in the right direction Laertes would have responded. But the outstanding fact is that Hamlet, in charity, in charitable justness, could go further and fails to do so. A confession of his repentance regarding Laertes' father is on the tip of his tongue, perhaps, when he declares, "I loved you ever"— Actually he proceeds, in sudden, testy self-justification,

> but it is no matter:
> Let Hercules himself do what he may,
> The cat will mew, the dog will have his day.

Hercules the demigod and humble friend, let alone Hamlet the

---

[14] The dramatist assumes that his audience will perceive that Hamlet cannot publicize the explanation given secretly to his mother (III. iv. 32) until he is in act of executing Claudius, and that his whole nature prevents him from committing regicide at the grave of Ophelia.

Dane, could do nothing with a courtier who will squall with
catlike complaint one moment and the next assume a sullen,
doglike muteness.[15]   Thus the superlative insult of Laertes'
silence is countered by the prince, as he strides from the scene,
with a superlative gibe.

The reconciling moment is past; fate goes on its way.   The
pride of the two young men who love Ophelia has triumphed
over her peace-making charity.   And Hamlet has unwittingly
played into the king's hands by mortally wounding the vanity
of Laertes.   He, as Claudius well perceives, has been stung by
the prince's parting thrust into a new impatience for revenge
(317 f.).   The king, after moments of fearful suspense, is
smoothly triumphant.   He can promise ambiguously that "This
grave shall have a *living* monument," i.e., the sacrifice of Hamlet—instead of the living monument that Ophelia's spirit desires, the ending of vengeful pride.   As in the preceding act,
but now more tragically, we think of *her* kind of "quiet" (321)
and "patience" (317, 322) while Claudius displays his.   And
when the sexton resumes his interrupted shoveling we may
recall, with changed and deepened irony, his query that opened
the scene, "Is she to be buried in *Christian* burial . . . ?"   This,
given her in the end by him, has been refused her, in spirit, by
her brother and her lover.

(d) *perfect conscience . . . ?*   V. ii

V. ii. 1-80

"So much for this, sir. . . ."   These words come from Hamlet slowly, in profound gravity.   He has just been unbosoming
himself to Horatio regarding Ophelia and her father.   But
now, of all times, he knows there must not be "too much of
this" (III. ii. 79): what he has to do would otherwise "want

[15] See the comment in the text, page 14 above, upon Hamlet's initial reference to Hercules (I. ii. 153).   In both cases the prince throws the heroic
simplicity of that demigod into contrast with the duplicity of his uncle's court.
In the present scene, as in I. ii, Hamlet pleads for honest simplicity in mourning and in piety.   In I. ii the court (including Laertes) listened in smooth
silence; now, by way of ironic sequel, the silent Laertes holds the foreground,
emblemizing for Hamlet the catlike and doglike attitude of the whole court.
Hence the prince's two closing lines are aimed not just at Laertes but at "the
uses of this world" (I. ii. 134), the world of Claudius's Denmark.

true colour, tears perchance for blood" (III. iv. 130). With a strong effort he turns his inward seeing from Ophelia's grave to the king's design for his own death: "now let me see the other. . . ."

Having just confessed to his friend, as we must suppose, the rashness of his fateful thrust through the arras at the supposed Claudius, he now relates how rashness, better employed, enabled him to discover Claudius's counterstroke:

> And praised be rashness for it: let us know
> Our indiscretion sometimes serves us well
> When our dear plots do pall; and that should teach us
> There's a divinity that shapes our ends
> Rough-hew them how we will.

His "dear plot" against the king (III. iii. 88 ff.)—"dear" in two senses of the word, fondly cherished and thereafter costly—did most dreadfully "pall": the killing of Polonius began a dark cortege of events leading up to the Graveyard scene.[16] But when we have learned by hard experience that "indiscretion" *generally* serves us ill, resulting as it usually does from the egoistic plots we cherish, then we can also "know" that it "sometimes," though rarely, "serves us well"; notably when inspired by the perfectly natural and healthy, in fact divinely designed, instinct for self-preservation.

Of course our instincts and inspirations, like our "dear plots," may also mislead us; we must not grant them a fatalistic trust. We have to use our minds and wills, weighing what can "come to good" (I. ii. 158), cherishing our "native hue of resolution" (III. i. 84), combining "blood and judgment" in our pursuit of justice (III. ii. 59, 74). We must try our best to shape our ends. But eventually we have to confess that even our very best efforts are mere rough-hewing under the supervision of the divine sculptor.[17] This is what, in the upshot—

[16] Thus the "dear" of the folios is richer dramatically than the "deep" of Q2. And the word "pall," coming so close upon the Graveyard scene, has a strong suggestion of death and fatality (as in *Macbeth* I. v. 52) along with its logical sense, which here is of course the same as in *Antony and Cleopatra* II. vii. 88.

[17] The reader may prefer "Maker" to "sculptor." In any case the implication of the metaphor is that it is mainly through our *work* in the largest

hence Shakespeare's stress upon it in this final scene—our experience "should teach us."

Horatio, not given to interrupting his prince, breaks in with an emphatic "That is most certain." The skeptical scholar of the opening scene of this drama has become very certain of one supernatural fact. He has learned it less from his own private life than from the life of his beloved prince.[18] Hamlet himself has learned from hard experience, particularly from the results of his own sins, that the "Everlasting" (I. ii. 131), whom he recognized at the first as the inflexible moral ruler of the universe, is also a personal Providence. After the first visit of the Ghost, "heaven" (I. v. 92) was impersonal, austere, and distant. But after the killing of Polonius, "heaven hath pleased it so To punish me with this and this with me" (III. iv. 174). And now, in the close, he is keenly aware of the "divinity" shaping the "ends" of every person.

The inspired "rashness" for which Hamlet expresses gratitude here was, though super-rational, obviously not irrational. We, like Horatio, are to "remember all the circumstance" (2). Hamlet had many good reasons for suspecting the intent of the king and of his two schoolfellows who bore the royal "mandate" (III. iv. 204) to England. Essentially rational, therefore, were the uneasy "fears" (17) that would not let him "sleep" (5) and that drove him "in the dark" to purloin and open the "grand commission" (18). And his strong sense, throughout the present episode and indeed throughout this last scene as a whole, of "heaven ordinant" (48) is no more significant than his belief that the Creator exacts from us the fullest possible use of His gift of "godlike reason" (IV. iv. 38). Hamlet's reason, along with inspiration, worked in countermining the plot of Claudius. It worked with inspired speed: "Ere I could make a prologue to my brains They had begun the play" (30). His "brain" (II. ii. 617) performed in precisely the same manner—

---

sense of the word, through our creative efforts, not through our schemes and ideals, that we come to know deity. Tennyson has the same viewpoint in *In Memoriam* cxxiv, using the world "moulding" instead of Hamlet's "shapes," and resuming the image in cxxxi with the words "will," "works," and "control."

[18] Horatio's private sufferings have taught him Stoic temperance (III. ii. 70 ff.); his prince's tragic trials have taught him (Horatio) "divinity."

blood and judgment and intuition all working well together—
when it planned the "play" (II. ii. 618, 624) that exposed the
king's initial crime.

Here, however, as not in the "peasant slave" soliloquy, the
prince's state of mind is firm and assured *throughout* because
he is fully determined, now, to execute Claudius. In speaking of
the "bilboes" (6), the "bugs and goblins" (22), the "earnest
conjuration" (38), etc., he uses increasingly that satiric, jocular,
objective tone, indicating fixed decision, which appeared in his
letter to the king (IV. vii. 42 ff.) and was dominant in the
first half of the Graveyard scene.

But when Horatio utters half a dozen mildly doubtful words
upon the doom of Rosencrantz and Guildenstern (56), the
prince's jocularity vanishes, leaving bare his underlying moral
severity:

> Why, man, they did make love to this employment,
> They are not near my conscience; their defeat
> Doth by their own insinuation grow:
> 'Tis dangerous when the baser nature comes
> Betwixt the pass and fell incensed points
> Of mighty opposites.

Whether or not his two schoolfellows guessed they were con-
ducting Hamlet to a designed sudden death is left to our imagination. But their elaborate assertion of loyalty to Claudius
when he promised them their commission showed us that they
were willing to go to any lengths in his service: their own
interests were completely "mortised and adjoined" to his (III.
iii. 20). This fact they had made sufficiently evident to Hamlet in the preceding scene after he had plainly hinted that he
would soon assume the throne (III. ii. 354 ff.), and despite his
repeated warnings to them that his overt madness was not, as
alleged by Claudius, "the heart" of his "mystery" (II. ii. 396-
398; III. ii. 382). His constant admonition to them was that,
if they would not continue their honest and "ever-preserved
love" for him (II. ii. 296), they should at least desist from
"insinuation" (59), from acting the part of go-betweens playing
Claudius's game against him. But they would not desist.
Therefore Hamlet became certain that any plot of the king

against him would be also theirs in spirit and responsibility (III. iv. 202-210). He is scrupulously careful not to adduce against them, in his present talk with Horatio, their very probable but unproved awareness of the ultimate aim of their voyage. It is sufficient that they "did make love to this employment": obviously they would have consented to the beheading of Hamlet (24) after the fact. Therefore they were *justly* condemned by their prince, under the "Danish seal" (50), to the execution designed for himself. No "leisure" (23), no "debatement" (45) nor "shriving-time" (46) could be allowed them, any more than it was to have been allowed him, because their tongues might well have saved them from their death.

Hamlet's legal logic, however, is far less impressive for Horatio, and for us, than the temperance and justice of his whole bearing here. He utters no bitterly violent words against his doomed schoolfellows, as he did against the dead Polonius, a far more innocent tool of the king. He might here have shouted that they also were "wretched, rash, intruding" fools who have found that "to be too busy is some danger" (III. iv. 31 ff.). Instead, he utters the above-quoted passage, similar in logic but radically different in spirit and tone: firm moral indignation has supplanted self-exculpating rage.

The great point is that his motive of *personal* vengeance, though not entirely obliterated (as it would be in a saint), is now, as it should be in the complete gentleman, above all in the gentleman-prince, subordinated fully to the principles of justice. If the doom of his two schoolfellows is just—and the just Horatio's silence upon Hamlet's declaration means acquiescence—what about their master, Hamlet's "mighty opposite," the king? This is the grand question to which the prince has been leading up in the course of the present episode. He keeps that question unspoken, with fine tact, prompting Horatio to put it to himself. The so far unnamed person behind Rosencrantz and Guildenstern, behind all the evil events that have happened—what should now happen to *him*, even though he is the nation's anointed sovereign?

"Why," Horatio exclaims intensely, hard upon Hamlet's mention of "mighty opposites," "what a *king* is this!" (62).

The damning emphasis is on the word "king." This word, this emphasis, has never hitherto escaped the wary lips of Horatio in reference to Claudius, not even when the latter was apparently proved to be the poisoner of the former sovereign (III. ii. 282-301). Hamlet's eminently just and prudent counselor, in whose mind never is "Antiquity forgot" (IV. v. 104), has now with his whole soul and mind passed judgment upon this wicked "king." Accordingly the prince, deeply satisfied, proceeds to put the hitherto unspoken question into words. His speech is the acme of honest and princely deliberation:

> Does it not, thinkst thee, stand me now upon —
> He that hath killed my king, and whored my mother,
> Popped in between the election and my hopes,
> Thrown out his angle for my proper life,
> And with such cozenage: is't not perfect conscience
> To quit him with this arm? And is't not to be damned
> To let this canker of our nature come
> In further evil![19]

The speaker's personal animus and ambition, frankly adduced in the three opening lines, are subordinate. Emphasized is the unquestionable right, particularly of a crown prince, to self-preservation. But the climactic point is the clear moral and religious call, stressed in the end-words "conscience" and "damned," which Hamlet now hears to prevent "this canker of our nature"—the plural "our" replacing the fourfold "my" above—from doing "further evil" to the commonweal and to humanity.[20]

---

[19] The speech rises, with the long rushing sweep of a wave, into a question at "this arm?" Then it plunges like a breaking wave to "further evil." The final sentence, beginning in F1 with a capitalized "And" and ending with a period, is more an exclamation than a question. I have changed the period to an exclamation point. Editors have generally changed it to a question mark and de-capitalized the "And."

[20] There are five first-person-singular pronouns in the first four lines of the speech; in the last four, none. That fact throws into strong relief, in the second half of the speech, the impersonal, social quality of the deed of regicide about to be performed by "this [not 'my'] arm." This arm that shall "quit" Claudius—"quit," I think, in the double sense of requite and dismiss—is now in the service of humanity, "our nature" (69), and of "divinity" (10) or "heaven ordinant" (48). The effect is heightened by depriving the word "conscience" of the possessive pronoun "my" which it had in Hamlet's preceding speech. The phrase "come In further evil" is suggestively

Thus Hamlet, in sharp contrast with his state of mind in the central scenes of the drama (III. ii, III. iii), has learned to be perfectly honest with himself, and with his friend, regarding his hard task of regicide. In this matter he has finally come to terms with his conscience and with Providence. Hence his vital temperance here. His "blood and judgment," which were "so well co-mingled" (III. ii. 74) during the acting of the Play but thereafter divided, are now again united, more vitally than ever, while he contemplates his imminent great deed. Past and gone is his intermittent, futile passion to fat "all the region kites With this slave's offal" (II. ii. 607) and to send his soul "damned and black" to "hell" (III. iii. 94). The thing he has to do is, now, plain duty. The anti-hero Laertes was recently ready to "dare *damnation*" by committing regicide in raging revengefulness (IV. v. 131 ff.). But the hero himself, freed now from such rage, is aware, on the contrary, that in his case *not* to commit the deed is to be "damned." For in this matter he is heaven's appointed "scourge and minister" (III. iv. 175). Divinity has shaped this "end." He has seen Providence at work in saving him from death and in sending Rosencrantz and Guildenstern to their deserved end. His virtual execution of them is "not near my conscience" (58). Therefore it is surely "perfect conscience" to "quit" their far more evil master "with this arm." Hamlet's spirit is now maturely honest, temperate, and firm because he knows that what he is about to do "can come to good" (I. ii. 158), because his "conscience" and best reason are at last completely convinced of the absolute need of this regicide, and because he believes he sees, in and through and above all, "heaven ordinant" (48).

The prince has put his final conviction before his friend Horatio in the form of a question, as he did his previous conviction regarding Claudius's first crime (III. ii. 298-300). In neither case does the question indicate any uncertainty on his

---

vague and inclusive. The reader may assume that Shakespeare, if not Hamlet himself, sees the merciful justness of preventing Claudius from bringing further evil upon his own soul as well as upon other persons. And the word "canker" applied to the sinful king (instead of to a single sin as in I. iii. 39) sums up climactically the imagery of diseased flesh, human, animal, and vegetable, that runs throughout this drama.

own part; it simply means that he desires the full concurrence of his alter ego. And Horatio gives it here, silently indeed but far more fully than before. The case against the king is so clear and complete that Horatio, with an affirmative nod, proceeds at once to the practical point: Hamlet must kill Claudius before the revealing news of the execution of his two schoolfellows arrives "shortly . . . from England" (71 f.). The prince rejoins with cool decisiveness:

> It will be short,
> The *interim's* mine, and a man's life's no more
> Than to say "one"—[21]

Presently Hamlet will appear before the "kingly eyes" to recount the "occasions" of his "sudden and more strange return" (IV. vii. 44 ff.). When he recounts the most urgent "occasion," namely the purpose of saving his own life, he will end the royal criminal as suddenly as that criminal planned to end him. A man can be killed as quickly as we can say "one." This recalls the prince's detached view of death in the first part of the Graveyard scene. If "Imperial Caesar" (V. i. 236 ff.) may be turned to "clay" to "patch a wall," Hamlet will not be squeamish in dispatching to clay a royal "politician" who has tried in so many ways to "circumvent God" (V. i. 88). The prince will kill this "man" (74) who is really no longer a king, he will excide "this canker of our nature" (69)—a creature not worth one of the "twenty thousand men" (IV. iv. 60) doomed in honorable warfare—without compunction and very soon.

> but I am very sorry, good Horatio,
> That to Laertes I forgot my self.

Ay, there's the rub—in the upshot, a fatal rub. No longer sorry for what he has to do to the king, Hamlet is all the more sorry, "very sorry," for what he has done to Laertes. New in the prince's vocabulary is the simple, pregnant phrase "for-

---

[21] In this passage I have reproduced the line-arrangement and also the italicizing of "interim" in F1. The first line, like its end-word, is "short." The rest of the passage has the press and thrust of a rapier. Hamlet probably makes a thrusting gesture at the word "one"; cf. his "One," below, when he first hits Laertes (291).

got my self." His just and temperate "self," evident at the
first (I. ii) but thereafter failing him on several crucial occasions, reasserted itself in the Closet scene with his mother (III.
iv), and has now attained an experienced, tried, religious quality
lacking at the first. But he "forgot" that nobler "self" for a
fateful minute in the close of the Graveyard scene (V. i. 313-
315). In a sudden, last outburst of intemperate anger, such as
he had not given way to since his blind thrust through the arras
in the Closet scene, he outraged the murdered councilor's son.
And now he sees Laertes' "cause" as vividly parallel with his
own (77 f.). "I'll court his favours." *Hamlet cannot proceed
with "perfect conscience" to end Claudius and assume his throne
until he has made reparation to Laertes.* "But sure the bravery
of his grief did put me Into a towering passion"—Here Horatio
exclaiming "Peace" at the entrance of Osric cuts short the
prince's expatiation upon his hard task of mollifying the an-
tagonized and conceited Laertes, so full of "bravery" (bravado).

V. ii. 81-235

Preparation for that task is afforded Hamlet unexpectedly
by *"young Osric,"* a sort of caricature of Laertes. This gull,
in a long dialogue, sorely tries the new charity and patience of
the prince. The gaudily dressed and more gaudily languaged
youngster is the latest and most blatant favorite of Claudius.
Wealthy in landed property, "spacious in the possession of
dirt" (90), he is endured at court because he supplies the royal
treasury. To such a pass has the smooth usurper come.
Polonius was succeeded by Rosencrantz and Guildenstern, and
these are now replaced by a "water-fly" (84) who reincarnates
their fatuity upon its lowest possible level. Osric is a comic
ephemerid; but he symbolizes the extreme growth of that dishonesty in manner and custom deplored by Hamlet at the
beginning of the present regime. Osric is the significant fluff
floating in the "unweeded garden" that has now fully grown
"to seed" (I. ii. 135). His mental stuff is composed of "the
most fond and winnowed opinions" (200). Though ridiculous,
he and "many more of the same breed" exemplify that purely
external notion of courtesy, of "encounter" between human

beings, that "the drossy age dotes on" (196-199). With genetic humor Hamlet places Osric as one that "did comply with his dug before he sucked it" (195). In such courtesy there is certainly "something . . . more than natural" (II. ii. 384). The prince meets it now, however, exactly as the complete gentleman should. His earlier personal bitternesses have fallen away. His satire here is keen but entirely impersonal as when he contemplated the courtier's skull in the graveyard (V. i. 90-101). The living specimen, Osric, is mocked to his face but in so indulgent and kindly a tone that, though nicely scratched all over by the prince, he is not at all wounded in his simple heart.[22]

And Osric is the best possible medium that the subtle king could use for securing Hamlet's consent to the fencing-match. By nature the prince is "Most generous and free from all contriving" (IV. vii. 136), but just now he has every reason to regard as "adders fanged" (III. iv. 203) all tools of Claudius— excepting only Osric. This fellow has not enough wit-sac to secrete one drop of poison. "Your lordship" (81), he begins, bowing deeply, sweeping the floor with his gorgeous "bonnet" (95), "is right welcome back to Denmark." That is not true; but the new Osric, alone of all the courtiers, can utter that greeting without the least touch of falsity or *double-entendre.* Hamlet, suddenly shaken with inward laughter, returns the greeting with responsive humility (83). And when Osric blows "hot" and "cold" regarding the weather (97 ff.) the prince can have no feeling of being fooled to "the top of my bent" as in the case of the "cloud" and the king's former emissaries (III. ii. 392 ff.). Osric can fool no one. When he praises the "absolute gentleman" Laertes, Hamlet (unlike us) has no reason to suspect the finger of the king behind all that colorful "arithmetic of memory" (119). In fact the recent "bravery" (79) of Laertes' grief at the grave was so extraordinary that the

---

[22] Osric, a rustic in origin, illustrates the fact noted by Hamlet in the preceding scene: "the age is grown so picked that the toe of the peasant comes so near the heels of our courtier he galls his kibe" (V. i. 148 ff.). The verbal fastidiousness of the upper class has influenced the whole nation: the countryman's affectation is now treading on the tender heels of the courtier's. But the important point is that Hamlet's humorous tolerance of the sexton's "equivocation" is extended in the present scene to the far more symptomatic and exasperating jargon of Osric.

linguistic "bravery" with which Osric now adorns him seems deliciously suitable: Hamlet (117 ff.) relieves his sore sense of Laertes' showiness by ironically outdoing Osric's encomium. He, bereft of all his "golden words" (136), comes lamely and very casually to the significant point, Laertes' excellence with "Rapier and dagger" (152); which skill, moreover, interests him far less than the magnificent "French rapiers" (156) which Laertes has wagered against the king's horses. Thus the proposed "dozen passes" (172) between Laertes and Hamlet seem, when Osric finally manages to mention them, nothing more than the flourishes of a passing court show.

And that ceremonial fencing-match is welcomed by Hamlet as a "happy" means of using "some gentle entertainment to Laertes" (214 f.), of courting his "favours" (78). But because the prince's time is "short" (73) he proposes, seizing upon the king's request for an "immediate trial" (175), that the match be held "here in the hall" at once: " 'tis the breathing time of day with me" (180-182). He glances at Horatio with significant irony. If the "king hold his purpose" (183), it will forward Hamlet's purpose. His recreation at the foils, as well as affording reconciliation with Laertes, will be the prelude to his turning an "incensed point" (61) against the king.

And now a nice bit of mental fencing takes place between the "mighty opposites" (62). Claudius, careful to avoid the suspicion that could be aroused by a too ready acceptance of Hamlet's proposal, sends a Lord to inquire if the prince's "pleasure hold to play with Laertes" at once, "or that you will take longer time" (205-207). Hamlet, again with an irony obvious to Horatio and us, replies: "I am constant to my purposes,[23] they follow the king's pleasure; if his fitness speaks, mine is ready: *now* or whensoever, provided I be as able as *now*." The nonchalance of that message to Claudius is carefully designed. Hamlet like his enemy will betray no suspicious eagerness for speed; in accord with court custom he will "follow the king's pleasure." But the casual "whensoever" is entirely submerged

---

[23] This is the counterpart to Hamlet's remark above, "let . . . the king hold *his* purpose" (182 f.). The plural "purposes" in his present speech may allude ironically to his double design of engaging in the fencing-match and of slaying Claudius. Cf. "occasions" in IV. vii. 47 and my note.

by the polite emphasis upon the iterated "now." Hamlet is fit, "ready," and "able" to engage in the play at foils "now"— and, as Horatio and we know, to kill Claudius immediately after the match: that stands upon Hamlet "now" (63).

Therefore he soon dismisses the "kind of gain-giving" (226) which assails his "heart" (222) now. But this premonition is so strong as to impress even the matter-of-fact Horatio. He, with all his watchfulness on behalf of his prince, has found in the proposed fencing-match not a single dubious feature. But now he urges Hamlet to obey his "mind" if it finds "anything" (227) doubtful: Horatio says he can easily postpone the match by informing the court that the prince has become on the sudden "not fit." "Not a whit," Hamlet rejoins, the rhyme cheerfully emphasizing his rebuttal, "we defy augury; there's a special providence in the fall of a sparrow":[24] we Christians must repel anything that savors of pagan divination, particularly in regard to death. Having found "heaven ordinant" (48) in the recent saving of his life, Hamlet accepts the possibility that heaven may now ordain his "fall." His killing of Claudius may involve his own death at the hands of the king's partisans. He faced that possibility in the "To be" soliloquy with resolution, yet not without a "dread of something after death" because his "conscience" (III. i. 83) at that time was doubtful and unfrank concerning his task of regicide. On that point he has now "perfect conscience" (67). Also the deepening of religious faith has had in him the effect of banishing romantic broodings upon the "undiscovered country." Death may come to anyone any time, he proceeds to declare, and "the readiness is all" (233). It is religious doctrine also that "no man has aught of what he leaves": we do not really possess the things we have in the visible world. That thought, which occupied Hamlet so much, so quizzically, and so objectively in the graveyard—notably in the case of the "great buyer of land" (V. i. 113)—grips his mind seriously and personally now. It strengthens him in facing the chance that death may "betimes" (235) deprive him of the kingdom of his ripened "hopes" (65). If death "be

---

[24] Christ's "sparrow" is thrown into contrast with the flocks of birds observed by the ancient Roman augurs.

now, 'tis not to come; if it be not to come, it will be now; if
it be not now, yet it will come" (232 ff.). Those three "now's"
echo his "now's" above (63, 211). With sober and firm cheer-
fulness he commends his fate to Providence, and prepares himself for decisive action, now.

V. ii. 236-321

The black hypocrisy of the king cordially putting Laertes'
hand into Hamlet's is foil for the prince's white magnanimity
here.[25] His great speech begins simply:

> Give me your pardon, sir, I've done you wrong,
> But pardon't as you are a gentleman.

That potent word "gentleman" was skilfully used by Claudius
(IV. v. 148; IV. vii. 83) in his efforts to appeal to all that is
superficial and false in Laertes' gentility. But this young
gentleman's deeper instincts will be aroused, we hope, by Hamlet's exemplification here of gentility at its best. The speech
is not an easy one for the proud prince to make. He humbles
himself in "This presence" (239), before "this audience" (251),
as never before. He has mastered—not eradicated—the "mind
impatient" (I. ii. 96) that played directly into Claudius's hands
by bitterly satirizing the dishonesty of this same court in the
opening ensemble (I. ii. 76 ff.). Patiently he now proceeds to
give Laertes the fullest public reparation possible at this juncture. Presently, after slaying the king, he can publicly explain
his error of killing Polonius instead. But he cannot kill the
king with "perfect conscience" (67)—nor with princely prudence, since he will need in the coming crisis all the favor he can
win from Laertes and others of the court[26]—until he has confessed openly, so far as may be, his own share of guilt. This

[25] Compare Spenser's depiction of the magnanimity of Prince Arthur
against the background of the foul treachery of Pyrochles and Cymochles in
a climactic scene of The Faerie Queene (Book II, canto viii). There as here
the gentleman-prince slays his two opponents, in the upshot, with a justness
all the more clear and complete because nobly delayed.

[26] The prudence of Hamlet was sadly slubbered by the Romantic critics,
who were not fond of that virtue. It was one of the most important qualities
of the gentleman, especially the gentleman as prince or ruler, in Renaissance
literature. See for instance Sir Thomas Elyot's The Governour, Book I,
chap. xxii.

tragic dilemma (so much more tragic in our knowledge than in his) he meets with superb political and moral skill; histrionic skill, maybe, but void of hypocrisy, inspired by real meekness:

> This presence knows,
> And you must needs have heard, how I am punished
> With sore distraction? What I have done
> That might your nature, honour, and exception
> Roughly awake, I here proclaim was madness.
> Was't Hamlet wronged Laertes? Never Hamlet.
> If Hamlet from himself be ta'en away
> And when he's not himself does wrong Laertes,
> Then Hamlet does it not, Hamlet denies it.
> Who does it, then? His madness? If't be so,[27]
> Hamlet is of the faction that is wronged,
> His madness is poor Hamlet's enemy.
> Sir, in this audience,
> Let my disclaiming from a purposed evil
> Free me so far in your most generous thoughts,
> That I have shot mine arrow o'er the house,
> And hurt my brother.

"I am punished With sore distraction": that is the keynote of his apologia. The word "distraction" can mean division and confusion of purposes; also, outright insanity: in either case a kind of "madness." And "madness" it was, the prince goes on to "proclaim," that caused whatsoever he has done—prudently he omits all the questionable particulars—that "might" in any way be considered as wronging Laertes. We know (and the public is to learn later) just how distracted, how mad, he was in his former ideal of "black" revenge (III. iii. 94) and how "heaven" did "punish" him therefor (III. iv. 174). And now the verb in the present tense, "am punished," while recalling to us his private confession to his mother in the Closet scene, also attests, for us, his private "gain-giving" (226) that his punishment is not yet ended; this feeling intensifies his contrition. Publicly, and veraciously, he confesses his *own* guilt in so far as it may be viewed fairly in isolation from the heavily

---

[27] The two question marks in this line (the second is not in the quartos), considered together with the ensuing "If," insinuate that something more than Hamlet's "madness" may be involved, namely the wickedness of Claudius.

contributing guilt of *others*. Certainly the *inward* cause of his sins (as Shakespeare has shown it to us throughout) was that he was "from himself" (245), that he "forgot" his true "self" (76), in certain fateful moments. He claims that the *real* Hamlet belongs to the "faction" (249) of Laertes, thus hinting, what he said outright to Horatio above, that the two young men have a common "cause" (78) against the "canker" (69), the king, who is the maximum source of all the "evil" (70). That common cause, Hamlet intends, will be made fully apparent to Laertes later. Meanwhile Hamlet entreats the other's "most generous thoughts" to accept his apology "so far" as to believe him guiltless of "a purposed evil" against—"my brother." This unexpected term, the acme of the prince's appeal, rescinds his recent outburst regarding "forty thousand brothers" (V. i. 292) and alludes poignantly to the "sister," the "ministering angel" (V. i. 264), whose union with Hamlet would have made Laertes actually the prince's "brother."

Laertes is much moved. The king and we, for opposite reasons, attend his reply in extreme suspense. He begins, "I am satisfied in nature, Whose motive in this case should stir me most To my revenge." My revenge! Employing unwittingly Hamlet's old phrase he confesses, to himself, his evil "motive" in the fencing-match. We have seen that Hamlet has learned to place retributive and preventive justice (63-70) far above the primitive lust of "my revenge" (I. v. 31; II. ii. 613). In a contrite moment he confessed to Ophelia, "I am very proud, revengeful, ambitious" (III. i. 126). But before he became really converted from revengeful pride, it drove him to the killing of Polonius, which resulted in arousing in the victim's son the very same evil passion. So that here we are shown by Shakespeare, beyond the seeing of Hamlet, the full working of the just "divinity that shapes our ends." The fatal phrase "my revenge," initiated by Hamlet and discarded by him too late, was unconsciously caught up in the preceding act and turned against him by Laertes: "my revenge will come" (IV. vii. 29). At present, however, it *seems* that this bad motif has been vanquished utterly by the eventual charity and magnanimity of Hamlet. His great nature has effectively appealed to the better "nature" of Laertes, especially through the climactic phrase "my brother," so opposite to "my revenge." Laertes declares himself satisfied in "nature" (255), responding to Hamlet's use of this word (242).

But the conventional and conceited part of Laertes' nature is *not* satisfied. Otherwise he would respond further to the other's generous words by making an apology of his own, confessing and asking pardon for his insulting treatment of his prince in the graveyard. Instead, he halts and falters, then goes on with embarrassment, "But in my terms of honour I stand aloof. . . ." His ensuing hasty chatter upon "known honour" (259), i.e., conventional correctness, is acceptable enough to the conventional court; but under the circumstances it is very insulting, really, to his prince, who, however, shows not the least sign of satirical impatience, let alone the "towering passion" (80) that the other's shallow showiness roused in him at the grave. Hamlet has resolutely buried with Ophelia all malice against her "brother." He controls himself perfectly in the face of the other's paltering; his mien is entirely tolerant and generous. Therefore Laertes is suddenly shamed into adopting, for a moment, a responsively generous attitude. With another quick change of tone, indicated by a second "But," he declares, "But till that time," the time of a formal reconcilement, "I do receive your offered love like love, And will not wrong it."

An extraordinary assertion! To us and to the king it means that the wavering Laertes has determined not to play foul with Hamlet, though without at all confessing that he had intended to do so. To the prince the assertion must mean that when he presently reveals the king's guilt Laertes will be wholeheartedly on his side, and that in the meanwhile he can discard entirely whatever vague uneasiness (222 ff.) he has felt regarding the fencing-match. Embracing "freely" (263) the other's responsive "love," throwing a brotherly arm about Laertes' shoulder, he declares he will play "this brothers' wager frankly," i.e., without the least dubiety and constraint. "Give us the foils." His tone is relaxed and cheerful. He adds lightly:

> I'll be your foil, Laertes; in mine ignorance
> Your skill shall like a star i' th' darkest night
> Stick fiery off indeed.

But Laertes rejoins, "You mock me, sir," in a suddenly acrid tone that gives Hamlet pause. "No, by this hand," he declares earnestly, searching the other's face. The king quickly intervenes. "Give them the foils, young Osric. Cousin Hamlet"—this hatefully intimate address, reminiscent of the opening ensemble (I. ii. 64), secures the prince's attention—"You know the wager?" Of course Hamlet knows it (271 f.). But recollection of the elaborate and ceremonious "wager" (154 ff.) serves to remind him that Laertes, unlike himself, takes the coming match very seriously as a trial of the prime accomplishment of a gentleman, the art of fencing; hence, apparently, his irritation at the prince's levity above. We, however, perceive a deeper cause. Laertes, who has been fluctuating between admiration and jealousy of Hamlet, is now yielding to the jealousy. The prince's steady graciousness, over against his own confused and weak emotionalism, does "like a star i' th' darkest night Stick fiery off indeed." The point is rubbed in by Hamlet's casual, bantering tone. Laertes feels humiliated. Vanity and self-interest, and the shrewd king's talk of the "wager," remind him of what he has secretly engaged to do—just the contrary of his public promise not to "wrong" Hamlet's love. Pulled one way by this promise, and the other way by the revived idea of "my revenge," the wretched youngster fumbles indecisively with the pile of foils, while Claudius distracts the attention of Hamlet—then desperately seizes the sharp one and, in feeling its heft, touches the point with his poison (275).

The watching Claudius is smoothly, deeply elated. His coming triumph over Hamlet shall be final, unlike the triumph he achieved in the opening ensemble. There he promised to drink many a "jocund health" (I. ii. 125). Here he declares equivocally, "The king shall drink to Hamlet's better breath" (282), i.e., Hamlet's transition to a better life. And this time his cosmic rhetoric is far more resolved and bold. At the first he said the "cannon" would resound to the "clouds" and "the heavens shall bruit again, Respeaking earthly thunder" (I. ii. 126 ff.). But this time there will be no "clouds," and "the heaven" will have a definitive meaning for "earth":

And let the kettle to the trumpet speak,
The trumpet to the cannonier without,
The cannons to the heavens, the heaven to earth,
"Now the king drinks to Hamlet."

In these lines Shakespeare tells us that Claudius is challenging "heaven ordinant" (47). The conscience that troubled him formerly he has managed to suppress, not entirely but almost, much to the advantage of his brilliant, plotting brain. He sincerely wishes Hamlet a "better breath," above in the "sweet heavens" (III. iii. 45), while he himself doth "shove by justice" effectually in the "currents of this world" (III. iii. 57 f.). His arts have been so successful that it seems they are condoned even by the supernal powers. He concludes, "Come, begin, And you the judges"—the earthly judges, Osric in particular, who do not see the "action" in its "true nature" (III. iii. 61 f.) —"bear a wary eye." With triumphant, exquisite irony Claudius wishes the ensuing match to be adjudged, by *earthly eyes,* perfectly fair and normal.

Laertes, however, is again hesitant. He does not try to hit Hamlet. To take in hand a sharp and poisoned foil in a moment of surging jealousy is one thing; quite another is to wound with it a noble, unsuspecting prince when the warmth of healthy sport has rearoused one's healthier emotions. Laertes now feels overwhelmingly that he must fulfil his promise not to "wrong" Hamlet's "love." This is clearly discerned by the king, and he dare not run the risk of Laertes' hesitancy developing into an explication with Hamlet. Claudius decides that he must do at once that which he had hoped to avoid except in case of extreme ill "chance" (IV. vii. 162): he must now murder with his own poison the son of the poisoned father. Mastering his reluctance he celebrates the prince's "very palpable hit" (292) by drinking his health, with all the preannounced ceremony, thereupon dropping the poison in the form of a "pearl" (283, 293) into the cup and sending it to Hamlet, who in commonest courtesy should acknowledge the royal toast if only by barely "sipping" the wine (IV. vii. 161).

But Hamlet, though for a moment he seems about to comply, does not do so; much to the scandal, we must assume, of Osric and the rest of the court. In thus offending the court wherein he is presently to become king the prince is well aware, in his present mood of prudent conciliation, that he is being very indiscreet. But "indiscretion sometimes serves us well" (8); in the present case, too, heaven is ordinant. No doubt for Hamlet, as for us, the blare of drum, trumpet, and cannon is darkly reminiscent. This braying out of the "triumph" of the king's "pledge" (I. iv. 11 f.) recalls the deadly chill of the air on the battlements just before the Ghost brought its revelation of the poisonous murder committed by this same king. Hamlet, with a passing far-off look, with conscious repugnance but not definite suspicion, draws back the hand he had extended for the cup. "I'll play this bout first," he declares brusquely; "set by awhile" (295).

The cup is set on a table near him, whither, at the same moment, Gertrude begins to move. Claudius grips the arms of his throne with desperate premonition, as when the phantasm of his first crime flickered before him in the Dumb-show (III. ii. 146 ff.). Then, in the pause after Hamlet's winning of a second "touch," his mother hands him her handkerchief to dry his brow (299). She is happy, happy in her son's final attainment of freedom from all his "madness" (V. i. 307), happy in the prevailing atmosphere of appeasement. She has loyally kept his secrets; but her soft mind, which shrank from facing her own sin until he compelled her, has avoided envisaging the coming tragic upheaval which he glimpsed and which he predicted to her (III. iv. 173-179). It seems to her now that all will be well, and that all's well that ends well. In the end, after much tribulation, her initial "prayers" (I. ii. 118) for harmonious happiness in Denmark have apparently been answered. In the course of nature—for "all that lives must die" (I. ii. 72)—Claudius will leave the throne to her beloved son, who, now so sane, will have the support of Laertes and of all. Therefore she will now take part genially, as royal consort, in the king's toast to the crown prince. "The *queen* carouses," she declares, stressing her rank, "to thy fortune, Hamlet." She lifts the cup ceremoniously.

While the prince bows to the "Good madam" with a dutiful politeness that he has refused to show to her husband, exactly

as in the opening court scene (I. ii. 120), the king is confronted
by a horrid dilemma. To save "my queen" he must lose "My
crown, mine own ambition" (III. iii. 55). In private she has
of late withheld herself from him, but still she is "conjunctive"
to his "life and soul" (IV. vii. 14). "Gertrude," he exclaims
intimately and poignantly, then covers his surge of feeling with
a brief royal command, "do not drink."

As "Gertrude," as wife and subject, she should certainly
obey him; she has never before publicly refused to do so. And
in courtly correctness, as all of her conventional self tells her
and as the whole court knows, she ought not, in defiance of the
king's express forbiddance, violate the cup so solemnly assigned
to the crown prince by the king. But, though she does not yet
suspect its contents consciously, her intuition, always quick, has
caught something ominous in Claudius's tone. And she is
strangely inspired. She now transcends the soft, conventional
"Gertrude." She becomes really, what in title and position she
has all along been, what she was when her son was born—long
years before her corruption by Claudius—the "queen, Th' imperial jointress of this warlike state" (I. ii. 9): here again the
final court scene returns full circle upon the first. "The queen,"
she says ceremoniously though also with deep affection, "carouses to thy fortune, Hamlet"; and to the astounded, wretched
king[28] she replies with inspired, firm, royal disobedience, "I will,
my lord; I pray you pardon me."

After drinking she stands for a moment as in a trance, holding the cup, then replaces it on the table. Hamlet, who in courtesy to her should lift and sip it now, says to her very gently,
in contrast with his response to Claudius (295), "I dare not
drink yet, madam; by and by" (304). She smiles. This is
her son who, when he so wills, can be extremely gentle, "patient as the female dove" (V. i. 309), but who enters very intensely into whatever action he has in hand, at present this
fencing-match. Dutifully but hastily he had applied her ker-
chief to his "brows" (299), which still, however, stream with
sweat. And now, for the last time, she does him the motherly

---

[28] Similarly Iago never anticipates his wife's disobedience to him and her
loyal love for Desdemona, the cause of his exposure and ruin in the last act
of *Othello*.

service which (we are impelled to imagine) she had often done him long ago when he engaged, after his very intense fashion, in childish sports, hating to be made to pause. She extends her hand and handkerchief towards him invitingly. He smiles and bends his head quickly as she urges tenderly, "Come, let *me* wipe thy face" (305).

Meanwhile the king has confessed to the conscience which he had outraged and silenced, but which is like a fiery poison in him now, "It is the poisoned cup, it is too late" (303). But he still has his dreadfully costly throne, and he is all the more determined to keep it. Certainly, far more than ever, his "offence is rank, it smells to heaven" (III. iii. 36). But now he repudiates heaven and conscience utterly. With superb evil self-control he pulls himself together and fixes his eyes significantly on Laertes. The miserable, confused youngster is struck with deep admiration of his master and filled with keen self-reproach. Because he has weakly refrained from wounding Hamlet his king has had to sacrifice his queen, and has done so with magnificent firmness, loyal to his fellow plotter. "My lord," cries Laertes loudly, imitating the king's aplomb, "I'll hit him now." Claudius replies, "I do not think't," with a quiet, steely scorn that pierces Laertes like a poisoned rapier.

Laertes has resolved to end Hamlet. "And yet," he broods heavily, aside, " 'tis almost 'gainst my conscience." His conscience, unlike his master's, is muddled and oscillating. It sways "almost" over to the side of the noble opponent now again facing him. And yet, this very "conscience" tells him that, in view of all that has happened, he must carry out his agreement with the king; else he is a false, disloyal weakling. And this feeling becomes for the moment overwhelming when Hamlet adjures him roundly:

> Come, for the third.
> Laertes, you but dally;
> I pray you, pass with your best violence;
> I am afeared you make a wanton of me.

With this slight, polite recrudescence of his old impatience the prince invites his own death. The jealous vanity of Laertes, sorely tried at the outset by the prince's public and superior magnanimity, swings him for a fatal minute entirely to the king's side: his emotional "conscience," balanced evenly a moment ago, "almost" inclining to Hamlet, swings in the opposite direction. He cannot let the prince win this public match by default. "Say you so?" he cries: do you actually, as though impelled by fate, urge me to hit you? "Come on."

But now Laertes, fencing his hardest for the first time since the match began, finds to his immense chagrin that his opponent is at least his equal. We remember Hamlet's confidence that he would "win at the odds"; off stage he has been "in continual practice" since "Laertes went into France" (220-222). And now when he is on the point of seizing the crown Hamlet is determined, underneath his gentlemanly nonchalance, to show Laertes and the court that, if the need shall arise, he can give a good account of himself with steel. In the third exchange he baffles his opponent, making him tire himself by thrusting with vain "violence" (309). The result, says Osric, is "Nothing, neither way" (312), in other words a signal defeat for the challenger, Laertes.

"Have at you now!" cries Laertes, suddenly and wrathfully, losing entirely his self-control. In *open* defiance of that better side of his "conscience" which he has been fighting *secretly*, he commits a gross foul. He attacks and hits the opponent who had lowered his sword, at the end of the third exchange, for the accustomed breathing-spell. Hamlet, parrying quickly, suffers only a minor wound. But this, together with the other's guilty face, brings to his mind with a rush the true explanation of the king's byplay above while Laertes hesitantly selected a foil (270-275)—a sharp one, too obviously. Very swift decision is demanded of the prince "thus be-netted round with villainies" (29). With perfect control he conceals from the court his discovery, thus gaining priceless seconds: he gives not the slightest sign that he is wounded; utters no exclamation; refrains from glancing at Claudius. Him the prince will kill presently. First he must kill or utterly disable the king's dangerous underling. Exerting his utmost skill, Hamlet disarms Laertes, seizes the fallen rapier, and hands him his own, urging ironically, "Nay

come, again" (314)[29]—fair warning for a foul opponent that
the final exchange is now really to begin. Before the watchful
king's command, "Part them, they are incensed" (313), can be
obeyed, Hamlet runs Laertes fairly through the breast.

Claudius has tried in vain to save his chief supporter, perceiving Hamlet's discovery and expecting now an attack upon
himself. The prince, silent even to the anxiously inquiring
Horatio (315), is listening intently for whatsoever words may
be uttered by the fallen Laertes. He, muttering that he has
entrapped himself like a vain and stupid "woodcock," confesses
he is "justly killed" with his "own treachery." The king's
treachery he will not yet reveal, still loyal to his master. Consequently Claudius believes himself safe from discovery. Therefore when Gertrude, who had seemingly fainted upon the young
men's violence (314), looks so lifeless that Hamlet cries, "How
does the queen?" (319), the king utters with confidence the
most heartless of all his lies, "She swounds to see them bleed."
Surely the soft lady cannot possibly betray him: she has never
done so hitherto whatever her suspicions; and now she seems
beyond speech; she doubtless does not comprehend what has
happened to her. So the king may well believe. But though
her mind, always dim, is overclouded now by quick-coming
death, her loving intuition regarding her son is still alert. He,
sparing her, never told her directly of the horrible poisoning
of his father; and she has all along, despite the Play scene,
avoided envisaging that crime—so long as her son was safe.
But Claudius's smooth voice, piercing her faint hearing now,
announcing that she has merely fainted, is the same smooth
voice that offered the cup with its "pearl" to her son. And so,

[29] The "Nay" is not mainly, if at all, a response to the king's command
in the preceding line. Hamlet's three words tell us that Laertes hesitates, for a
moment, knowing he faces death from the poisoned point of his own rapier.
His hesitation is due less to physical fear than to the horror of his "conscience"
(307) at having poisoned his prince, a horror that weakens his defense against
Hamlet's deadly thrust, and prepares for his repentance below. The word
"come," uttered at the beginning of each of the three previous bouts and
here introducing the fourth, indicates that Laertes' sudden, unfair onset was
an appendage to the third bout. With that onset compare the still fouler tricks
of Prince Arthur's opponents cited in note 25 above. There, too, the unfair
conduct is due to weakness of character and to violent exasperation at un-
success—and to the author's desire for utmost dramatic effect in a climactic
situation.

the poisonous present and the poisonous past blend, for her dying mind, in one black flash. With toxic energy her last words warn and try to save her son:

> No, no, the drink, the drink!
> O my dear Hamlet, the drink, the drink,
> I am poisoned.[30]

V. ii. 322-414

Thus the poisoner is publicly accused by her who gave public support to him, her "lord" (III. ii. 278), at the end of the accusing poison-scene of Hamlet's Play. That was immediately after the prince's abortive cry, "You shall see anon how the murderer gets the love of Gonzago's wife." The Ghost told us "how" he got it (I. v. 41-57). And recently Claudius himself told us why he lost it: the quality of this sort of love is such that in "time" it must burn low; the "kind of wick" that "lives within the very flame," supplying it, will in the end "abate it" (IV. vii. 111-116). But he cynically asserted this to be true of all love whatsoever. He believed it was true of Gertrude's mother-love for Hamlet. He knew, indeed, that "The queen his mother Lives almost by his looks" (IV. vii. 11 f.), but he was sure that if those "looks" were removed by Hamlet's death in England she would fully recover, as she recovered from the death of Hamlet's father, in "time." He could not see that her maternal love had a different, a timeless kind of "wick" and "flame"; that it had in it something real, eternal, which her other loves had not. Hence the king could not conceive that the wife who had supported her "lord" at the end of the Play's poison-scene would desert him in the present poison-scene because of her love for her son.

And Hamlet's resolution is—like his heart in the byplay of the "napkin" above (299-305)—concordant here with his mother's. He whose mind so confusedly shrank from regicide after the Play is clear and ready now: "Oh villainy! How?[31]

---

[30] This convulsive cry, in three shortened verses—in Q2 there are just two lines, the first ending with the word "Hamlet"—takes the form of a rising and descending curve with a sustained pitch in the second and longest verse.

[31] Q2 and the folios have "How"; Q1, "ho." The locking of the door against the escape of the king is the decisive practical deed that Hamlet left undone at the close of the Play episode in III. ii.

Let the door be locked. Treachery! Seek it out." He wants
all the method of the "villainy," the "How" of it, to be fully
uncovered and displayed to the court. Pointing his rapier at
Claudius, the prince is about to brand him as the "serpent" (I.
v. 36) who hiddenly stung his father's as well as his mother's
life. But Laertes exclaims, with his hand on his pierced breast:
"It"—the "Treachery"—"is here, Hamlet. Hamlet thou art
slain. . . . The treacherous instrument is in thy hand, Unbated
and envenomed. . . ." He seems determined to take all the
"foul practice" (328) against Hamlet upon himself, falsely
loyal to his king. But the true example of the queen's dying
speech is working strongly in the dying Laertes. And so,
breathing hard, he concludes: "Thy mother's poisoned; I can
no more: the king—the king's to blame." The woman whom
Claudius secretly debauched at the beginning has become at the
last the chief cause of his public exposure. Her first speech in
the drama did much to make everyone "look like a friend" (I.
ii. 69) on the usurper; her last speech has had exactly the opposite effect, especially upon the king's chief supporter, Laertes.

Hamlet, transfixed for a moment by horror and dismay on
his own account, whispers hoarsely, "The point *envenomed*,
too!"—not only unbated, as he already knew, but also poisoned.
About to take his throne, he is about to be taken by death. But
beforehand he was prepared for this (230-235). And now his
thought instantly passes, as it has passed more and more during
the second half of the tragedy, from himself to his "work."
Exclaiming, "Then, venom, to thy work," he rushes upon the
king, beating aside with the help of Horatio the opposing swords
which some of the courtiers, despite the revelations of the queen
and Laertes, are still ready to draw on their wicked master's
behalf. Hamlet thrusts the poisoner through and through.

"Treason! treason!" (334) is the general outcry, so awful
is the killing of the anointed head of the realm, the "cease of
majesty" (III. iii. 15), even when the king is a proved criminal.
Some continue to aid him though they know he is ended. And
he, clinging desperately to this life in dreadful fear of the other
life, of the justice of "heaven" (288, III. iii. 36)—confessing
thus the hidden weakness wrought by conscience under all his

superficial strength—gasps out in his very dying words a false
hope that he can still live. He who told his first falsehoods
(I. ii. 1 ff.) only to others tells his last to himself also: "O, yet
defend me, friends, I am but hurt." Immediately he breathes
his last, while his own gorgeous, poisonous cup is thrust to his
lips, symbolically, by Hamlet. That "chalice" (IV. vii. 161)
is a dreadful last sacrament, contrary to that of which his murdered brother was deprived (I. v. 77). But Hamlet is thinking
now of the poisonous communion of Claudius with his mother
and with Denmark:

> Here, thou incestuous, murderous, damned Dane,
> Drink off this potion. Is thy "union" here?
> Follow my mother.

The "union"—Hamlet plays upon the king's term for his poisonous "pearl" (283, 293)—of his mother and Claudius, establishing a false harmony in the state, could not, as Hamlet saw
from the first, "come to good" (I. ii. 158). And the public
good is the prince's dominant thought now, not the fulfilment
of his old passion of personal revenge. He does not call his
mortal enemy a "slave" and "villain" (II. ii. 608, III. iii. 77)
but, for the first and last time, "Dane"—the royal cognomen
which he gave to his dead father (I. iv. 45) and lately to himself (V. i. 281). Hamlet thus intimates, in answer to the general cry of "treason," that not himself but the vile *king*, Claudius, the "damned Dane" whose dead body he has now thrust
away from the throne, has committed treason, against the royal
name and power; against Denmark; and, especially, against
every *honest* Dane.

The cry of "treason" is silenced. Hamlet, uncrowned and
dying monarch, assumes his throne. Laertes, near to death,
pronounces upon Claudius now, "He is justly served." Laertes
has ultimately learned the true meaning of "justly." And the
justice which Hamlet has always loved in spirit (III. ii. 59 ff.)
has now been achieved by him in act and, above all, in character.
The fencing-match in this final scene has symbolized the whole
drama, the drama of a struggle between two "mighty opposites"
(62): growing dishonesty and growing justice. Dishonesty has

been a diseased, spreading growth in Denmark, a nation typical, as Shakespeare has made us feel, of human society at large. Hamlet has succeeded in weeding "this world" of "things rank and gross in nature" (I. ii. 134-137). But in certain crucial moments he himself was tainted with that dishonesty; and, no matter how much of the blame belongs to others, his own responsibility is supreme because of the greatness of his personality and position. He is now greatly just in character and deed. But, as Laertes' final words remind us, this "noble Hamlet" has done fatefully unjust deeds:

> Exchange forgiveness with me, noble Hamlet:
> Mine and my father's death come not upon thee,
> Nor thine on me.

"*Heaven* make thee free of it," Hamlet responds devoutly, stressing the first word and making the sign of the Cross over his expiring opponent; "I follow thee." Having finally obtained from the other a full *gentlemanly* pardon (238, 257-261) he invokes for him *heavenly* pardon, which he needs also for himself, about to "follow" Laertes. "I am dead, Horatio—wretched *queen*, adieu." To God he commends her also, with this "adieu";[32] terming her "queen" here because he feels so poignantly all of his mother's wretched, empty queenship.

But his "time" (346) is short, and his last thoughts are for his kingdom, this world of Denmark, for which he has been "heaven's scourge and minister." He has been able to "catch the conscience" and punish the wrong deeds of the nation's chief representatives, one after another. Even the shallow rank and file of the court, the "mutes or audience" (345), who sided with Claudius and smiled at the supposedly idealistic crown prince at the first (I. ii.)—even they now "look pale and tremble" (344). They have at length been given some perception, dim and horrified, of the cost of "smiling" villainy "in Denmark" (I. v. 105-109). At tragic cost this noble prince has done what he was "born" to do: he has purged the "time" that was "out of joint" and has "set it right" (I. v. 189 f.). But he

---

[32] In Shakespeare's time "adieu" had often a conscious allusion to the deity, as in I. v. 91, 111. Compare the "good-bye" of Ophelia in IV. v. 199 f. and see the note.

cannot live to keep it right. Therefore he is intent that his whole story, truly told, shall live after him so that the "pith and marrow" of his reputation may have its right effect "in the general censure" (I. iv. 22, 35): "Horatio, I am dead, Thou liv'st, report me and my causes right To the unsatisfied."

"Never believe it" (351). For once the temperate Horatio entirely loses his temperance, for a minute, in his passionate devotion to his dying friend. He is overpowered (like us) by the final, fully tempered, beautiful magnanimity, transcending death, of his prince, now his king. He has not known till now the full nobility of Hamlet. The skeptical Horatio "might not this believe" but for the "true avouch" of his "own eyes" (I. i. 56-58). In the beginning he was almost shaken out of his self-command by the supernatural appearance of the late king, whom he so much admired (I. ii. 176, 186). In the end, he is more shaken by the glory of "young Hamlet," a dying "god of day" (I. i. 152, 170). Horatio will follow and serve this new king even beyond death. He snatches up the poisoned cup, dropped by Hamlet beside the throne, and is about to drain its last drops.

Hamlet, exerting all his remaining strength, gets to his feet and seizes his friend's arm. "As th' art a man, give me the cup. Let go, by heaven I'll have it." We recall how he over-mastered his friend after a struggle when determined to follow the Ghost alone (I. iv. 85); now, the prince will follow death alone. He appeals to Horatio as a "man." It is the task of "as just a man" as Horatio (III. ii. 59) to live on, for the sake of his prince's "name," in this "harsh world." In the word "harsh" Hamlet is pitying Horatio, not at all himself. His beautiful words pulse with harsh pain, to be sure, but, above that, with the heavenly joy of tried and true and perfected friendship:

> O good Horatio, what a wounded name,
> Things standing thus unknown, shall live behind me!
> If thou did'st ever hold me in thy heart,
> Absent thee from felicity a while,
> And in this harsh world draw—thy breath—in pain—
> To tell my story.

Drawing agonized, spasmodic breath, Hamlet, with Horatio's arm about him, sinks back upon his throne, then hears faintly a "warlike noise" (360)—a *"March afar off,"* and a responsive *"shout within."* He rouses himself, with a prophetic light in his face. He sees that his successor will be Fortinbras, a narrow and too impetuous prince but honest, able, and ever ready to act "When honour's at the stake" (IV. iv. 56). He will do his best for Denmark when he has learned from Horatio all that Hamlet has done and willed to do: "he has my dying voice, So tell him. . . ." No further can Hamlet "rough-hew" Denmark's or his own "ends" (10 f.). But though his life is imperfect—what man at the end can have "perfect conscience?" —he has "readiness" (234), and peace at the last: "The rest is silence."

"Good night, sweet prince. . . ." Horatio, weeping, has echoed unconsciously a phrase he heard when this symphonic drama opened in *spiritual* darkness, "Give you good night" (I. i. 16, 18). But his parting verse for his friend's soul is: "And flights of angels sing thee to thy *rest!*" That lovely line, soaring quietly into the "undiscovered country," takes up Hamlet's dying word "rest" (a word suggesting both the remainder of his earthly story and his imminent peace in heaven)[33] and at the same time recalls his initial invocation in Horatio's presence to the heavenly powers: "Angels and ministers of grace defend us!" (I. iv. 39).

Horatio, rapt for a moment with Hamlet's peace, exclaims, absently and aloofly, "Why does the drum come hither?" (372) —then rouses and grips himself to obey effectually the prince's dying behest. First he lets Fortinbras and the English ambassador take in all the "woe" and "wonder" (374) that confront their eyes. Then, prudently, he sums up the tragedy in general, impartial terms (383-397).[34] Later, when Fortinbras

---

[33] Compare the pun on "rest" in Romeo's final speech (V. iii. 110)—so much surpassed by the fine *double-entendre* in Hamlet's final speech.

[34] By stating that it was *not* Claudius (383) who gave order for the execution of Rosencrantz and Guildenstern, Horatio captures the acute attention of Fortinbras (as indicated by the opening words of his reply) and prepares him for learning, later and fully, of Hamlet's "new commission" (32) and of the just reasons for it. In that context Horatio will hand over to Fortinbras the "commission" (26) of Claudius dooming the prince.

shall have assumed supreme control (398-401) and re-established public order (405),[35] Horatio will speak words "from
his mouth whose voice will draw on more" (403): he will impart the *inward* truth of Hamlet and his "story" (360) with
the aim of influencing the policy and proceedings of the new
king of Denmark, Fortinbras.

In the closing lines Fortinbras, who has known Hamlet only
by reputation, pronounces truths that Hamlet's Ophelia knew
well. The prince, distinguished as courtier, gentleman, and
thinker, was at the same time a "soldier" (III. i. 159). Above
all, as we of the audience were made to feel in the opening
scenes of the drama, he was of royal character, the "expectancy
and rose of the fair state" (III. i. 160). He was a prince who
would have become a great king, martial and commanding, but
courteous, wise, and just. Actually, however, his kingship and
his soldiership were of inward, not outward, nature: his warfare
was, and remains for us, deeply spiritual. That light is beyond
Fortinbras. But in his way he can recognize Hamlet's martial
and royal traits and his great potentiality:

> Bear Hamlet like a soldier to the stage,
> For he was likely, had he been put on,
> To have proved most royally; and for his passage,
> The soldiers' music and the rites of war
> Speak loudly for him.

[35] Compare Horatio's concern for public peace and order in IV. v. 8 ff.
The same concern, continually present to the mind of Hamlet, was shown
emphatically in his dying speech.

INDEX